An Indian Trinitarian Theology of *Missio Dei*

American Society of Missiology Monograph Series

Series Editor, James R. Krabill

The ASM Monograph Series provides a forum for publishing quality dissertations and studies in the field of missiology. Collaborating with Pickwick Publications—a division of Wipf and Stock Publishers of Eugene, Oregon—the American Society of Missiology selects high quality dissertations and other monographic studies that offer research materials in mission studies for scholars, mission and church leaders, and the academic community at large. The ASM seeks scholarly work for publication in the series that throws light on issues confronting Christian world mission in its cultural, social, historical, biblical, and theological dimensions.

Missiology is an academic field that brings together scholars whose professional training ranges from doctoral-level preparation in areas such as Scripture, history and sociology of religions, anthropology, theology, international relations, interreligious interchange, mission history, inculturation, and church law. The American Society of Missiology, which sponsors this series, is an ecumenical body drawing members from Independent and Ecumenical Protestant, Catholic, Orthodox, and other traditions. Members of the ASM are united by their commitment to reflect on and do scholarly work relating to both mission history and the present-day mission of the church. The ASM Monograph Series aims to publish works of exceptional merit on specialized topics, with particular attention given to work by younger scholars, the dissemination and publication of which is difficult under the economic pressures of standard publishing models.

Persons seeking information about the ASM or the guidelines for having their dissertations considered for publication in the ASM Monograph Series should consult the Society's website—www.asmweb.org.

Members of the ASM Monograph Committe who approved this book are:

Robert Gallagher, Associate Professor of Intercultural Studies
        and Director of M.A. (Intercultural Studies),
    Wheaton College

Margaret Guider, O.S.F., Associate Professor of Missiology, Boston College

RECENTLY PUBLISHED IN THE ASM MONOGRAPH SERIES

Clive S. Chin, *The Perception of Christianity as a Rational Religion in Singapore: A Missiological Analysis of Christian Conversion*

Matthew Friedman, *Union with God in Christ: Early Christian and Wesleyan Spirituality as an Approach to Islamic Mysticism*

An Indian Trinitarian Theology of *Missio Dei*

Insights from St. Augustine and Brahmabandhab Upadhyay

P. V. JOSEPH

FOREWORD BY
JOHN JEFFERSON DAVIS

American Society of Missiology Monograph
Series vol. 39

☙PICKWICK *Publications* · Eugene, Oregon

AN INDIAN TRINITARIAN THEOLOGY OF *MISSIO DEI*
Insights from St. Augustine and Brahmabandhab Upadhyay

American Society of Missiology Monograph Series 39

Copyright © 2019 P. V. Joseph. All rights reserved. Except for brief quotations in critical publications or reviews, no part of this book may be reproduced in any manner without prior written permission from the publisher. Write: Permissions, Wipf and Stock Publishers, 199 W. 8th Ave., Suite 3, Eugene, OR 97401.

Pickwick Publications
An Imprint of Wipf and Stock Publishers
199 W. 8th Ave., Suite 3
Eugene, OR 97401

www.wipfandstock.com

PAPERBACK ISBN: 978-1-5326-5940-9
HARDCOVER ISBN: 978-1-5326-5941-6
EBOOK ISBN: 978-1-5326-5942-3

Cataloguing-in-Publication data:

Names: Joseph, P. V., author.

Title: An Indian trinitarian theology of *missio dei*: insights from St. Augustine and Brahmabandhab Upadhyay / by P. V. Joseph.

Description: Eugene, OR: Pickwick Publications, 2019 | American Society of Missiology Monograph Series 39 | Includes bibliographical references and index.

Identifiers: ISBN 978-1-5326-5940-9 (paperback) | ISBN 978-1-5326-5941-6 (hardcover) | ISBN 978-1-5326-5942-3 (ebook)

Subjects: LCSH: Theology, Doctrinal—India. | Trinity. | *Missio Dei*. | Augustine, of Hippo, Saint, 354–430. | Upadhyay, Brahmabandhab, 1861–1907.

Classification: LCC BT30.15 J6 2019 (print) | LCC BT30.15 (ebook)

Unless otherwise stated, biblical quotations are taken from the New Revised Standard Version Bible: Anglican Edition, copyright © 1989, the Division of Christian Education of the National Council of the Churches of Christ in the United States of America. All rights reserved.

Manufactured in the U.S.A.   07/11/19

To
Rev. Dr. George Kuruvila Chavanikamannil
in deep appreciation for his invaluable contributions to my life

Contents

Foreword by John Jefferson Davis | ix
Acknowledgments | xiii

Introduction | 1
1. Renewal of Trinitarian Theology and *Missio Dei*: Historical Trajectories | 10
2. Contours of Indian Christian Theology and Mission Discourse | 52
3. The Trinitarian Theology of Brahmabandhab Upadhyay | 90
4. St. Augustine and Trinitarian *Missio Dei* Theology | 128
5. Towards an Indian Trinitarian Theology of *Missio Dei* | 168
Conclusion | 206

Sanskrit Glossary | 211
Bibliography | 215
Author Index | 235
Subject Index | 239
Scripture Index | 245

Foreword

It is a well-known fact in the West that the Indian subcontinent has been the birthplace of some of the world's most ancient religious traditions: Hinduism, Jainism, and Buddhism. In later centuries, the religions of Islam and Sikhism made their homes in India as well. It is not quite as well known that Christianity, especially as represented by the Syrian Christian tradition, has ancient roots in India as well.

In the last several centuries scholars and theologians in the Christian churches of India have done pioneering work in seeking to express the Christian faith in the thought forms and traditions of Indian culture so as to make Christianity a more truly indigenous Indian religion. These efforts, however, have remained, for the most part, little known in the West.

It is for this reason that the publication of Paolil Varghese Joseph's *An Indian Trinitarian Theology of Missio Dei: Insights from St. Augustine and Brahmabandhab Upadhyay* represents such an important event not only for current theological scholarship, but perhaps even more importantly, for the growth, influence, and maturity of Indian Christian theology and the mission of the Christian churches in India.

P. V. Joseph is a very gifted emerging Indian Christian theologian who has written a very important monograph that deserves the attention of Christian theologians, theological educators, missiologists, missionaries, and pastors in both Western and Asian contexts. The author has taken up the important and difficult task of expounding and applying to the task of mission one of the most central doctrines of the Christian faith—the Trinity—as understood by Augustine and by Brahmabandhab Upadhyay, a

Foreword

pioneering Indian theologian of the nineteenth and early twentieth centuries. As yet little known in the West, Upadhyay was one of the earliest and most significant of Indian theologians to attempt to formulate the Christian doctrine of the Trinity, heretofore formulated in the language of Augustine and the Graeco-Roman categories of the Christian West, in the Sanskritic thought forms of the Advaita Vedanta philosophy, as classically expressed in the work of Shankara.

The author demonstrates an accurate and scholarly mastery of the primary sources of Trinitarian theology, in both its Western and Indian expressions. He expounds the seminal work of Augustine's *De Trinitate* with a view to unfolding its contributions to a missiological theology of the *missio Dei*, showing how God's mission to the world is founded in the eternal, internal relations of Father, Son, and Holy Spirit, and in the relations of love existing among them.

The reader will find in this substantive volume concise histories and expositions of the doctrines of the Trinity as they unfolded both in Western and Indian contexts, down to the present. These chapters would serve as valuable readings on the doctrine of the Trinity for seminary students and other students of Christian theology. The chapters expounding the teachings of Upadhyay and his predecessors would provide valuable introductions for Western readers who have little previous exposure to Indian Christian theology.

A notable feature of Joseph's work is his convincing argument that the doctrine of the Trinity, incorporating insights from both Augustine and Upadhyay, can not only be expressed in thought forms indigenous to India, but also in ways that are socially and ethically much needed and relevant to current challenges that face the Indian church and society. Joseph argues—convincingly, in my estimation—that the doctrine of the Trinity, properly understood as grounded in the *communion of equal persons* in loving and harmonious relationships, and in respect for and recognition of the inherent *differences* existing among those persons—should constitute a way forward for addressing the situation of the Dalits and other marginalized social groups in India, who have long been disadvantaged by the traditional caste system. Joseph argues that an orthodox, biblical Trinitarian theology can be a truly *liberating* theology for the masses in India today.

His work should be seen as an essential starting point for all those who would seek to advance the work of developing an indigenous Indian Christian theology in the days and years ahead.

Foreword

It is now increasingly recognized that the demographic center of gravity of the world Christian movement has shifted from Europe and North America to the Global South—to Asia, Africa, and Latin America. Mission is no longer "from the West to the rest," but "from everywhere to everywhere." Christian scholars in the West, in our now globalized environment, need to hear and learn from the emerging scholars of the Global South—scholars such as P. V. Joseph. The author has demonstrated that he has learned from the Western/Augustinian tradition of Trinitarian thought. It is now time for those of us in the West to learn from and partner with our colleagues in the new Majority churches as we engage together in the *missio Dei*.

I congratulate Joseph on this excellent and important contribution to Trinitarian theology, in cross-cultural perspective, and heartily recommend it to my fellow teachers and students, pastors, missionaries, and to all those who seek to know and serve the Triune God more deeply and effectively.

John Jefferson Davis, PhD

Professor of Systematic Theology & Christian Ethics
Chair, Division of Christian Thought
Gordon-Conwell Theological Seminary
S. Hamilton, MA

Acknowledgments

It is a simple fact of life that no one person alone can achieve success in life, and it is true for a monograph of this kind as well. This book has come out in this shape through the efforts of so many people who have contributed in substantial ways to its making.

At the outset, I extend my sincere thanks and appreciation to Boston University School of Theology; to all my professors, the Dean, and the Academic Dean for the opportunity to pursue my doctoral program in this prestigious institution, particularly for the award of doctoral fellowship, which helped in the timely completion of my work. I owe deep appreciation to my mentor, Dr. John Jefferson Davis, Professor of Systematic Theology & Christian Ethics, for his excellent guidance, encouragement, and advice throughout the writing of this book. I wish to express my gratitude to Dr. John H. Berthrong, Associate Professor of Comparative Theology, who extended all possible help and assistance towards the successful completion of this project. I am especially indebted to Dr. Dana L. Robert, Truman Collins Professor of World Christianity and History of Mission, for her constant support at each step of the program. I must also appreciate Dr. Robert C. Neville, Professor of Philosophy, Religion, and Theology; Dr. Thomas Thangaraj, Visiting Professor of World Christianity; and Dr. Rady Roldan-Figueroa, Associate Professor of the History of Christianity, for being part of the dissertation committee and for their perceptive suggestions.

I have a profound sense of indebtedness to two remarkable couples who stood with me throughout this arduous academic journey. Rev. Dr. George and Mrs. Leela Chavanikamannil, the founders of New Theological

Acknowledgments

College in Dehradun, India, and Dr. Timothy Tennent, President of Asbury Theological Seminary, and Mrs. Julie Tennent have contributed to the completion of my doctoral work in ways beyond words. My special thanks go to late Mr. Frank Doll and to Mrs. Anne Doll as well as to Dr. Daniel and Mrs. Lita Schlueter, who extended their prayerful support and were a great source of encouragement. I am also grateful to Mr. Dave and Mrs. Marilyn Sweet; Rev. Dorington Little; and Ms. Elizabeth Jones, who have extended their help in so many different ways.

My association with Westgate Evangelical Church (Weston, MA), and its pastors, elders, and members, has been a great blessing. I extend my thanks to the church, especially to Rev. Dr. Bruce Daggett; Rev. Brandon Levering; Mr. Steve and Mrs. Natasha Hope; Mr. George Rideout; and the board of elders. The Walker Center (Newton, MA) was my home away from home for long five years. I remember with gratefulness the friendship and warm fellowship of the Walker Center staff as well as the Barton House residents. I must express my special thanks to Rev. Francis Graham, who has been a wonderful friend and brother. I also express my thanks to late Mrs. Lorraine Holcomb, Mrs. Robyn Davis, and Julia Hynes for their help with the editing of my book. I appreciate the great help extended by the staffs of the School of Theology Library and Mugar Memorial Library of Boston University, Goddard Library of Gordon-Conwell Theological Seminary, and Andover-Harvard Theological Library of Harvard Divinity School.

I am grateful to Pickwick Publications and the American Society of Missiology for having accepted and published this monograph under the ASM series. Special thanks are due to Dr. James R. Krabill, Chair, ASM Scholarly Monograph Series Editorial Committee, and to the staff at Wipf and Stock Publishers: Mr. Matthew Wimer, Assistant Managing Editor; Mr. Daniel Lanning, Editorial Administrator; and to my editors, Dr. Chris Spinks and Mr. Zane Derven. I also extend my special thanks to Dr. Simon Samuel, Principal of New Theological College, Dehradun, India, for his support and encouragement. A special word of thanks to my friend, Mr. Abraham Kattil, who spent many days on proofreading and other assistance.

Finally, I must thank my mother and siblings for their constant prayers and support. Perhaps nobody has been more important to me in the pursuit of this research than my wife, Lissy, and our daughters, Sneha and Abia, who have made huge sacrifices to see that my efforts bear fruit in the form of this publication. I am deeply indebted to my wife for her commitment, persistent

Acknowledgments

prayers, support, and for being both father and mother to our children during the long period of my absence. It has been quite a journey of perseverance, hope, and faith where I have experienced both the presence and the provisions of the Triune God in ways words cannot express!

Introduction

THE MODERN REDISCOVERY OF the doctrine of the Trinity over half a century has left a great impact on the thought and life of the Christian Church. With this reinstatement, the Trinity, which was left out for a long time as an esoteric mystery, has captured the imagination of theologians and church leaders resulting in a plethora of literature on the subject. The new development has forced the Church to review its dogma, spirituality, and Christian practices through the lens of this central doctrine of the Christian faith. One of the important and essential upshots of the doctrine has been the reclamation of a theocentric and trinitarian understanding of mission as the *missio Dei*. This book attempts to point the way toward developing an Indian trinitarian *missio Dei* theology within this larger horizon of the renewal of trinitarian theology drawing perspectives from the trinitarian interpretations of St. Augustine and Brahmabandhab Upadhyay.

THE TRINITY, AUGUSTINE, AND BRAHMABANDHAB UPADHYAY

"God is always going forth from God, into the world, creating and redeeming and sustaining it."[1] This idea of God's movement out of himself into the world and humanity has been rediscovered in the modern renaissance of trinitarian theology and in the subsequent development of the *missio Dei* concept. While this concept is a more recent development, the idea of *missio* as the sending forth and the outward movement of the Triune God could

---

1. Cunningham, *These Three Are One*, 336.

be traced back to the trinitarian doctrine of St. Augustine. In Augustine's trinitarian theology, the idea of divine missions emerges in the inner trinitarian relation of the Godhead and in the outward movement of God—the Father's sending forth of the Son, and the sending forth of the Holy Spirit by the Father and the Son. Augustinian theology of the Trinity is seen as paving the way for a trinitarian foundation of mission, signaling a shift from Christocentric mission to a trinitarian approach. The emphasis has been that if mission is the *missio Dei*, it must relate to all three persons of the Trinity and be seen as patrological, Christological, and pneumatological—of the Father, of the Son, and of the Holy Spirit.[2] As Moltmann has put it, "It is not the church that has a mission of salvation to fulfil in the world; it is the mission of the Son and the Spirit through the Father that includes the church."[3] This understanding of mission as *missio Dei* and the rediscovery of its trinitarian foundation marked a significant development in recent theological and mission discourse. The concept of the *missio Dei* with its emphasis on the doctrine of the Trinity signaled a shift from the traditional *ecclesiocentric* view of mission to a *trinitarian-centric* approach. This study is undertaken in an attempt to contextualize the *missio Dei* theology for an Indian context informed by trinitarian theology. It seeks to explore Augustine's concept of trinitarian *missio* as well as the Indian restatement of the doctrine of the Trinity represented in the work of Brahmabandhab Upadhyay and draw their insights for an Indian trinitarian mission theology.

Brahmabandhab Upadhyay (1861–1907), a Brahmin convert, was an Indian theologian, savant, journalist, and freedom fighter who made the first and most important interpretation of the Christian doctrine of the Trinity from the perspective of Hindu philosophy. Upadhyay sought to restate the doctrine of the Trinity from within the framework of the Vedanta category of *saccidānanda* with a view to indigenizing the Christian faith and thus to build Christianity on Indian philosophical and cultural foundations. He believed that the Christian faith brought to India from the West had come in Graeco-Roman and scholastic thought forms, and hence, was not fully intelligible to the Indian mind. In order to make the Christian gospel more comprehensible in the Indian context, Upadhyay found it was essential to express the Christian faith through Indian philosophical and cultural categories. He believed that the Advaita Vedanta expounded by the renowned

---

2. See Newbigin, *Trinitarian Faith and Today's Mission*, 31.
3. Moltmann, *Church in the Power of the Spirit*, 64.

Introduction

Hindu philosopher Shankara (also written Śankara or Shankaracharya) provided an appropriate framework for this task.

Upadhyay was searching for a foundation for the indigenous expression of Christian faith in India. He discovered this in his reinterpretation of Advaita Vedanta within the context of a Thomistic worldview, where he essentially replaced Thomas Aquinas's use of Aristotelian philosophy with that of Shankara's. Upadhyay's exposition of the Christian doctrine of the Trinity in terms of *saccidānanda* was an important step in this direction. In this endeavor, he sought to bring Christian theology and mission together, thereby demonstrating a great "insight into the dynamic relationship between good theology and good missiology."[4] The appropriation of the Advaita Vedanta concept of *saccidānanda* in the trinitarian theology of Upadhyay offers terminology for contextualizing a Christian understanding of God for an Indian setting. This will also demonstrate how bringing into relationship the trinitarian theologies of Augustine and Upadhyay can provide conceptual resources for the future construction of a trinitarian theology of *missio Dei* in a form appropriate for the Indian context.

TRINITARIAN REDISCOVERY, INDIAN THEOLOGY, AND MISSION

This study is placed within the larger context of trinitarian renewal as well as the emergence of Indian Christian theology. The twentieth century witnessed a renaissance of trinitarian theology, particularly within the Protestant and Roman Catholic traditions, initiated respectively by Karl Barth and Karl Rahner. This retrieval of the central role of the doctrine of the Trinity subsequently helped reclaim the trinitarian foundation of Christian mission. It is important to note that until the sixteenth century, the term "mission" was used solely in relation to the trinitarian doctrine, for the Father's sending of the Son and the Holy Spirit.[5] However, the term "mission," which was primarily used to refer to the Triune God and the inner life of God's action, gradually came to signify a wide range of activities of the Church and even Christian institutions, and thus mission assumed a more anthropocentric meaning. Consequently, there has been a shift in the use of the term "from a theocentric connotation to a more anthropocentric one."[6] Gradually, the term lost its original distinctiveness and identity as God's

---

4. Tennent, *Building Christianity on Indian Foundations*, viii.
5. Bosch, *Transforming Mission*, 1.
6. Tennent, *Invitation to World Missions*, 54.

An Indian Trinitarian Theology of *Missio Dei*

mission. The revitalization of trinitarian theology has played a significant role in reclaiming the meaning of "mission" as God's mission by seeking to ground mission in the Triune God.

The emergence of trinitarian understanding of mission has gained great momentum globally and drawn much attention and reflection from theological and mission circles. While one may not speak of a trinitarian revival in India, the doctrine of the Trinity became one of the launching grounds for the development of Indian Christian theology, as will be expounded later in the book. It is quite significant that discourse on theology in India developed in the context of the mission pursuit and in the attempt to indigenize the Christian faith. Much of the early theological discourse could be seen as efforts towards formulating an indigenous theology as part of the attempt to express Christianity in the native cultural thought forms. Therefore, it is perhaps appropriate to term Indian theology as Indian indigenous theology as termed by the Danish theologian, Kaj Baago.[7]

Trinitarian theology that played a crucial role in the beginning of the theological indigenization process—as seen in the critical reaction and responses to the Trinity from Raja Ram Mohan Roy and Keshub Chunder Sen—since then has not received a central place in theological discourse in India. Given the renaissance of the doctrine of the Trinity and the extensive responses it has elicited in the global theological landscape, one might feel that the aloofness of Indian theology would only deprive it of the rich dividends of this important theological development. In this respect, it will be a fruitful exercise to initiate a study of the *missio Dei* theology in relation to the doctrine of the Trinity in the Indian context. A study of the *saccidānanda* concept of Brahmabandhab Upadhyay in relation to Augustine's trinitarian theology and the *missio Dei* concept is an important step in this direction. Given the vast body of literature on Augustinian studies and the growing interests in the theology of Upadhyay in India and beyond, such a study could open up possibilities for further research and discourse in Indian mission and theology, and hopefully, at a global level as well. This is also important in view of the remarkable growth of Christianity in the non-Western world and the increasing globalization of the Church's identity. Significantly, in this global milieu, the non-Western theological articulations are beginning to be taken seriously. Indian Christian theology, in spite of being less than two centuries old, has made significant contributions to global theology and mission. Regrettably, these

---

7. See Baago, "Indian Indigenous Theology."

Introduction

theological insights have not been brought sufficiently into the theological landscape worldwide. There is need for more earnest research in Indian Christian and mission theologies, bringing the Indian contribution within the broader spectrum of Christian theology and missiology. In the East and the West, there is a sense of disquietude over the continuing hegemony of Western theology in World Christianity, and the inadequate recognition of non-Western theologies and mission discourse at the global theological enterprise. One of the answers to this problem may be sought in bringing non-Western indigenous theologies and mission discourses into conversation with Western thought.

CONTRIBUTION OF THIS STUDY

The present study is a unique project in the Indian theological and mission context since there has not been any significant study in the area of the *missio Dei* and Trinity, especially in bringing together Indian and Western trinitarian theologies. There have been numerous studies and writings undertaken on Brahmabandhab Upadhyay's theological thought. However, a mission theology from Upadhyay's works remains to be explored more carefully and in detail. Among the several studies undertaken on Brahmabandhab Upadhyay, two very significant works are those of the Cambridge Professor, Julius Lipner's *Brahmabandhab Upadhyay: The Life and Thought of a Revolutionary* and *Building Christianity on Indian Foundations: The Legacy of Brahmabandhav Upadhyay* by Timothy Tennent, Professor of World Christianity and President of Asbury Theological Seminary. The former is a critical, historical, and theological biography of Upadhyay. Lipner's straightforward and persuasive work examines the multifaceted life of Upadhyay and his complex theological trajectory. Tennent's work is perhaps the most comprehensive and in-depth analysis of Upadhyay's theology and its implications for an indigenous Christianity undertaken as a doctoral research at Edinburgh University. This present study moves in a different direction as it seeks to bring together the trinitarian thought of Upadhyay and Augustine in association with *missio Dei* as well as to draw from their trinitarian perspectives that could enrich the theological and mission thoughts in India. This is an area hitherto unexplored, and in this sense, I hope that this project could be a significant contribution to current theological and mission conversation in India.

It is hoped that this study will advance scholarship in the fields of Indian Christian theology, Trinity and missiology, and dialogue in the pluralistic setting of India. The theological and missiological concepts dealt with in the book have particular relevance to the religious communities influenced by the Sanskrit tradition as well as to the subaltern communities and their counter-theologies in opposition to the Sanskrit paradigm. This could also motivate the Indian Christian community to enter the thought-world of Hinduism and the larger Indian culture and tradition, and to engage in meaningful dialogue for the task of mission. In the present Indian context, which is religiously and socially fragmented, a meaningful dialogical engagement with the Sanskrit tradition and non-Christian religions could also help the Christian churches to address the widespread perception of Christianity as a "foreign" religion.

This study is confined to an examination of the trinitarian theologies of Augustine and Brahmabandhab Upadhyay with a view toward the future development of a trinitarian theology of mission in an Indian context. Therefore, this study does not propose to undertake a comprehensive examination of Augustine's trinitarian theology. Hence, it is limited to the first four chapters of the *De Trinitate* as they form the primary source for Augustine's theology for mission and Trinity in terms of the divine sending (*missio*), the Father's activity of sending the Son and the Holy Spirit. Similarly, this study is restricted to examining Upadhyay's thought in relation to the concept of *saccidānanda* without moving into other areas of his Vedantic exposition, for instance, his interpretation of the doctrine of creation as *Maya*. A more comprehensive dialogue between other Western trinitarian theologies and the Vedanta concept of *saccidānanda* could also be undertaken. However, a detailed project is beyond the scope of this study.

In attempting to explore the trinitarian thoughts of two theologians—Augustine and Upadhyay—this book brings together the thoughts of such diverse figures whose contexts were quite different. However, I believe that in spite of these differences, both Augustine and Upadhyay provide important insights for the development of an Indian *missio Dei* theology grounded in the doctrine of the Trinity. The doctrine of the Trinity is foundational for Christian faith and mission, as much as the very being of the Church and its mission flow from the Trinity. Upadhyay endeavored to show the importance of contextualizing the Christian faith in the Indian context for its mission and how the expression of the Christian doctrine of the Trinity through the use of the Advaita Vedanta terminology of *saccidānanda* could contribute to this end.

Introduction

THE STRUCTURE OF THIS BOOK

In this historical and theological investigation, the primary method of investigation involved is a review of primary sources in relation to the doctrine of the Trinity as expounded by Augustine and Upadhyay with a view to bringing out their implications for the subsequent development of an Indian trinitarian *missio Dei* theology. Furthermore, the interpretations of the major trinitarian theologians as well as the literature in Indian Christian theology will form part of this exploration. This study attempts to discover the dimension of mission involved in Augustine's work on the Trinity and how Upadhyay undertook to discover the meaning of the Christian doctrine of the Trinity through the lens of Hindu philosophy with an obvious mission objective. This is being undertaken within the larger context of the trinitarian renaissance and the emergence of the *missio Dei* concept as well as the development of indigenous theology in India.

In order to provide background to the major topic of this study, the first and second chapters place in perspective a brief review of the recovery of trinitarian theology and the historical development of the *missio Dei* concept as well as an overview of Indian Christian theology and mission thought. The first chapter is a brief review of the development of trinitarian theology until the modern period followed by an engagement with the writings of scholars on the trinitarian renewal—Karl Barth, Karl Rahner, and Vladimir Lossky—representing the three major Christian confessions.[8] The second section of the chapter examines the historical development of the *missio Dei* concept and its trinitarian foundation which first began with the IMC conference in Willingen 1952 and the post-Willingen discourses.

An overview of the development of Indian Christian theology in a mission context is offered in the second chapter, especially the engagement between Christian missionaries and progressive Hindus such as Raja Ram Mohan Roy, Keshub Chunder Sen, and others.[9] This situates the study in the Indian context and provides a background for the investigation of Brahmabandhab Upadhyay's trinitarian theology in the following chapter. From its beginnings, Indian Christian theology had a strong underlying mission concern and, in fact, it emerged from the Hindu-Christian theological conversation in a missionary setting. While these theological developments took place within the framework of the Sanskrit tradition,

---

8. See Barth, *CD* 1/1; Rahner, *Trinity*; Lossky, *Mystical Theology of the Eastern Church*.

9. See Roy, *Precepts of Jesus*; Sen, *Keshub Chunder Sen's Lectures in India*; Mozoomdar, *Oriental Christ*.

An Indian Trinitarian Theology of *Missio Dei*

an attempt has been made in this chapter to highlight the emergence of Indian counter theologies in opposition to the Sanskrit paradigm that has dominated Indian theological reflection.

The following two chapters examine the trinitarian theologies of Brahmabandhab Upadhyay and Augustine of Hippo, respectively. As will be shown in the third chapter, Upadhyay was the first Indian theologian to attempt an indigenous interpretation of the Christian doctrine of the Trinity from the Advaita Vedanta perspective. In fact, he was the first Indian Christian theologian to recognize the importance of "a positive dialogue with the indigenous theological and (Hindu) philosophical tradition" of India.[10] This chapter expounds Upadhyay's restatement of the trinitarian doctrine from within the framework of *saccidānanda*. In order to provide clarity to Upadhyay's thought, I have attempted a study of the prominent Hindu philosophical concept of "Brahman" and how Upadhyay sought to understand it in terms of *saccidānanda* in view of his larger objective of interpreting the Christian doctrine of the Trinity. This is followed by a detailed study of Upadhyay's use of *saccidānanda* for expressing the trinitarian doctrine in an Indian context. The major sources on Upadhyay are the two collections of his articles, as well as two important works undertaken on Upadhyay's thought.[11] In order to furnish a background to Upadhyay's exposition of *saccidānanda*, I have drawn from several Hindu texts as well as from Shankara's writings from which Upadhyay has taken the Vedanta concept of *saccidānanda*.[12]

The fourth chapter offers a comprehensive study of Augustine's doctrine of the Trinity in relation to *missio Dei* in his engagements with his Arian opponents. In undertaking a detailed examination of Augustine's trinitarian teaching, the study attempts to show that God's mission takes place in the outward movement of the Godhead, in the sending of the divine persons, in the incarnation of the Son, and the Pentecost of the Holy Spirit. Thus, theologically, mission refers to the *economic* activity of the trinitarian sending in the New Testament where the Father sends the Son and the Father and the Son together send the Holy Spirit. The study of Augustine is focused on his exposition on the doctrine of the Trinity as found

---

10. Tennent, *Building Christianity on Indian Foundations*, 7.

11. See Upadhyay, *Writings*; Lipner, *Brahmabandhab Upadhyay*; Tennent, *Building Christianity on Indian Foundations*.

12. See Radhakrishnan, *Principal Upaniṣads*; *Brahma-Sūtra-Bhāṣya of Sri Śaṅkarācārya*.

in his seminal treatise, *On the Trinity* (*De Trinitate*), which is the primary source for the trinitarian *missio*.[13]

An attempt has been made in the fifth chapter to bring in perspectives from the trinitarian thoughts of Augustine and Upadhyay and to draw their implications for formulating a *missio Dei* theology informed by the doctrine of the Trinity. This chapter seeks to show the significance of the reception of a trinitarian *missio Dei* theology for a more holistic vision of mission in the diverse and pluralistic settings of India. It is important to recognize the trinitarian image of the Church and its mission as well as the need to bring this aspect to bear upon the life and mission of the emerging indigenous church movements in India. Capturing the trinitarian imagination is of great consequence to the Church's mission to the poor and the marginalized, and for continued dialogue in the pluralistic context of India. This chapter also attempts to argue, especially in view of Upadhyay's use of Advaita Vedanta philosophy, for the usefulness of the Sanskrit tradition as an instrument for contextualizing the Christian faith in India, particularly in view of the rising objections to it from Indian counter-theological paradigms. This chapter concludes with a call for the recognition of the need for majority world voices, including Indian Christian ones, to be heard in global theological and missiological conversations in light of the continuing expansion of the world Christian movement.

---

13. Augustine, *De Trinitate*.

1

Renewal of Trinitarian Theology and *Missio Dei*: Historical Trajectories

INTRODUCTION

THE TRINITY IS ARGUABLY the most central and foundational of all the doctrines of the Christian faith. The Trinity, which assumed an important place in the early development of Christian doctrine during the patristic and medieval eras, suffered a significant degree of marginalization during the Enlightenment and post-Enlightenment periods. The resurgence of trinitarian doctrine in the twentieth century was a significant development in the history of Christian theology. This modern renewal and articulation of the doctrine did not confine itself to the traditional interpretation followed in the ancient creeds. There has been a broadening of the horizon of trinitarian doctrine's implications into wider spheres of ecclesial and social concerns. One such striking development has been the rediscovery of the trinitarian foundation of Christian mission and its integration with the concept of the *missio Dei*. This new understanding of mission led to a shift from the traditional *ecclesiocentric* view of mission to a *trinitarian-centric* approach. This chapter attempts to trace the rebirth of trinitarian theology as well as the development of the idea of the *missio Dei* that developed alongside the modern trinitarian restoration.[1] The first part of this chapter reviews the trinitarian renewal as presented in the works of selected theologians from major Christian confessions. This study intends to serve

---

1. A shortened version of this chapter was published in *Dharma Deepika: A South Asian Journal of Missiological Research*. See Joseph, "Resurgence of Trinitarian Theology."

Renewal of Trinitarian Theology and Missio Dei: Historical Trajectories

as a historical context for the larger objective of this study to bring into conversation the Western and Indian traditions of trinitarian theology with reference to the concept of the *missio Dei*. The second part of the chapter will examine the expansion of the concept of the *missio Dei* in its broader trinitarian foundation.

TRINITARIAN THEOLOGY: FROM THE PATRISTIC PERIOD TO THE ENLIGHTENMENT

The first five centuries of the Christian Church were foundational for the development of trinitarian theology. Crucial christological foundations for trinitarian doctrine were formulated at Nicea in 325 in response to the christological controversies ignited by Monarchianism, Modalism, and Arianism. The debate set off by the fourth-century Christian heresy of Pneumatomachism (Macedonianism) led to the formulation of the Nicene Creed at the Council of Constantinople in 381, which became the benchmark of trinitarian orthodoxy. After the council, the Synod of Constantinople held in 382 affirmed in its synodical letter the consubstantiality and co-eternity of the Father, the Son, and the Holy Spirit.[2] The Council's affirmation in the full deity and equality of all the three persons of the Godhead marked a definitive chapter in the history of the development of trinitarian doctrine, which would serve as the norm for the future articulations of the Christian doctrine of God.[3] The doctrine of the Trinity received its classic formulations at the hands of the Cappadocian Fathers, Basil the Great, Gregory of Nyssa, and Gregory of Nazianzus.[4] While the Cappadocians represented primarily the Greek formulation of the doctrine of the Trinity, it was St. Augustine who was most influential in the development of the doctrine of the Trinity in Latin theology.[5]

---

2. See Tanner, *Decrees of the Ecumenical Councils*, 25, 28.

3. Grenz, *Rediscovering the Triune God*, 8.

4. See Gregory of Nyssa, *On the Holy Spirit*; *On the Holy Trinity*; *On "Not Three Gods"* (NPNF2/5:315–336); Gregory of Nazianzen, *Third Theological Oration*; *Fourth Theological Oration*; *Fifth Theological Oration* (NPNF2/7:301–328); Basil, *Letter 38* (NPNF2/8:137–141). The work of St. John of Damascus is considered the classic orthodox formulation of the doctrine of the Trinity in the Eastern Church. Drawing on the idea of perichoresis (circumincession or interpenetration, the mutual inter-penetration and indwelling within the threefold nature of the Trinity—God the Father, the Son, and the Holy Spirit) from Gregory of Nazianzus, John explored the concept more fully. See his *Exact Exposition of the Orthodox Faith* (Louth, *St. John Damascene*, 89–117).

5. Augustine, *The Trinity (De Trinitate)*, henceforth cited as Augustine, *De Trinitate*.

An Indian Trinitarian Theology of *Missio Dei*

Trinitarian thought was further developed and expressed in the Tome of Pope Damasus, the Athanasian Creed, and the council of Toledo. The *Tome of Pope Damasus* issued by Pope Damasus in 382 contains unequivocal affirmation of the deity and equality of the three persons of the Godhead.[6] The Athanasian Creed has exerted a great influence on the doctrine of the Trinity and became the standard for trinitarian orthodoxy in the West. It remarkably summarizes the affirmations of the councils of Nicea (325) Constantinople (381) Ephesus (431) and Chalcedon (451), and asserts the equality and deity of all the persons of the Trinity in the strictest Augustinian form.[7] The teaching of the Athanasian Creed is reflected in the creed of the local council of Toledo (Spain) held in 675 which has one of the clearest statements on the doctrine of the Trinity affirming the deity, equality, and the unity of the persons of the Trinity.[8] The doctrine of the Trinity continued to remain central in Christian thought and received further development through the works of Richard of St. Victor, St. Bonaventure, St. Thomas Aquinas, and the Reformers.[9]

The rise of rationalism and empirical science during the Enlightenment had a great impact on the Christian understanding of the doctrine of the Trinity. Although emphasis on human reason became the hallmark of this period, it was not considered inimical to theology at least in the early phase of the Enlightenment. In fact, human reason was understood to be an aid for the articulation of theology and for the defense of the

---

See also Clark, "De Trinitate," 91–102; Ayres, *Augustine and the Trinity*. An important Latin father who made a remarkable contribution to the development of the Western doctrine of the Trinity is Hilary of Poitiers often referred to as the "Athanasius of the West." Hilary, along with Marius Victorinus, contributed significantly to Augustine's mature pneumatology. See Barnes, "Latin Trinitarian Theology," 77; Beckwith, *Hilary of Poitiers on the Trinity*; Weedman, *Trinitarian Theology of Poitiers*. For Hilary's work on the Trinity, see his *De Trinitate* (NPNF2/9:40–233).

6. Rahner, *Teaching of the Catholic Church*, 90–91.
7. Schaff, *Creeds of Christendom*, 2:34–42.
8. Rahner, *Teaching of the Catholic Church*, 92, 95.
9. For original discussion of these theologians on the Trinity, see Richard of St. Victor, *Twelve Patriarchs*, 373–97; Richard of St. Victor, *On the Trinity*; Bonaventure, *Works of Bonaventure*, 1:49–54, 2:33–65; Aquinas, *Trinity*, 1a. 27–32; *Summa Theologiae*, 6; Calvin, *Institutes of the Christian Religion*, 64–88. See also Olson and Hall, *Trinity*, 67–79. It is not the purpose of this study to examine the issue of the filioque. For the filioque controversy, see Heron, "Who Proceedeth," 49–166; Meyendorff, *Byzantine Theology*, 91–102.

biblical revelation.[10] During the latter phase of the Enlightenment, reason increasingly became the guiding principle of life and the ultimate arbiter of truth. One of the consequences of this development was the rejection of the belief about revelation and inspiration of the Bible. The doctrine of the Trinity, which hitherto had been grounded firmly in this faith and conviction of the Scripture, was relegated to the realm of the irrational and was regarded as incompatible with modernity.[11] Another major development during this period was the rise of Unitarianism in the sixteenth century in Europe and later spread to America in the eighteenth century. Unitarianism rejected the Trinity as it found the unity of God incompatible with the plurality of the Trinity.[12]

Enlightenment philosophy reached its pinnacle in the thought of Immanuel Kant, who sought to understand religion in terms of morality. The Christian faith, according to Kant, makes sense only "if we read a moral meaning into [its] article of faith."[13] In such a scheme of thought, the doctrine of the Trinity had no place, and it served no practical purposes. Therefore, for Kant, "the doctrine of the Trinity, taken literally, has *no practical relevance at all*."[14] Similarly, Herman Samuel Reimarus's application of the historical-critical method in the study of the New Testament as a mere historical document bereft of any supernatural components eliminated divine revelation and reduced Jesus to merely an exemplary moral teacher. Reimarus understood the Holy Spirit not as person, but as the extraordinary gift of God and the Trinity as irrational.[15] This reductionist stance towards the Christian faith rejected traditional approaches to the doctrine of the Trinity.

---

10. Powell, *Trinity in German Thought*, 60–61; Marmion and Nieuwenhove, *Introduction to the Trinity*, 142.

11. Powell, *Trinity in German Thought*, 61.

12. Welch, *In This Name*, 23–29. See also Channing, "Unitarian Christianity," 371–75; Wilbur, *History of Unitarianism*, 1:337–49. For a treatment of the trinitarian doctrine by Reformed theologians between 1520 to ca. 1725, see Mueller, *Post-Reformation Dogmatics*. For the rise of deistic and Unitarian attack on the Trinity, see Mueller, *Post-Reformation Dogmatics*, 103–35.

13. Kant, *Religion and Rational Theology*, 264. See also, Grenz, *Rediscovering the Triune God*, 16.

14. Kant, *Religion and Rational Theology*, 264; see also 167.

15. Reimarus, *Fragments*, 91–98; Marmion and Nieuwenhove, *Introduction to the Trinity*, 143–44. See Powell, *Trinity in German Thought*, 64–69.

An Indian Trinitarian Theology of *Missio Dei*

In this context, it is important to note the impact of the theology of Friedrich Schleiermacher. Many have seen the apparent relegation of the classical doctrine of the Christian faith to the end of Schleiermacher's magnum opus *The Christian Faith* as evidence of his rather short treatment of the Trinity.[16] Moltmann maintains that this marginalization of the Trinity reflects Schleiermacher's understanding of "Christianity as a 'monotheistic mode of belief.'"[17] Yet, there are those who believe that one need not take Schleiermacher's fragmentary treatment of the Trinity in *The Christian Faith* as an oversight on his part. In fact, they see the trinitarian discussion at the end to be important as a conclusion to the entire delineation on the Christian faith.[18] Interestingly, Schleiermacher himself calls the Trinity "the coping-stone of Christian doctrine."[19] He is averse to distinguishing between the being of God in himself (immanent Trinity) and the being of God in relation to the world (economic Trinity). For Schleiermacher, God as revealed in history and related to the world ought to be the object of theological study. He is reluctant to indulge in speculative thinking about the internal distinctions within the being of God. Therefore, he finds misplaced the orthodox separation of the immanent and economic aspect of the Godhead.[20] Does this imply that Schleiermacher posits a stance beyond the immanent and economic Trinity? Claude Welch finds in Schleiermacher a third alternative, namely essential Trinity, which includes the essential "character of the divine distinctions" of "*homoousios*, coeternity and coequality, and such terms as *hypostasis* and *persona*."[21]

Ironically, unlike the theologian Schleiermacher, it was philosopher George W. F. Hegel who is believed to have played a significant role in preserving the doctrine of the Trinity in the nineteenth century. Hegel's

---

16. Schleiermacher, *Christian Faith*, 738–51.

17. Moltmann, *Trinity and the Kingdom*, 3.

18. Williams, *Schleiermacher the Theologian*, 139; Fiorenza, "Schleiermacher's Understanding of God as Triune," 176; Grenz, *Rediscovering the Triune God*, 18–20. For a recent strong defense of Schleiermacher as a trinitarian theologian, see Poe, *Essential Trinitarianism*.

19. Schleiermacher, *Christian Faith*, 739.

20. Grenz, *Rediscovering the Triune God*, 22; Williams, *Schleiermacher the Theologian*, 153; Schleiermacher, *Christian Faith*, 748.

21. Welch, *In This Name*, 294. According to Schleiermacher, the essential fact of the doctrine of the Trinity is the coexistence of the being of God revealed to us and the being of God in himself. In his own words, it is "to equate as definitely as possible the Divine Essence considered as thus united to human nature with the Divine Essence it itself" (Schleiermacher, *Christian Faith*, 739).

interpretation of the Trinity is closely linked with his teaching on God as Spirit (*Geist*). God's nature is fundamentally spiritual, which according to Hegel, is found in the Christian revelation of God as the Father, the Son, and the Spirit. The whole of the Godhead is essentially Spirit. "It is this doctrine of the Trinity which raises Christianity above the other religions."[22] Hegel's description of the inner relationships of the Trinity has had a significant influence on the renewal of trinitarian theology, particularly on the immanent Trinity.[23] "God is thus grasped as what he is for himself within himself; God [the Father] makes himself an object for himself (the Son); then, in this object, God remains the undivided essence within this differentiation of himself within himself, and in this differentiation of himself loves himself, i.e., remains identical with himself—this is God as Spirit."[24] While the immanence of God is important, the historical aspect of God is equally important. Therefore, as noted by Samuel Powell, for Hegel, "the being of God cannot be separated from the historical process of the world."[25] From this understanding, flows the integral relation of the Spirit with the world, and consequently the economic Trinity, God as manifest in history. Powell succinctly depicts Hegel's contribution to trinitarian renewal: "Hegelian motifs in Trinitarian thought have survived and have resurfaced in the twentieth century in unexpected ways . . . looking back, it is clear that the fact that there is any contemporary interest in the doctrine of the Trinity at all owes a great deal to Hegel."[26]

MODERN RENEWAL OF TRINITARIAN THEOLOGY

One of the most remarkable developments in the theological landscape of the twentieth century was the rehabilitation of the doctrine of the Trinity. Contrary to the marginalization of Trinity that characterized theological trends of the Enlightenment era, the revitalization of this classic doctrine was propelled by significant contributions by Protestant, Catholic, and Orthodox theologians. This section examines briefly the contributions of Karl Barth, Karl Rahner, and Vladimir Lossky. These theologians are important

---

22. Hegel, *Lectures on the Philosophy of World History*, 51; Grenz, *Rediscovering the Triune God*, 27–28.

23. Grenz, *Rediscovering the Triune God*, 28.

24. Hegel, *Lectures on the Philosophy of Religion*, 1:126.

25. Powell, *Trinity in German Thought*, 139–40; Grenz, *Rediscovering the Triune God*, 29.

26. Powell, *Trinity in German Thought*, 140.

for the historical roles they played in the revitalization of the trinitarian doctrine in modern times.

Karl Barth

Karl Barth stands out among those who sought to restore the central role of trinitarian thought in Christian theology. He was, arguably, the single most influential Protestant theologian of the twentieth century and a trailblazer of the renewal of trinitarian theology in the modern period. Significantly, Barth made the doctrine of the Trinity central to his *Church Dogmatics*, and he sought to construct his doctrinal expositions on the basis of this fundamental dogma of the Christian faith.[27]

Barth developed his theology of revelation in the context of Protestant liberalism which, he says, "fell prey to the absolutism with which the man of that period made himself the centre and measure and goal of all things."[28] Here theology was subjected to all that pertains to humanity which became the reference point in discourse on God and revelation. This theological method originated, "in medieval mysticism and the humanism of the Renaissance," and was developed in Descartes (1596–1650). It thrived in Protestantism under the influence of the Enlightenment, "in the anthropological and humanistic theology of the nineteenth century," and found its highpoint in Schleiermacher and his adherents.[29] The task ahead of Barth was to liberate theology from this anthropocentrism of the day and ground it in the self-disclosure, the revelation of God. In seeking to restore the theocentrism of theology, Barth reasoned that it is from God and God's prior act and the divine self-disclosure that theology emerges, and not from the initiative of human being who is merely the recipient of the divine revelation, the Word of God. The Word of God forms the only foundation for all theological formulation which takes place "in the life and the activity of the church."[30] Thus, Barth seeks to recover the foundation (the Word of God) as well as the context (the Church) of theologizing.

Barth's seminal thoughts on the Trinity are found in its relation to revelation. He begins his exposition of the doctrine of the Trinity from the premise that "the biblical concept of revelation is itself the root of the

27. At the outset of his exposition of the Trinity, Barth explains the importance of the doctrine in the *Church Dogmatics*. See Barth, *CD* 1/1:295–304.

28. Barth, *CD* 1/2:293; Mueller, *Karl Barth*, 51.

29. Mueller, *Karl Barth*, 51.

30. Grenz, *Rediscovering the Triune God*, 35–36. Barth, *CD* 1/1:17.

doctrine of the Trinity."³¹ Trinity is grounded in the self-disclosure of God. Barth asserts, "God reveals Himself as the Lord, or what this statement is meant to describe, and therefore revelation itself as attested by Scripture, we call the root of the doctrine of the Trinity. . . . The doctrine of the Trinity is the interpretation of revelation or that revelation is the basis of the doctrine of the Trinity."³² How is revelation the foundation for the doctrine of the Trinity? The three forms of the Word of God: the Revealed Word, the Written Word, and the Proclaimed Word in its indissoluble unity are central to Barth's discussion on the doctrine of the Word of God. He employs the triune form of revelation as an analogy to Trinity about which he states thus: "the doctrine of the Word of God is itself the only analogy to . . . the doctrine of the triunity of God. In the fact that we can substitute for revelation, Scripture and proclamation the names of the divine persons Father, Son, and Holy Spirit and *vice versa*."³³ This correspondence between revelation and the Trinity, for Barth, stems from the fact that God, the subject of revelation, the Revealer is "identical with His act in revelation and also identical with its effect." Thus, to use Barth's ternary, God is the *Revealer* (the subject), *Revelation* (the act), and *Revealedness* (the effect).³⁴

Barth applies the distinction between the Father, the Son, and the Holy Spirit of the Trinity to the triune form of revelation. The Revealer, the ground of revelation, is distinct from Revelation—signifying "absolutely something new in relation to the mystery of the revealer"—corresponding to the distinction between the Father and the Son. Just as the Spirit is distinct from the Father and the Son, so is Revealedness differentiated from the Revealer and Revelation "as the result of the first two" and constitutes the third distinction of the three-fold form of revelation. Thus, in Barth's analogy, the Father is the speaker, "the word which is the word of the speaker" is the Son, and the Holy Spirit is the meaning of both the speaker and the speaker's Word.³⁵

While Barth makes a clear distinction within the Trinity, he prefers to use "mode (or way) of being" instead of "person."³⁶ Barth's preference for

---

31. Barth, *CD* 1/1:334. See Mueller, *Karl Barth*, 63.

32. Barth, *CD* 1/1:307–12. See Bromiley, *Introduction to the Theology of Karl Barth*, 14.

33. Barth, *CD* 1/1:121.

34. Barth, *CD* 1/1:295–96.

35. Barth, *CD* 1/1:363–64. See also Marmion and Nieuwenhove, *Introduction to the Trinity*, 158.

36. Barth, *CD* 1/1:359.

mode of being has elicited strong criticism, and he has often been accused of modalism. However, the emphasis on the *mode of being* is seen as a counter to subordinationism and underlines the unity of the Trinity without sacrificing the distinctions. Barth says, "we mean by the doctrine of the Trinity the proposition that He whom the Christian Church calls God and proclaims as God, the God who has revealed Himself according to the witness of Scripture, is the same in unimpaired unity and yet also the same thrice in different ways unimpaired distinction."[37] Both the unity (oneness) and triunity (threeness) of God are paramount for Barth. "The God who reveals Himself according to Scripture is One in three distinctive modes of being subsisting in their mutual relations: Father, Son, and Holy Spirit."[38] There is within the Trinity the communion, the perichoresis "according to which all three, without forfeiture or mutual dissolution of independence, reciprocally interpenetrate each other and inexist [sic] in one another."[39] This demonstrates a clear distinction within the Trinity and it should shield Barth from the charge of modalism. Barth's trinitarian theology has been subjected to criticism for the seeming tendency to modalism and for being more monotheistic than trinitarian.[40] Despite these criticisms, Barth's contribution as an initiator of the modern trinitarian renewal is undeniable.

Karl Rahner

Karl Rahner was perhaps one of the most prolific and influential Roman Catholic theologians of the twentieth century. Rahner, although, did not write as extensively as Karl Barth did on the doctrine of the Trinity, his trinitarian writings have nevertheless been influential enough to make Rahner one of the great catalysts in twentieth century trinitarian revitalization.[41] His single most historic contribution to the contemporary

---

37. Barth, *CD* 1/1:307. See Mueller, *Karl Barth*, 65–66.

38. Barth, *CD* 1/1:348.

39. Barth, *CD* 1/1:396.

40. For criticism of Barth for what appears to be modalistic tendencies in his trinitarian theology, see Hodgson, *Doctrine of the Trinity*, 229; Baillie, *God was in Christ*, 134–35; Moltmann, *Trinity and the Kingdom*, 141–44. For Barth's own rejection of modalism, see Barth, *CD* 1/1:382.

41. Rahner's most important work on the Trinity remains his *Trinity*. The other works that deal with the Trinity or are relevant to the doctrine are: Rahner, *Foundations of Christian Faith*, 133–37; "Theos in the New Testament," in *Theological Investigations* (*TI*), 1:79–148; "Remarks on the Dogmatic Treatise 'De Trinitate,'" *TI*, 4:77–102; "Observations on the Doctrine of God in Catholic Dogmatics," *TI*, 9:127–144; "Oneness and

Renewal of Trinitarian Theology and Missio Dei: Historical Trajectories

trinitarian resurgence is what has come to be known widely as *Rahner's Rule*: "The 'economic' Trinity is the 'immanent' Trinity and the 'immanent' Trinity is the 'economic' Trinity."[42] In this context, Peter Phan observes that Rahner's trinitarian theology emerges from the human experience of God's revelation in history, what he calls "an ascending or 'from below' theology." Methodologically, says Peter Phan, our understanding of the inner being, the trinitarian life of God (immanent Trinity) is made possible in formulating a trinitarian theology through the self-disclosure of the Father in history through the incarnation of the Son and the bestowal of the Holy Spirit (economic Trinity).[43]

Rahner deplores the isolation of the doctrine of the Trinity from the life of the Church. The fact of God as triune in God's being and God's relation to the world seemed to have lost its resonance in the lived Christian experience. The doctrine of the Trinity was driven away from the centrality of the Church's life and was consigned to the rather isolated domain of Christian dogma. Consequently, the Trinity was banished, as it were, from Christian life, faith, and practice.[44] This, according to Rahner, has led Christians to be practically "almost mere 'monotheists.'" The marginalization of the Trinity from Christian faith and practice is such that Rahner concedes, "should the doctrine of the Trinity have to be dropped as false, the major part of religious literature could well remain virtually unchanged."[45]

Rahner attributes the irrelevance of trinitarian doctrine in Christian life to the influence of Neo-Scholasticism that "had produced a 'unitarian' Christology and theology of grace."[46] He also holds the influence of Augustine and Thomas Aquinas responsible for the isolation of the Trinity. Aquinas treated God under two treatises, *On the One God* and *On the Triune God*, and assigned primacy to the divine essence in his study of God. This method of apparent distinction between the two treatises later prevailed in Neo-Scholasticism leading to greater emphasis on the being of God (immanent Trinity) and lesser importance on the divine persons

---

Threefoldness in Discussion with Islam," *TI*, 18:105–121; "Trinity, Divine," 295; "Trinity in Theology," 308.

42. Rahner, *Trinity*, 22. For an exposition on Rahner's Rule, see Phan, "Mystery of Grace and Salvation," 197–201.

43. Phan, "Mystery of Grace and Salvation," 194. See also Holzer, "Karl Rahner, Hans Urs von Balthasar," 319.

44. Rahner, *Trinity*, 10–15. See also LaCugna, "Introduction," ix.

45. Rahner, *Trinity*, 10–11.

46. LaCugna, "Introduction," ix.

An Indian Trinitarian Theology of *Missio Dei*

and relations (economic Trinity). This, according to Rahner, has led to an abstract approach that separated the Trinity from salvation history. Augustine's psychological analogy of the Trinity, according to Rahner, "neglects the experience of the Trinity in the economy of salvation in favor of a seemingly almost gnostic speculation about what goes on in the inner life of God."[47]

Rahner opposes positing any gap between God *in se* (immanent Trinity) and God *pro nobis* or God *for us* (economic Trinity). As noted above, excessive concentration on the immanent Trinity (the eternal being of God) has resulted in disconnection between the Trinity and the economy of salvation. Rahner, through his axiom, seeks to revitalize the Trinity and establish the relationship between the Trinity and Christian life. The revelation, he maintains, points to the fact that Trinity is "a mystery of *salvation*," and salvation has meaning only when it is related to "this primordial mystery of Christianity."[48] Rahner seeks to recover the integral relation of the Trinity and salvation history and to counteract the marginalization that he believes the doctrine suffered in the development of scholastic theology. He seeks to "show how the mystery of the Trinity is for us a mystery of salvation." Rahner's Rule is the "*basic thesis* which establishes this connection between the treatises and presents the Trinity *as* a mystery of salvation."[49] Thus, Rahner contends that God's self-disclosure in salvation history is "*no other than* or *exactly the same* as the Trinity of Father, Son, and Spirit in their eternal mutual relations," the immanent Trinity. There is no God behind the God who is revealed in history, rather there is only one Triune God revealed "to us as Father, Son, and Spirit, exactly as they are related to each other in themselves."[50] The influence of Rahner's Rule upon contemporary trinitarian thought is reflected in the wide-ranging responses it has received. Rahner's attempt to retrieve the place of Trinity in salvation history has helped to set the agenda for much of the subsequent work in this area.[51]

---

47. Rahner, *Trinity*, 16–18; Rahner, *Foundations of Christian Faith*, 135; LaCugna, "Introduction," ix; Ables, "Decline and Fall of the West?," 164. For Augustine's psychological analysis of the Trinity, see Augustine, *De Trinitate* 9.2–3 (272–74); 10.17–19 (300–2); 14.21 (388).

48. Rahner, *Trinity*, 21; Olson and Hall, *Trinity*, 98.

49. Rahner, *Trinity*, 21–22.

50. Phan, "Mystery of Grace and Salvation," 197–98; Linicum, "Economy and Immanence," 113.

51. A discussion on the critical responses to Rahner's Rule is beyond the scope of

Renewal of Trinitarian Theology and Missio Dei: Historical Trajectories

Vladimir Lossky

The contribution of both Protestantism and Roman Catholicism in the modern trinitarian revival represented by Karl Barth and Karl Rahner, as discussed above, has been widely acknowledged. Regrettably, the historic trinitarian theological tradition of the Eastern Church has not at times been given adequate recognition in the modern Western discussions of the trinitarian renaissance.

Since the fall of the Soviet Union in the late 1980s and early 1990s, the Orthodox Church and its theological tradition have become more visible and widely known in the West. Trinitarian doctrine, for the Eastern Orthodox Church, has been "the unshakable foundation of all religious thought, of all piety, of all spiritual life, of all experience."[52] Therefore, it is not quite accurate to speak of a "renewal" of trinitarian theology in the Eastern Church, since the Trinity has always been one of the most fundamental aspects of Eastern theology. Given this indispensability of the doctrine of the Trinity in the Eastern tradition, no study on trinitarian renewal can overlook the rich and profound trinitarian thoughts of Eastern theology. Fred Sanders, in this regard, points out two reasons for the recognition of Eastern theology in trinitarian revival: "Frist, no other Christian tradition is so explicit, even flamboyant, on matters trinitarian as are the Orthodox, and second, the churches of the East and West have the vexed matter of the *filioque* clause to settle."[53]

The name that stands out in Eastern trinitarian thought of the twentieth century and the one that befittingly deserves mention along with Barth and Rahner is that of Vladimir Nikolayevich Lossky. Lossky was an influential theologian of the Eastern Orthodox Church who died rather early at the age of 54. Having been exiled from Russia in 1922 along with his family, Lossky received his education in medieval philosophy in Prague and in Paris. He was well-grounded in contemporary philosophy, the spirituality of the fathers and in the Orthodox theological tradition.[54] Two aspects in the thought of Lossky are significant for current trinitarian discussions: apophasis and the Eastern emphasis on the trinitarian persons.

---

this brief survey. For more on this, see Jowers, "Exposition and Critique of Karl Rahner's Axiom," 165–200; Rauser, "Rahner's Rule," 82–94; Cary, "On Behalf of Classical Trinitarianism," 365–405.

52. Lossky, *Mystical Theology of the Eastern Church*, 65.
53. Sanders, *Image of the Immanent Trinity*, 49.
54. See Schmemann, "In Memoriam," 47–48.

An Indian Trinitarian Theology of *Missio Dei*

Apophasis (negative theology), an essential feature of Eastern theology, occupies a central place in Lossky's trinitarian thought. Apophasis is grounded in the assumption of the fundamental incomprehensibility of God through any positive attributes. Rational exercises, human language, and logic *cannot* fully express the mystery of God. The only way one can speak about God and divine mystery is in apophatic terms. Lossky asserts that one can approach the mystery of the Trinity, only with a "change of spirit" and penitence (*metanoia*), and in a spirit of humility and ignorance (*ignorantia*). Therefore, what is essential is a return to a Christian apophaticism, which would transform "rational speculation into a contemplation of the mystery of the Trinity."[55]

Does the apophatic affirmation of the unknowability of God completely rule out the possibility of knowing God in any sense whatsoever? Lossky advances an answer to this dilemma through the well-known Eastern theology of *essence* (*ousia*) and *energies* (*energeia*). God in God's essential nature (in divine essence) is inaccessible. Following the Greek fathers, especially the theology of Gregory of Palamas, Lossky contends that there is "in God an ineffable distinction, other than that between His essence and His persons, according to which He is, under different aspects, both totally inaccessible and at the same time accessible."[56] This distinction is between what the Eastern fathers called *divine essence* and *divine energies* (divine operations) both of which are inseparable from each other in the being of God. While God is inaccessible and unknowable in God's *essence*, God is both accessible and communicable in God's *energies* "in which He goes forth from Himself, manifests, communicates, and gives Himself."[57] The distinction between the essence and energies reveals the two aspects of the Trinity. The immanent Trinity is God in God's essence. The energies represent the economic Trinity, "that mode of existence of the Trinity which is outside of its inaccessible essence."[58] The divine energies demonstrate the accessibility and knowability of God. In the economic manifestation of the Trinity, "the Father appears as the possessor of the attribute which is manifested, the Son as the manifestation of the Father, the Holy Spirit as He who manifests."[59]

---

55. Lossky, *Mystical Theology of the Eastern Church*, 48–50.
56. Lossky, *Mystical Theology of the Eastern Church*, 70. For Gregory Palamas's distinction between the theology of *essence* and *energy*, see Palamas, *Triads*, 93–96.
57. Lossky, *Mystical Theology of the Eastern Church*, 70.
58. Lossky, *Mystical Theology of the Eastern Church*, 73.
59. Lossky, *Mystical Theology of the Eastern Church*, 82–83.

Second, in consonance with Rahner's concern as well as following the Greek trinitarian thought, Lossky stresses the plurality of the Trinity. Over against "the unity of the divine essence" emphasized by the West, Eastern theology starts with the three hypostases "seeing in them the one nature" and thus emphasizing the plurality of the Trinity.[60] Drawing on St. Basil's judgment, Lossky attempts to show that the Eastern position is consistent with the Scripture and the triune distinctions in the baptismal formula.[61] Interestingly, he is prepared to concede equal legitimacy to the stance of both the West and the East so long as caution is exercised in each paradigm. Accordingly, he insists that the West should "not attribute to the essence a supremacy over the three persons, nor the [East] to the three persons a supremacy over the common nature."[62] Lossky warns that disruption of "the balance of this antinomy between nature and persons, absolutely different and absolutely identical at the same time," could potentially generate propensity either towards Sabellian Unitarianism of rational speculations or towards tritheism.[63] Nevertheless, Lossky grants more primacy to the Greek Fathers's articulation of the "relationship between the divine persons" which would restore "our deifying relationship with the life of the Trinity [to] its rightful place."[64] Following the Eastern Fathers's insistence on the monarchy of the Father, Lossky argues that the Eastern trinitarian doctrine is more concrete and personal than the Western stance. The Eastern emphasis of absolute equality in every respect and "the infinite connaturality of Three Infinite Ones," rules out subordination and preserves the "mysterious equivalence" in the Godhead.[65] Lossky's work has contributed

---

60. Lossky, *Mystical Theology of the Eastern Church*, 52, 56. Ables, "Decline and Fall of the West?," 165.

61. For the views of Basil the Great on *hypostases* and *essence*, see *Letter* 38 and *Letter* 125 (NPNF2/8:137–141, 194–96).

62. Lossky, *Mystical Theology of the Eastern Church*, 56.

63. Lossky, *Mystical Theology of the Eastern Church*, 57.

64. Ables, "Decline and Fall of the West?," 165. The trinitarian relationship here has an underlying sense of the doctrine of co-inherence or perichoresis of the divine persons, which is an important teaching of the Eastern Church. Although the concept of perichoresis was developed at a much later time by John of Damascus (675–749), the idea (co-inherence) is found in Gregory of Nazianzen and Basil the Great. See Gregory of Nazianzen, *Fifth Theological Oration* 31:14 (NPNF2/7:322); Basil, *Letter* 38:8 (NPNF2/8:141).

65. Lossky, *Mystical Theology of the Eastern Church*, 62–63; *Orthodox Theology*, 46–47. See Giles, *Trinity & Subordinationism*, 98–99. For Cappadocian Fathers' views on the monarchy of the Father, see Basil the Great, *Letters* 38:4; 236:2, 6 (NPNF2/8:138–39,

significantly to the retrieval of the Eastern trinitarian theological tradition by Western theologians.

CONTEMPORARY TRINITARIAN DEVELOPMENTS

The period from the second half of the twentieth century until today, roughly seventy years, has witnessed a remarkable variety of approaches to and engagements with the doctrine of the Trinity. The movement of trinitarian renewal that began with Barth, Rahner, and Lossky subsequently gained momentum through the works of theologians across many Christian traditions. In critical engagement with the theology of these three, new trajectories were opened up, bringing trinitarian theology into a wider theological landscape. Karl Barth remains the most dominant figure whose thoughts continue to stimulate reflection on the doctrine of the Trinity across confessional boundaries. Noting Barth's influence, Ted Peters writes, "The major contributors to the contemporary rethinking of the doctrine of the Trinity either extend principles already proffered by Barth or else follow lines of thought that parallel his *Church Dogmatics*."[66] The ensuing section will discuss trinitarian theology from a cross-section of theologians who have made significant contributions to our understanding of God's relation to the world in God's trinitarian nature, and thereby to the contemporary trinitarian renaissance. The following section will explore the trinitarian thoughts of Wolfhart Pannenberg, Robert Jenson, John Zizioulas, and Colin Gunton. This will be followed by a rather detailed discussion on the thoughts of Jürgen Moltmann, Eberhard Jüngel, Leonardo Boff, and Catherine LaCugna whose thoughts, in my view, have significant bearing on the contemporary discourse on a trinitarian theology of mission.

Wolfhart Pannenberg and Robert Jenson

Wolfhart Pannenberg pursued his trinitarian discourse in continuation with the modern trinitarian conversation initiated by Karl Barth and Karl Rahner. Pannenberg makes a case for the universal orientation of theology and views it as a public task.[67] He attempts to base his trinitarian teaching on revelation and contends that our knowledge about Trinity is derived from revelation in history. The Triune God is revealed in God's revelation

---

276–78); Gregory of Nazianzen, *Oration* 40:43; 42:15 (NPNF2/7:375–76, 385).

66. Peters, *God as Trinity*, 82.

67. Pannenberg, *Systematic Theology*, 1:x–xi; *Basic Questions in Theology*, 1:199–200.

Renewal of Trinitarian Theology and Missio Dei: Historical Trajectories

through Christ in history as the economic (historical) Trinity. Further, in seeking to ground the doctrine of the Trinity in revelation, Pannenberg bases it on Christ, more importantly, on Christ's message of the rule of God.[68] Elsewhere, he notes that "God's being and existence cannot be conceived apart from his rule."[69] The execution of God's rule takes place in the Son, the Risen Lord, who is given lordship over all. This lordship is marked by mutuality in the relationship of the Father and the Son where there is a handing over and handing back of lordship from the Father to the Son and from the Son to the Father. This reciprocity of the divine relations has implications for the being of God and self-distinction within the being of God.[70] Pannenberg further traces this divine mutuality in the passion, resurrection, and lordship of the Son where all the trinitarian persons are at work.[71] As concluded by Powell, "the ground of the doctrine of the Trinity" is found in this relation of the Son to the Father and the Spirit.[72]

The leading American Lutheran theologian Robert Jenson, like Jürgen Moltmann and Pannenberg, attempts to locate trinitarian theology in salvation history. According to Jenson, God's self-disclosure has a historical foundation in the biblical narratives of God's work displayed in history and in the Christ event. Here God is not only identified *by* events in Israel's history (Exodus) and in the resurrection of Christ, but God is also identified *with* those events as the Triune God named specifically as Yahweh in the Old Testament and Father, Son, and Holy Spirit in the New Testament.[73] God's self-disclosure is characterized by a temporal character evidenced in God's identification by "specific temporal actions" within certain "temporal communities," and in the possibility of God in Christ and the participation of the Son in human history.[74] This participation, for Jenson, is un-

---

68. Pannenberg, *Systematic Theology*, 1:304.

69. Pannenberg, *Theology and the Kingdom of God*, 55.

70. Pannenberg, *Systematic Theology*, 1:312–13; Powell, *Trinity in German Thought*, 206

71. Pannenberg, *Systematic Theology*, 1:313–15.

72. Powell, *Trinity in German Thought*, 204, 206; Pannenberg, *Systematic Theology*, 1:312–15.

73. Jenson, *Systematic Theology*, 1:59–60. See also Jenson, *Systematic Theology*, 42–46; Jenson, *Triune Identity*, 5–16; Grenz, *Rediscovering the Triune God*, 108. God is identified by proper names and God's acts in history both in the Exodus and in the Resurrection. Thus, for Jenson, God is "the one who rescued Israel from Egypt" and "whoever raised Jesus from the dead" (Jenson, *Systematic Theology*, 1:44).

74. Grenz, *Rediscovering the Triune God*, 110; Jenson, *Systematic Theology* 1:46.

like the teaching of divine immunity to temporality as found in Hellenic metaphysics.[75] The biblical God is open to relation beyond himself and, therefore, can "accommodate other persons" to himself without distorting his life or losing his triune identity as the Father, the Son, and the Spirit.[76]

John Zizioulas and Colin Gunton

The ontology of the personhood grounded on the Trinity formulated by the Cappadocian fathers forms an important premise for the trinitarian thought of John Zizioulas, the Eastern Orthodox metropolitan of Pergamon. In this ontological revolution of the fathers, says Zizioulas, "the being of God is identified with the person" through the concept of hypostasis.[77] Zizioulas notes that the "experience of *ecclesial* being" of the fathers played a vital role in their articulation of the ontology of the Trinity. This experience revealed to them the fact that "the being of God could be known only through personal relationships and personal love. Being means life, and life means *communion*."[78] The Cappadocians discovered that communion (*koinonia*) signifies the unity of the Godhead because the trinitarian oneness "lies in the *koinonia* or communion of the three persons."[79] The dimension of *otherness* reflected in the *threeness* (distinction) of the Trinity, for Zizioulas, is *constitutive* of unity. This otherness in the Trinity is *absolute*, where the three persons of the Godhead are absolutely different. The "otherness is *ontological*" with the Trinity. Yet, "communion and otherness" are reconciled within the Trinity.[80] The dimension of communion and otherness in Trinity, Zizioulas maintains, offers a model for peace and reconciliation in a world of difference, respect for creation (ecological concerns) and its preservation.[81] This understanding of the Trinity has implications for the life of the Church and the wider areas of human society. Zizioulas is a leading Orthodox voice ecumenically, and his works have been very significant in the renewal of modern trinitarian theology.

The late British systematic theologian Colin Gunton adopted Zizioulas's trinitarian insights "as a comprehensive paradigm for

75. Peters, *God as Trinity*, 129.
76. Jenson, *Systematic Theology* 1:225–26.
77. Zizioulas, *Being as Communion*, 41.
78. Zizioulas, *Being as Communion*, 16–17.
79. Grenz, *Rediscovering the Triune God*, 138.
80. Zizioulas, "Communion and Otherness," 352–53.
81. Zizioulas, "Communion and Otherness," 352–53, 359.

developing relationally based visions of personhood, Church community, and politics."[82] Taking his cue from Zizioulas, Gunton holds that a Christian ontology grounded in the doctrine of the Trinity is essential for the Church as a community. This ontology will be an alternative to the monistic and hierarchical models of the philosophical world and the challenges posed by modern conditions. Gunton is in full agreement with the Cappadocian fathers that the most fundamental thing about God's being is the personal communion of the Godhead. For him, the personal communion within the Trinity is the ontological foundation of the Church.[83] Gunton identifies four essential concepts in the doctrine of being as communion which are integrally bound to each other: *person, relation, otherness,* and *freedom.* These dimensions are located in the Trinity, in the communion of the Father, the Son, and the Holy Spirit. The institution that is called to reflect this divine communion on the earth is the Church.[84] Given his social approach to the doctrine of Trinity in *The Promise of Trinitarian Theology,* Gunton extends the significance of the communion and relational (otherness) aspects of the Trinity beyond the religious domains to the social spheres of life in human society and creation.[85]

Jürgen Moltmann

One of the most remarkable developments has been in the area of Trinity and God's relation to the world represented in God's mission. God's relation to the world seen in the context of God's mission in the sending of the Son and the Holy Spirit engenders the question of God's impassibility and relationality. Divine impassibility (*apatheia*) is a Greek philosophical concept according to which suffering, feelings, and passivity are incompatible with the nature of God. The Greek philosophical concept of divine impassibility influenced early Christian theology from the second century on, and the Church has historically affirmed this doctrine. However, the twentieth century witnessed a growing abandonment of the early Christian inheritance of the doctrine of divine impassibility and the advocacy of the doctrine of divine suffering and relationality across theological traditions.[86] The relationship of the Tri-

---

82. Ables, "Decline and Fall of the West?," 169.
83. Gunton, "Church on Earth," 53, 66. See Chia, "Trinity and Ontology," 453.
84. Gunton, *Promise of Trinitarian Theology*, 11, 12.
85. Gunton, *Promise of Trinitarian Theology*, 12, 13.
86. Bauckham, "'Only the Suffering God can Help,'" 6–8. See also Mozley, *Impassibility of God*, 127–66, 167–72.

An Indian Trinitarian Theology of *Missio Dei*

une God to the world and humanity received a new impetus in the works of contemporary trinitarian theologians.

Rejecting the metaphysical concept of divine *apatheia*, the German theologian Jürgen Moltmann makes divine pathos central to his delineation of the doctrine of the Trinity. He takes the history of Jesus—salvation history—as his point of departure in developing the doctrine of the Trinity. The history of Jesus is part of the history of the trinitarian persons and is related in trinitarian terms in the New Testament. Therefore, Moltmann begins from the presupposition that the "*New Testament talks about God by proclaiming in narrative the relationships of the Father, the Son and the Spirit, which are relationships of fellowship and are open to the world.*"[87] God's relation to the world as well as God's trinitarian fellowship is situated in the cross and the suffering of God, what Moltmann calls "a doctrine of *theopathy*."[88] The cross, for him, is the key to understanding the Trinity, and the cross "stands at the heart of the trinitarian being of God."[89] This is an innovative idea that stems from Moltmann's theology of the pathos of God.

Moltmann sees the cross as signifying the abandonment of the Son to suffering by the Father as well as the separation of the Father and the Son. The separation of the Father from the Son in the divine forsakenness (godforsakenness) is something that takes place in the inner being of God himself, a "stasis within God" which sets "God against God."[90] Here both godforsakenness (of the Son) and godlessness (of the world) meet at the cross. Humanity is not *godforsaken* in their godlessness, because the Father has forsaken his Son in order that the godless would be justified and accepted into the communion of the Trinity.[91] Yet, "in the forsakenness of the Son the Father also forsakes himself. In the surrender of the Son the Father also surrenders himself," albeit not in a *patripassian* sense.[92] One can understand what happened on the cross between the Father and the Son only in trinitarian terms.

In trinitarian interpretation of the cross event, love and unity become the underlying principle, as it were, in the passion of the Triune God. The cross represents God's self-communication in which God goes out of himself

---

87. Moltmann, *Trinity and the Kingdom*, 64. Emphasis in original.
88. Moltmann, *Trinity and the Kingdom*, 24–25, 75.
89. Moltmann, *Crucified God*, 207.
90. Moltmann, *Crucified God*, 151–52.
91. Moltmann, *Crucified God*, 242–43, 276.
92. Moltmann, *Crucified God*, 243.

Renewal of Trinitarian Theology and Missio Dei: Historical Trajectories

and gives God's own self to the world. This is the *self-giving* of the Son as well as the Father's *giving up* of the Son. God's self-communication is the disclosure of God's own being which God does out of "the inner pleasure of his eternal love."[93] This love is understood only in trinitarian terms because it is part of the very being and nature of the Triune God. The trinitarian persons love each other out of the necessity of their being, which Moltmann calls as inner-trinitarian love, necessary love. This is the same love with which "God creatively and sufferingly loves the world."[94] Thus, the inner-trinitarian love between the Father, the Son, and the Holy Spirit is united with God's love for the world, and the cross bears witness to this trinitarian reality. One cannot perceive this trinitarian dimension of love apart from the unity of the trinitarian persons in the event of the cross.

There is unity of will and purpose in the Triune God in the cross. Moltmann notices "a deep conformity between the will of the Father and the will of the Son in the event of the cross," because just as the Father delivers up the Son to die, the Son willingly gives himself to die.[95] Therefore, dialectically, in the separation of the Father and the Son in the latter's godforsakenness, they are inwardly united to each other in their surrender and suffering for the godless world. Out of this union of the Father and the Son proceeds "the Spirit which justifies the godless, fills the forsaken with love and even brings the dead alive."[96] In this salvation history, the Father, the Son, and the Spirit are co-active, and their unity lies in their union and their fellowship. This unity of the trinitarian persons, Moltmann maintains, is a communicable unity, an open and inviting unity that is inclusive.[97] He brings in the Eastern theological concept of "*perichoresis*" to explain the inner trinitarian unity. *Perichoresis* is the reciprocal indwelling or the coinherence of the persons of the Trinity (cf. John 17:21; cf. 16:14; 17:1). Accordingly, the trinitarian persons reciprocally dwell *in* each other and *with* each other sharing in the eternal love. "The doctrine of the perichoresis links together in a brilliant way the threeness and the unity, without reducing the threeness to the unity, or dissolving the unity in the threeness."[98] The eternal perichoresis of the triune persons is open and in-

---

93. Moltmann, *Trinity and the Kingdom*, 57–58.
94. Moltmann, *Trinity and the Kingdom*, 58–59.
95. Moltmann, *Crucified God*, 243.
96. Moltmann, *Crucified God*, 244.
97. Moltmann, *Trinity and the Kingdom*, 95, 149.
98. Moltmann, *Trinity and the Kingdom*, 174–75.

An Indian Trinitarian Theology of *Missio Dei*

viting to the whole creation for its reception and communion in the divine life. God who enters into and relates himself to the world in the divine pathos invites humanity and creation into the trinitarian communion to share and participate in the divine life. Behind this grand vision of eschatological fellowship of the Trinity with the world and humanity lies the mission of God. At a more practical sphere, the reciprocal (perichoretic) indwelling of the Trinity can be linked to Moltmann's social doctrine of the Trinity, according to which perichoresis points to a trinitarian vision of human society characterized by mutual relationship, equality, and love.[99] Moltmann remains one of the most influential theologians of our time who has sought to integrate theology with Christian praxis.

Eberhard Jüngel

The question of correspondence between the divine aseity (ontological independence of God) and relationality (God's relation to the world) has been an important issue in the modern trinitarian theology. Eberhard Jüngel is one of those who sought to bring together the aseity of God and God's relationality through his interpretation of the trinitarian theology of Karl Barth. The issue at hand is how to affirm God's relationship to the world without endangering the aseity of God.[100] The historical Christian affirmation of the personal dimension of God—God being personal—necessarily raises the question as to God's relation outside of God's being. Insistence on God's ontological independence would amount to a denial of relationality as being essential to God's being. Conversely, asserting relationality as fundamental to the being of God would negate the aseity of God since it makes God's dependence on relations outside of God's being necessary. Jüngel seeks to resolve this dilemma by bringing to focus the internal relatedness that is constitutive to the being of the Triune God.[101] This premise provides Jüngel with the ground to develop his thesis that "God's being *ad extra corresponds* essentially to his being *ad intra*." Here in "God's *self*-interpretation (revelation) . . . God corresponds to himself."[102] One could notice in Jüngel's thesis an agreement with Rahner's axiom on the immanent and economic Trinity.

---

99. Moltmann, *Trinity and the Kingdom*, 19, 157–58. For more on Motlmann's social trinitarianism, see *Trinity and the Kingdom*, 198–202.

100. See Jüngel, *God's Being is in Becoming*, 36, 114–23.

101. Peters, *God as Trinity*, 91.

102. Jüngel, *God's Being is in Becoming*, 36.

Renewal of Trinitarian Theology and Missio Dei: Historical Trajectories

Jüngel's burden is to recapture the importance of the doctrine of Trinity in avoiding a wedge between the immanent and economic Trinity. He finds a solution in Barth's treatment of trinitarian doctrine the correspondence between what God is in himself and what God is in revelation. Therefore, by bringing together the *ad extra* and *ad intra* being of God, Jüngel attempts to "avoid setting God's being for himself in opposition to his being for us." Thus, for him, "the essence of God is nothing other than the essence of the one who works and reveals."[103] This correspondence between the *economic* and *immanent* being of God, according to Jüngel, signifies the "relationally structured being" of God. The self-relatedness of God (*ad intra*) becomes the ground for the expression of God's *ad extra* being in revelation.[104] Revelation bears witness to the fact that God's being is a relational being, which implies that God is related within himself as well as related to the world. Thus, God, who is internally related in God's trinitarian being, is able to enter into relation outside of God's being, making God as a "*doubly relational being.*" In this relation outside of God's being, God's being can "exist ontically, *without* thereby being ontologically dependent on this other being."[105] God's revelation and relatedness outside of God's being are not out of necessity, but it is God's freedom, grace, and love.

God's relatedness to the world is not comprehensible apart from God's passion and obedience in the Christ event where, according to Jüngel, "God abandons himself to death." In Jesus Christ, God hands himself over to suffering that is an opposition to God.[106] An important factor one must bear in mind is the underlying principle in predicating suffering to God which, as indicated earlier, is God's freedom and love. Suffering and death are not foisted upon God; rather they are chosen and willed in divine freedom by God for himself. Jüngel, therefore, maintains that "passion and death are not a metaphysical piece of misfortune which overtook the Son of God who became man. God chose this 'fate.'" It is a trinitarian act where the Father "participates with the Son in the passion . . . God persists in the historicality of his being."[107] In the abandonment of the Son, the Father takes upon himself the "alien suffering" of humanity and suffers it in the humiliation of

---

103. Webster, *Eberhard Jüngel*, 17.

104. Jüngel, *God's Being is in Becoming*, 37.

105. Jüngel, *God's Being is in Becoming*, 114.

106. See Jüngel, *God's Being is in Becoming*, 101–2; *God as the Mystery of the World*, 299, 387–88.

107. Jüngel, *God's Being is in Becoming*, 102.

An Indian Trinitarian Theology of *Missio Dei*

the Son. In this suffering, God "gives himself away because he will not give up humanity."[108] In this "death-accepting separation" of the Father and the Son, God did not abandon God's deity, but was *supremely* God. The loving Father abandons his beloved Son for the sake of people who are under death and takes upon their death into God's eternal life. Thus, even in separation, the Father is united with the Son in love through the Holy Spirit "in such a way that man is drawn into this love relationship."[109] The Triune God goes beyond himself in the Holy Spirit to the world of humanity which is not "loveworthy." Here God is not "only a love which *radiates* into lovelessness" but it "*involves itself* with that lovelessness" and "it makes what is totally unloveworthy into something worthy of love . . . *by* loving it."[110] God has demonstrated this love for humanity in the sending and the giving up of the Son for the world. For Jüngel, the suffering of the Son symbolizes the loving inner-relatedness of God's being as well as God's radical relatedness to the world and humanity which is God's selflessness demonstrated in the *sending* of the Son to death. Here one must be careful to note that this divine selflessness does not end the trinitarian self-relatedness, rather implements and affirms it to the utmost.[111] God's freedom to suffer in God's love for the world is very crucial for Jüngel's trinitarian thought since it disproves the doctrine of divine impassibility. God's relation to the world is founded on God's love manifested in God's suffering for the godless world. Therefore, in God's freedom to relate with the world, God choses to suffer in Jesus Christ, and thereby brings humanity to himself. One cannot be oblivious of the dimension of mission woven into the very fabric of Jüngel's dogmatic thoughts on the eternal being of God.

Leonardo Boff

The concepts of trinitarian relationality (communion) and social trinitarianism are given specific cultural application by the Brazilian Catholic liberation theologian Leonardo Boff in light of his own Latin American context. He has broadened Moltmann's idea of the doctrine of social Trinity by projecting Trinity as the model for a sense of community, equality, and

---

108. Jüngel, *God's Being is in Becoming*, 102.

109. Jüngel, *God as the Mystery of the World*, 328.

110. Jüngel, *God as the Mystery of the World*, 329. See Kline, "Participation in God and the Nature of Christian Community," 52.

111. Jüngel, *God as the Mystery of the World*, 371–72. See also Jüngel, *God as the Mystery of the World*, 373.

interrelationship in human society. Taking the Greek concept of *perichoresis* as the structural axis of his trinitarian explication, Boff believes that it speaks to those who seek justice and freedom from their oppression and suffering. For them, the trinitarian community of the Godhead serves as a model for an ideal human community of freedom and justice that would reflect "the image and likeness of the Trinity."[112] Reflecting further on this archetypal correspondence between the Trinity and human society, Boff has this to say: "Human society is a pointer on the road to the mystery of the Trinity, while the mystery of the Trinity, as we know it from revelation, is a pointer toward social life and its archetype."[113] He is convinced that an ideal human society that accords with God's plan is the one that is shaped after the trinitarian model of societal relationship grounded in the perichoretic communion in the Triune God.[114] Boff regards ideology that emerges from strict monotheism as being opposed to this trinitarian model of relationship, because it provides a conceptual underpinning for concentrating power in one hand, be it in society, religion, politics, or family. Strict and rigid monotheism and divine monarchy have potential for inequality and hierarchical ordering and dominance in the Church, nations, society, and family.[115] Boff contends that perfect sense of love, unity, equality, and self-giving that characterize the communion of the Trinity provide a corrective when these ideals are realized in human society in order to establish an egalitarian society founded on freedom and justice.[116]

Therefore, moving beyond the paradigms of trinitarian plurality and unity, the starting points of Greek and Latin theologies respectively, Boff takes trinitarian communion as his point of departure in constructing his trinitarian theology. The profundity of this communion within the Godhead, the interrelatedness of the Father, the Son, and the Holy Spirit, Boff believes, is best expressed by perichoresis.[117] Perichoretic communion implies the eternal and reciprocal indwelling of the Father, the Son, and the Holy Spirit "communicating life and love" to each other. Boff discovers in this eternal interpenetration and mutual indwelling of the divine persons, what he calls, "a mystery of inclusion," according to which no one person

---

112. Boff, *Trinity and Society*, 7.
113. Boff, *Trinity and Society*, 119.
114. Boff, *Trinity and Society*, 11.
115. Boff, *Trinity and Society*, 20–21.
116. See Boff, *Holy Trinity*, 63–64.
117. Boff, *Trinity and Society*, 4–5.

of the Trinity can be conceived in isolation.[118] This trinitarian inclusion, which he also calls "union-communion-perichoresis," is quite germane to Boff's construction of a social doctrine of the Trinity.

Perichoretic communion, the trinitarian inclusion, is an open one which invites "human beings and the whole universe to insert themselves in the divine life."[119] This trinitarian communion is extended to humanity and creation in the mission of God where the life and love of the Trinity are poured out into the world.[120] The mission of the Father, according to Boff, has to do with the mysteriousness of creation and the ineffableness of the Father's presence in that creation. Yet the Father through the Son and the Spirit creates, and this creation is "an expression of the intimate, perichoretic life of God, a life that expands outwards, creating different beings with whom God can communicate and enter into communion."[121] The mission of the Son begins with his sending by the Father, which is the *hypostatic* (personal) communication of the Triune God, God's self-giving to the world. The incarnational mission of the Son demonstrates the eternal design of the Trinity, which is to gather all beings into trinitarian communion "through the mediation of the Son and the driving force of the Holy Spirit" (cf. John 1:3; Eph 1:10; Col 1:16).[122] One must note that Boff's social trinitarianism takes an important turn in his positioning the mission of the Holy Spirit in actions and revolutions that seek liberation of the oppressed and transformation of society. He maintains that the Holy Spirit is present in these "painful processes of structural change" and brings about unity and new creation. The work of the Spirit is specifically found in the Church, the sacrament, which the Holy Spirit makes a community in the image of the Trinity.[123] Mission of the Father, the Son, and the Holy Spirit represents the openness of God's communion which goes "beyond the existence of the three Persons by including creation."[124] It is a communion which is characterized by *koinonia*, ecclesial communion, equality, relationship, and recognition of diversity and plurality. These ideals

---

118. Boff, *Holy Trinity*, 15.
119. Boff, *Trinity and Society*, 6.
120. Boff, *Trinity and Society*, 95.
121. Boff, *Trinity and Society*, 174–75.
122. Boff, *Trinity and Society*, 186.
123. Boff, *Holy Trinity*, 94–95.
124. Boff, "Trinitarian Community and Social Liberation," 304.

Renewal of Trinitarian Theology and Missio Dei: Historical Trajectories

constitute the pointers towards a society and Church that best approximate the trinitarian communion and image.

Catherine Mowry LaCugna

Sharing the social trinitarianism of Moltmann and Boff, as well as taking lead from Rahner's axiom, yet with her own distinctive emphasis, the late Catholic theologian, Catherine LaCugna, seeks to bring to focus the economic Trinity and its relevance for Christian faith and life. Her opening statements in her acclaimed work, *God for Us: Trinity and Christian Life*, capture the essence of LaCugna's treatment of the Trinity: "The doctrine of the Trinity is ultimately a practical doctrine with radical consequences for Christian life. . . . The life of God—precisely because God is triune—does not belong to God alone."[125] For LaCugna, "the central theme of trinitarian theology is the relationship between the pattern of salvation history (*oikonomia*) and the eternal being of God (*theologia*)."[126] She regrets that excessive emphasis on the metaphysical approach to the doctrine of Trinity since Nicea (325) created a wedge between the immanent and economic Trinity and thus reduced the doctrine to an abstraction.[127] The extreme preoccupation with the *intradivine self-relatedness* of the divine persons (substance ontology) in effect has made the Trinity unrelated to the world.[128] LaCugna attempts to retrieve the economic dimension of the Trinity with special emphasis on its relational (relational ontology) aspect and its application in Christian faith and praxis. The essentially personal and relational (communion) dimension of the Trinity provides vision for a society where communion with each other, sharing in love, and the sense of equality would prevail.[129] Thus, LaCugna calls for a rehabilitation of the doctrine of the Trinity by seizing its mystery *for us* and making it central to our faith and life.

Taking her point of departure from Rahner's rule as well as his insistence on the self-communicating nature of God, LaCugna reiterates the essential relation between God in God's eternal being (*theologia*) and God who is revealed in history (*oikonomia*) as the fundamental framework for the doctrine of the Trinity.[130] The essential idea of God's self-communi-

125. LaCugna, *God for Us*, 1.
126. LaCugna, *God for Us*, 230.
127. See LaCugna, *God for Us*, 217.
128. LaCugna, "Practical Trinity," 681.
129. LaCugna, "Practical Trinity," 681–82.
130. See LaCugna, *God for Us*, 211.

cating nature is foundational for the revitalization of trinitarian doctrine. This self-communication of God takes place only in soteriological terms, in God's self-expressiveness in the mission, in the sending of the Son and the Holy Spirit in history. It is God's mission in the Son—*God-with-us* (*oikonomia*)—that provides humanity access to the knowledge of *God-with-God* (*theologia*). It may be summed thus: "*theologia* is fully revealed and bestowed in *oikonomia*, and *oikonomia* truly expresses the ineffable mystery of *theologia*."[131] However, LaCugna brings in a necessary caveat: God's self-communication of himself in the economy of salvation does not exhaust the incomprehensibleness and ineffableness of the divine mystery. This God, in God's essential being, is personal and relational, and hence, open to the world. God, who is personal and existing as "the mystery of persons in communion," shares the divine communion with the world and humanity in the Son.[132] The Triune God has come to us through the Son and the Holy Spirit in the economy of salvation, inviting us into the trinitarian communion and into communion with one another. God and creation in communion forms the *oikonomia*, the household of God, the reign of God.

TRINITARIAN RENEWAL AND MISSION

The preceding appraisal of the trinitarian resurgence demonstrates not only a consistent development for more than half a century, but also deepening reflection on this vital Christian doctrine, drawing on insights from across confessional boundaries. Observing this significant progress of trinitarian theology, the Lutheran theologian Carl Braaten writes: "At no point in contemporary theology do we find such trans-confessional unity as in the new construction of the doctrine of the Trinity."[133] An important hallmark of this trinitarian development, alongside the dogmatic inquiry, as noted above, has been the retrieval of its practical implications for the life of the Church and society. There is, perhaps, no other place where both dogmatic inquiry and practical implications of Trinity have played out as in mission. Perhaps more than any other period in the modern history of Christian doctrine, the trinitarian revitalization recaptured the integral relation between the doctrine of the Trinity and the practice and theory of mission. It is quite pertinent to take note of the fact that the earliest historical formulations of the doctrine of the Trinity were initiated in a

---

131. LaCugna, *God for Us*, 221.
132. LaCugna, "Practical Trinity," 681–82.
133. Braaten, "Triune God," 416.

Renewal of Trinitarian Theology and Missio Dei: Historical Trajectories

missionary context. Speaking about this, Lesslie Newbigin says the proclamation of the gospel in the pagan world necessitated an articulation of a fully trinitarian doctrine of God:

> It is indeed a significant fact that the great doctrinal struggles about the nature of the Trinity, especially about the mutual relations of the Son and the Father, developed right in the midst of the struggle between the Church and the pagan world. These trinitarian struggles were indeed an essential part of the battle to master the pagan worldview at the height of its power and self-confidence. The Church had to articulate the Christian message of God's Kingdom in a world which interpreted human life mainly in terms of the interaction of "virtue" and "fortune." . . . It is significant that the Church found itself driven to articulate the Christian message in this situation in terms of trinitarian doctrine, and that, during the period in which the intellectual struggle took place to state the Gospel in terms of Graeco-Roman culture without thereby compromising its central affirmation, it was the doctrine of the Trinity which was the key to the whole theological debate.[134]

The trinitarian foundation of mission in the modern renewal of the doctrine of the Trinity was brought to a focus with the emergence of the concept of mission as *missio Dei*, the mission of God, in the mid-twentieth century. The *missio Dei* essentially views God as the source and initiator of mission and the Church is privileged to participate in the divine mission. In a trinitarian sense, it means that God sends "the church to the world [as] a continuation of the Father's sending of the Son and the Spirit."[135] The baptismal formula in the Matthean mission-command (Matt 28:18–20), as noted by Robert Jenson, demonstrates the divine sending and the triune nature of mission. According to Jenson, "the rubric for baptism contained in this sending stipulates the triune name, for the mission itself, as here commanded, is triune."[136] Thus, in *missio Dei* the Triune God is the ground of Christian mission. The following section of this chapter will examine the emergence of the *missio Dei* in relation to the doctrine of the Trinity since the second half of the twentieth century.

---

134. Newbigin, *Trinitarian Faith and Today's Mission*, 32.
135. Braaten, "Triune God," 425; Bosch, *Transforming Mission*, 10.
136. Jenson, *Triune Identity*, 30.

An Indian Trinitarian Theology of *Missio Dei*

THE TRINITY AND *MISSIO DEI*

The *missio Dei* has, in recent times, become a contested theological/missiological term. Historically, the concept of the *missio Dei* is rooted in St. Augustine's *De Trinitate* in relation to the divine sending within the Trinity—the Father sends the Son, the Father and the Son send the Holy Spirit, and the Triune God sends the Church into the world in mission.[137] Since *missio Dei* in Augustine will form the subject matter of the fourth chapter of this book, we will not attempt a full exposition of Augustine's trinitarian thought at this point. The *missio Dei* as a paradigm in theology of mission has assumed significance and entered into mission studies as a new approach only after the fifth conference of the International Missionary Council at Willingen, Germany in 1952, where the idea of the *missio Dei* was originally introduced. Accordingly, in the Willingen conference,

> mission was understood as being derived from the very nature of God. It was thus put in the context of the doctrine of the Trinity, not of ecclesiology or soteriology. The classical doctrine on the *missio Dei* as God the Father sending the Son, and God the Father and the Son sending the Spirit was expanded to include yet another "movement": Father, Son, and Holy Spirit sending the church into the world. As far as missionary thinking was concerned, this linking with the doctrine of the Trinity constituted an important innovation.[138]

The Latin "missio" (mission) was used until the sixteenth century only in the context of trinitarian relations, referring to the sending of the Son by the Father, and the sending of the Holy Spirit by the Father and the Son. The traditional expression for Christian mission until then was "propagation of the faith." It was the Jesuits who used the term "missio" to refer to the dissemination of the Christian faith among non-Catholics which included not only non-Christians, but Protestants as well.[139] The introduction of the *missio Dei* concept marked a transformation in the way mission was traditionally perceived. Mission now has come to be viewed as being grounded in God who is the origin of mission and not in the Church. "When Christian communities speak about God, by definition they have

---

137. See Augustine, *De Trinitate*, 4.25 (178). A detailed discussion of mission as divine sending within the Trinity is found in Books II–IV. Bosch, *Transforming Mission*, 390. See also Poitras, "St. Augustine and the *Missio Dei*," 28–46.

138. Bosch, *Transforming Mission*, 390.

139. Bosch, *Transforming Mission*, 1; O'Malley, "Mission and the Early Jesuits," 3.

Renewal of Trinitarian Theology and Missio Dei: Historical Trajectories

to speak about Father, Son and Holy Spirit. There simply is no other God. Therefore to speak about the *missio Dei* is to indicate, without any qualification, the *missio Trinitatis*."[140] Mission receives specificity as far as its foundation is concerned, i.e., it is grounded in God who is a triune being and thus it assumes a trinitarian nature. Hence, Willingen 1952 necessitated a shift from an *ecclesiocentric* model of mission to a *theocentric* one, or more specifically, a *trinitarian-centric* approach. According to Bosch, in the post-Willingen period the *missio Dei* concept was broadly affirmed by conciliar Protestants, Evangelicals, and the Eastern Orthodox, as well as by Roman Catholics in the documents of Vatican II.[141] This section will trace the trajectory of the *missio Dei* in its relation to trinitarian theology with respect to its historical beginning and subsequent development.

Karl Barth, Karl Hartenstein, and Missio Dei

The origin of the concept of the *missio Dei*—not the phrase itself—has often been traced back to Barth's "Theology and Mission in the Present Situation" which he presented at the Brandenburg Missionary Conference in Berlin in 1932.[142] Although there are no unequivocal evidences that relate the phrase, "missio Dei" to Barth, his influence on the *missio Dei* theology is nonetheless considered significant. In a remarkable study on the *missio Dei*, Trinity and Karl Barth, John Flett has refuted the attribution of the origin of the *missio Dei* to Karl Barth. Even so, Flett observes that "references to the missionary task emerge at the most decisive points throughout the *Church Dogmatics*."[143] Mission, for Barth, is part of the Church and an activity of the Church. It is addressed to those who are *inside* the Church as well as to those *outside* the Church. Mission as evangelization is aimed at those within the church "in theory but not in practice [as] nominal Christians." "Evangelisation serves to awaken this sleeping Church."[144] Mission in "the true and original sense [as the] sending or sending out to the nations to attest the Gospel is at the very

---

140. Kirk, *What is Mission?*, 27.

141. Bosch, *Transforming Mission*, 390–91.

142. Barth, "Die Theologie und die Mission," 189–215. See also Richebächer, "*Missio Dei*," 590. Guder, "From Mission and Theology to Missional Theology," 42.

143. Flett, *Witness of God*, 30. For a detailed discussion of Flett on his rebuttal of the attribution of the origin of the *missio Dei* to Barth, see Flett, *Witness of God*, 11–17. For details on the origin on the concept of the *missio Dei* and its historical development, see Flett, *Witness of God*, 35–77, 78–122, 123–62.

144. Barth, CD 4/3:872–73. See Rössel, "From a Theology of Crisis," 207.

An Indian Trinitarian Theology of *Missio Dei*

root of the existence" of the church.[145] This task of mission is committed to the Church and it must engage in mission, and it "is alive only when it is engaged as such" in mission. The Church is "as such a missionary community or it is not the Christian community."[146]

Barth found that the early church's understanding of mission signified the sending aspect within the Trinity. Mission emerges from the Triune God's sending activity. The Church, as a missionary community, is called to participate in mission in obedience to God's command.[147] As Darrell Guder observes, by linking this "missionary vocation of the church . . . with the mission or sending of God, Barth gave a profound and shaping impulse to the re-orientation of western ecclesiology that was already fermenting in the mission discussion."[148] The following text from Barth's Brandenburg lecture is worth noting: "the concept *missio* in the early church was a term derived from the doctrine of the Trinity, namely for the description of God's sending of himself in the Son and the Holy Spirit into the world. Is it possible to understand it in any other way?"[149] In contexts where mission was interpreted in soteriological, cultural, and ecclesiological categories, Barth's attempt to relate mission to the doctrine of the Trinity is significant. Thus, as Bosch notes, Barth became perhaps the earliest theologian to introduce mission as the activity of the Triune God, hence contributing to the idea of the *missio Dei*, albeit in an unintended manner.[150]

The Latin phrase, *missio Dei* itself was coined at a later stage, and is attributed to Barth's friend, the German missiologist Karl Hartenstein. More specifically, the phrase *missio Dei* initially appeared in an essay by Hartenstein in 1934 where he says that "therefore mission is called today in all aspects to always test before God anew, to examine if it is what it should be: *missio Dei*, the sending of God, yes, from Christ the Lord, the necessary sending of the apostles: "As the Father has sent me, so I send you"—and answer to the call passed on to the church of all ages on the basis of its Word from the apostles: "Go out into all the world.""[151]

---

145. Barth, *CD* 4/3:874.
146. Barth, *CD* 3/4:504–5.
147. Barth, "Die Theologie und die Mission," 204.
148. Guder, "From Mission and Theology to Missional Theology," 43.
149. Barth, "Die Theologie und die Mission," 204.
150. See Bosch, *Transforming Mission*, 389.
151. Hartenstein, "Wozu nötigt die Finanzlage," 217. See also Schuster, "Karl Hartenstein," 65.

Johannes Aagaard erroneously claims that the term *missio Dei* "appears for the first time" in Hartenstein's article on the Willingen Conference of IMC in 1952. The following passage that Aagaard cites from Hartenstein's 1952 document to substantiate his claim is a much later one than the statement of Hartenstein cited above: "Mission is not only the conversion of individuals, it is not only obedience to a word of the Lord, it is not only the obligation to gather the congregation; it is participation in the sending of the Son, the *missio Dei*, with the all-embracing aim of establishing the Lordship of Christ over the whole redeemed creation."[152]

While Hartenstein based his understanding of mission on the Trinity, there is a strong sense of integration between the *missio Dei* and *missio ecclesia* in him. Mission is grounded in God who is the Lord of mission who calls the Church to service in the world.[153] Mission of God and mission of the Church are related "in the context of salvation history." The Triune God who sends himself in the Son and in the Spirit sends the Church. Therefore, while emphasizing the close integration of the Church and mission, Hartenstein unmistakably upholds mission as the mission of the Triune God. Hence, "the *missio dei* is always more than the *missio ecclesiae*."[154]

Missio Dei *and the Trinity at Willingen*

The idea of the *missio Dei* surfaced at the International Missionary Conference at Willingen in 1952, albeit with a sense of ambiguity that surrounded its presence there. As indicated above, Karl Hartenstein, who was credited with the invention of the phrase *missio Dei*, also played a vital role at the Willingen conference. However, there is no evidence to suggest that the phrase *missio Dei* itself was introduced in Willingen.[155] In his critical literary study of the *missio Dei*, Rosin contends, "neither [Hartenstein], nor his

---

152. Hartenstein, "Theologische Besinnungen," 54, cited in Aagaard, "Trends in Missiological Thinking," 12.

153. Hartenstein, "Wozu nötigt die Finanzlage," 65. See also Hartenstein, "*Augsburg Confession*," 40–41.

154. Schuster, "Karl Hartenstein," 67. See also Schuster, "Karl Hartenstein," 65, 79. Hoekendijk charges Hartenstein with assigning the Church "too central a role in the development of the idea of the *missio Dei*" (Schuster, "Karl Hartenstein," 75).

155. The following two primary sources of the Willingen conferences make no mention of the term "*missio Dei*." See Goodall, *Missions Under the Cross*, 188–92; Lehmann, "Missionary Obligation of the Church," 20–38. This article is an abridged version of the North American report on Aim I of the Study of the Missionary Obligation of the Church undertaken by the International Missionary Council.

friends brought [*missio Dei*] with them to Willingen as a watchword." He further maintains that the phrase was not found in the Willingen Conference's "discussion Group 1, or during the meetings of the commission, in which [Hartenstein] played an important part."[156] Even so, the concept of the *missio Dei* was adopted in Willingen and the idea became prevalent in the discussion of the trinitarian foundation of mission at the conference.

The significance of the idea of the *missio Dei* may be seen in how it "brings out very effectively the historical and theological importance of the Willingen conference."[157] The Willingen conference in 1952 was a momentous one in the history of mission theology. It was held in an environment of disenchantment fomented by crucial events in the socio-political spheres of the time which had significant implications for Christian mission. The two World Wars involving the Christian West seemed to raise serious questions about the credibility of the Christian faith and mission. The decline of Western colonialism also had important consequences for Western Christian mission as they were perceived to be bound together. These factors created a sense of apprehension regarding the future of mission in the erstwhile-colonized nations. Perhaps the greatest concern was the future of mission in China in the aftermath of the communist revolution in 1949 under Mao Tse-tung. Consequent to the communist takeover, China remained closed to foreign mission, generating fear about its effect spilling over to neighboring nations.[158] These challenges are sounded in the words of M.A.C. Warren spoken at Willingen: "At Whitby, in 1947, we hoped that the most testing days of the Christian mission, at least for our generation, lay behind us.... But here at Willingen, clouds and thick darkness surround the city, and we know with complete certainty that the most testing days of the Christian mission in our generation lie just ahead."[159] Given the challenges posed by these changed circumstances, what was the legitimacy of Christian mission?

The challenges paved the way for a new understanding of mission, and more importantly, for seeking a theological foundation for mission in the changing environments. It is quite significant here to note that the

---

156. Rosin, "*Missio Dei*," 7–8.

157. Richebächer, "*Missio Dei*," 590.

158. Günther, "History and Significance of World Mission," 528; Richebächer, "*Missio Dei*," 590; Sundermeier, "*Missio Dei* Today," 560.

159. Goodall, *Missions Under the Cross*, 40. See also Philip, *Edinburgh to Salvador*, 26–54.

responses to this crisis brought out in the Willingen Conference to justify mission were grounded on the centrality of God. As observed by Theo Sundermeier, "Willingen 1952 was the first time that mission was so comprehensively anchored in the doctrine of God."[160] This anchoring of mission in God as its source and originator is seen in each of the three models of mission proposed in Willingen. The eschatological and salvation history approach brought to the conference by the Germans (Karl Hartenstein and Walter Freytag) saw mission as proclamation of the gospel to the whole world between the period of the ascension and Parousia. This is the mission of the Church as the divine instrument to lead to the ultimate goal of fulfillment of God's salvific plan.[161] The Dutch model represented by J. C. Hoekendijk proposed the objective of mission as being world-centered, "a model based on the history of the promise."[162] Mission is the establishment of *shalom* in the world through the apostolate, where Hoekendijk does not appear to see much significance for the Church.[163] According to this model, the Church is merely an instrument for mission in *the world* where the latter sets the agenda for the former. The mission of the Church is to discern the signs of the kingdom that God is making in the world, "to bear witness to them, and participate in them."[164]

The American report, in its most extensive treatment on mission, emphasized that the "missionary obligation of the Church is grounded in the outgoing activity of God, whereby, as Creator, Redeemer, Governor, and Guide, God establishes and includes the world and men within his fulfilling purposes and fellowship."[165] The objective of mission is seen as "the transformation of individual lives and of cultural and social patterns."

160. Sundermeier, "*Missio Dei* Today," 560.

161. Günther, "History and Significance of World Mission," 528–29.

162. Günther, "History and Significance of World Mission," 529; Engelsviken, "*Missio Dei*," 488.

163. Hoekendijk, "Church in Missionary Thinking," 334; Bassham, "Development and Tensions," 54. In his book, *The Church Inside Out*—written a decade after Willingen 1952—Hoekendijk reaffirms the objective of mission as the establishment of *shalom*, which is "at once peace, integrity, community, harmony, and justice." The apostolic preaching was "shalom through Christ." He insists that this "concept in all its comprehensive richness should be our leitmotif in Christian work. God intends the redemption of the whole of creation" (Hoekendijk, *Church Inside Out*, 21–22). Hoekendijk's views were to exert great influence in the subsequent study on "The Missionary Structure of the Congregation."

164. Berkhof, *Christian Faith*, 411–13.

165. Lehmann, "Missionary Obligation of the Church," 20.

An Indian Trinitarian Theology of *Missio Dei*

Here the Church is called to be sensitive and respond to "what the triune God has done and is doing in the world."[166] More importantly, the report calls for a shift from a *Christo-centric mission* to the *trinitarian-centric mission*. The report points out that the Great Commission which "has gathered up the core of missionary aim and motivation, links the explicit mandate of Jesus, the Lord, with the triune name of God."[167] The commonality that underlies all these different approaches, as indicated earlier, was the centrality of God in mission. This signifies a move from an anthropocentric model of mission to theocentric one—*missio hominum* to *missio Dei*—known today as the *Copernican revolution of mission*. God is the ground of mission which ultimately belongs to God. The Church is called to participate "in that mission which remains, always, *God's mission*."[168] The trinitarian emphasis of the American report left an indelible mark on the final statement of the Willingen Report, capturing the trinitarian foundation of mission as follows:

> The missionary movement of which we are a part has its source in the Triune God Himself. Out of the depths of His love for us, the Father has sent forth His own beloved Son to reconcile all things to Himself, that we and all men might, through the Spirit, be made one in Him with the Father in that perfect love which is the very nature of God. . . . We who have been chosen in Christ, reconciled to God through Him, made members of His body, sharers in His Spirit, and heirs through hope of His Kingdom, are by these very facts committed to full participation in His redeeming mission. There is no participation in Christ without participation in His mission to the world. That by which the Church receives its existence is that by which it is also given its world-mission. "As the Father hath sent Me, even so I send you."[169]

This "trinitarian foundation of mission" is regarded as "one of the most striking achievements" of the Willingen conference.[170] Wilhelm Andersen sums up "Willingen's approach to a theology of the missionary enterprise" as "trinitarian in character" where "the triune God Himself is declared to be the sole source of every missionary enterprise." He further

---

166. Lehmann, "Missionary Obligation of the Church," 22.

167. Lehmann, "Missionary Obligation of the Church," 21. See also Günther, "History and Significance of World Mission," 529.

168. Günther, "History and Significance of World Mission," 529. Emphasis added.

169. Goodall, *Missions Under the Cross*, 189–90. See also, Vicedom, *Mission of God*, 5.

170. Rosin, "*Missio Dei*," 10.

says, "the theological statement of Willingen confesses, in the plainest possible terms, a trinitarian basis for the missionary enterprise."[171] This remarkable development in mission theology has given Willingen a very significant place both historically and theologically. What was achieved in Willingen was just a beginning, and the concept of the *missio Dei* and its trinitarian foundation outlined here would be subsequently developed and integrated in a variety of ways.

Post-Willingen Developments

The *missio Dei* theme emerged prominently during the post-Willingen period. In his post-Willingen writing, Hartenstein says, "the sending of the Son to reconcile the universe through the power of the Spirit is the foundation and purpose of mission. The *missio ecclesiae* comes from the *missio Dei* alone. Thus, mission is placed within the broadest imaginable framework of salvation history and God's plan of salvation."[172] This evidently echoes the Willingen consensus on mission and the Trinity.

The important development to which Willingen 1952 contributed was a move from an *ecclesiocentric* mission to a *trinitarian-centric* mission. The church-centered mission framework of the nineteenth century was felt to be inadequate "for dealing with the problems facing churches engaged in mission . . . in the post-colonial era."[173] To those problems, the *missio Dei* came as a response "with a clearer understanding of the trinitarian basis and nature of the church's mission, and an openness and sensitivity to the eschatological character of the kingdom, and the church's subordinate relationship to it."[174] In the post-Willingen discourses, the *missio Dei* as a theological and missiological category underwent significant changes and interpretations exemplified in two models in the *missio Dei* theology, namely, the *salvation history* model and the *history-of-the-promise* model.

The *missio Dei* concept found one of its classical formulations in the work of the German missiologist Walter Freytag, one of the leading representatives of "Salvation History" model. According to Freytag, mission is carried out with a view to the end, the *Parousia*. It is "'part of God's own eschatological action,'" 'as' "'the sign of the coming end set up by Him.'"[175]

171. Andersen, "Towards a Theology of Mission," 47, 52.
172. Hartenstein quoted in Richebächer, "*Missio Dei*," 589–90.
173. Scherer, "Church, Kingdom, and *Missio Dei*," 85.
174. Scherer, "Church, Kingdom, and *Missio Dei*," 85.
175. Freytag, *Reden und Aufsätze*," 189.

An Indian Trinitarian Theology of *Missio Dei*

Mission as *missio Dei* is meaningful only in the context of the *eschaton*, which gives "mission the proper perspective."[176] Therefore, the Church "is called to take part in the responsibility of God's outgoing into the whole world . . . and that the Church has its life towards that end, the goal of God in the coming again of Christ."[177] Since mission is *missio Dei*—"part of God's own eschatological action" and the "responsibility of God's outgoing into the whole world"—it undercuts the undue emphasis on human action in mission. Thus, the *missio Dei* comes as a corrective to the anthropocentrism of mission (*missio hominum*), and "its overestimation of human missionary action and its achievements."[178]

The person who systematically developed and popularized the *missio Dei* concept was the German missiologist Georg Vicedom. He affirms the theocentricity of mission against the tendency that holds the Church as the subject of mission. Vicedom does not negate the place of the Church in mission, rather sees both mission and Church as "God's very own work." Both the Church and mission are divine "instruments through which God carries out His mission." The Church remains the Church "in the divine sense" only insofar as, she participates in God's mission to the world.[179] In *missio*, the sending of God, according to Vicedom, God is the subject as well as the object—God sends himself in mission: "God sends His Son; Father and Son send the Holy Ghost." In this trinitarian mystery of *missio*, God is not only "the One sent," but also "the Content of the sending," and it does not dissolve "the equality of essence of the divine Persons." The significance of this "intra-divine sending" for the church's mission is seen in that "the church's commission is prefigured in the divine. . . . The meaning and content of her work is determined by the *missio Dei*."[180] God's revelation in *missio Dei* always has human redemption as its object. This saving act of God is extended through the *missio*, the "sending" of God, which is "the sum and substance of God's creativity and activity." "Thus the entire *Heilsgeschichte*," contends Vicedom, "exhibits itself as a history of *missio Dei*."[181] Nevertheless, Vicedom extends his understanding of the *missio Dei* beyond divine sending and human redemption to the creation and God's

---

176. Gensichen, "Walter Freytag," 439.
177. Freytag, "Changes in the Patterns of Western Missions," 146.
178. Gensichen, "Walter Freytag," 439.
179. Vicedom, *Mission of God*, 5–6.
180. Vicedom, *Mission of God*, 8.
181. Vicedom, *Mission of God*, 9; Engelsviken, "*Missio Dei*," 483.

preservation of it (*missio Dei generalis*): "[God] exemplifies Himself as a God who has not excluded His creation from His care."[182] In the subsequent development of the *missio Dei* and its concept, *missio Dei generalis* came to assume the dominant place in missiological discourse which is clearly reflected in the history-of-the promise model.

The Willingen concept of the *missio Dei* was affirmed in the next International Missionary Council conference in Accra, Ghana in 1958.[183] The New Delhi Assembly in 1961 further upheld the *missio Dei* and mission's theocentrism. Mission is affirmed as belonging to God and not to the Church "because mission is a predicate of God." "God is a missionary God. . . . *Missio Dei* is active in the whole of history."[184] In the Uppsala conference of 1968, the *missio Dei* assumed the center stage reaffirming the trinitarian anchoring of mission. The conference also sought to distinguish the *missio Dei* from *missio ecclesiae*. Thus, in the Willingen and post-Willingen conferences *missio ecclesiae* paved the way for *missio trinitatis*, "in which mission is understood as a participation in *missio Dei*. Mission thereby is seen as a movement from God to the world, and the church is seen as an instrument for that mission—the church as a function of the mission."[185]

There was another development, as mentioned earlier, in the history of the *missio Dei* which widened the ambit of the phrase, signifying an obvious shift away from the original intention of the *missio Dei*. The ambiguity that surrounded the *missio Dei* right from its inception led to the possibility of what Rosin calls "theological exploitation." The phrase, gradually, came to assume wide-ranging interpretations depending on "its theological context," giving "it enough elasticity as a symbol of short formula . . . to allow it to function in the most divergent trains of thought."[186] Thus, the scope of the *missio Dei* was expanded in the early part of the twentieth century where not only the Church, but the world also becomes the participant in God's mission. God's mission "takes place in ordinary human history, not exclusively in and through the church. . . . The *missio Dei* is God's activity, which embraces both the church and the world, and in which *the church may be privileged to participate*."[187] The establishment

---

182. Vicedom, *Mission of God*, 10; Engelsviken, "*Missio Dei*," 484.
183. Orchard, *Ghana Assembly*," 180–84, 207; Rosin, "*Missio Dei*," 24.
184. Birkeli, "Svenska Prästforbundet," 28.
185. Aagaard, "Trends in Missiological Thinking," 13.
186. Rosin, "*Missio Dei*," 25; see also, 14–15.
187. Bosch, *Transforming Mission*, 391. Emphasis added.

An Indian Trinitarian Theology of *Missio Dei*

of *shalom* became the objective of the *missio Dei* and thereby the world was brought into the focus of mission. Accordingly, the Church's task was redefined, as it were, so as to bear witness to this new dimension of mission. The Church is called to "join it in the sense of working with movements in the world that further shalom, whether or not these movement[s] have any Christian basis. The order is therefore not God-church-world, but God-world-church. Or one might rather say: God-world-shalom . . . while the church does not really have any important place in this sequence of *missio Dei*."[188] Bosch feels "this wider understanding of the scope of the *missio Dei*" is quite removed from the original intentions of the concept as envisaged by Hartenstein. He says that Hartenstein, through the use of the *missio Dei*, "had hoped to protect mission against secularization and horizontalization, and to reserve it exclusively for God." Bosch laments that the radicalization of the *missio Dei* tends to undermine the Church's involvement where the Church is seen "unnecessary for the *missio Dei*."[189] This tendency towards secularization and horizontalization of mission was evident at the Willingen conference in the vision of the American report, which was received, but not adopted as final statement. The American report at Willingen called for recognizing that "God is carrying out His judgment and redemption in the revolutionary movements of our times."[190] The ambiguity of the *missio Dei* from its very inception and the resultant possibility of divergent and radical interpretations and modifications in the post-Willingen period made the *missio Dei* "the Trojan horse through which the (unassimilated) 'American' vision was fetched into the well-guarded walls of the ecumenical theology of mission."[191]

An important figure behind the development of the wider understanding of the *missio Dei* was the Dutch missiologist Johannes Christiaan Hoekendijk. According to Hoekendijk, as noted earlier, *shalom* is the key word that characterizes mission as well as the goal of mission. Hence, the focus of the *missio Dei* shifted from the Church to the world.[192] Church's role is to serve the *missio Dei*, to set up *signs of shalom*, which are expressed in secular

---

188. Engelsviken, "*Missio Dei*," 489. See also Engelsviken, "*Missio Dei*," 487–89. Hoekendijk, *Planning for Mission*, 43–47.

189. Bosch, *Transforming Mission*, 392.

190. Goodall, *Missions Under the Cross*, 240. See also Newbigin, "Recent Thinking on Christian Beliefs," 260–61.

191. Rosin, "*Missio Dei*," 26.

192. Hoekendijk, "Notes on the Meaning of Mission(-ary)," 43; Engelsviken, "*Missio Dei*," 489; Skreslet, *Comprehending Mission*, 33.

movements that seek transformation, justice, and freedom in the world. It is important to observe the place of the Church in the *missio Dei*, that is of service and witness to this mission.[193] Hoekendijk's idea of the secular world as the locus of the *missio Dei* was further developed through the Western European study group which was part of a study project of WCC on "The Missionary Structure of the Congregation" (1962–1966). The study focused on mission primarily in relation to the world and world history. Here God is seen as "active in the secular political and social events of the world, through people of good will, whether Christians, people of other religious convictions or atheists. The Church's mission is to discern the signs of the times and join God (or Christ) where God is active to transform the world towards shalom."[194] This secularized interpretation of the *missio Dei* has to be seen in the wider context of transformation taking place in the Christian West. The 1960s and 1970s witnessed a secularizing trend in theology and mission as evidenced in the emergence of liberation theologies. In this context, much of Protestant theology was interested in secular themes where mission was primarily sought to be understood in terms of emancipation from economic, political, and social injustices.[195]

Obviously, the broadening and secularization of the *missio Dei* and the marginalization of the Church which have come as a consequence of Willingen and post-Willingen debates on Church-centered mission generated reverberations among those who assigned a central space to Church and salvation history in the *missio Dei*.[196] An important development in this context was the emergence of the evangelical movements like Lausanne Committee for World Evangelization and World Evangelical Fellowship. These movements arose in reaction to the conciliar and ecumenical view of mission and sought to retrieve the classical understanding of the *missio Dei*.[197] It must also be noted that while the missionary conferences

---

193. Wieser, *Planning for Mission*, 51–52; Engelsviken, "Missio Dei," 489.

194. Matthey, "Missiology in the World Council of Churches," 429. See also Hoedemaker, "Legacy of J. C. Hoekendijk," 168.

195. The following works represent the secular understanding of mission and theology during this period: Cox, *Secular City*; Metz, *Emergent Church*; Metz, *Faith in History and Society*; Gutiérrez, *Theology of Liberation*.

196. See Schultz, *Mission from the Cross*, 97; Scherer, *Gospel, Church, and Kingdom*, 113–17; Bosch, *Transforming Mission*, 385, 392.

197. See Stott, *Making Christ Known*, xi–xvii. The 1982 Grand Rapids Report on Evangelism and Social Responsibility affirms that "evangelism and socio-political involvement are both part of our Christian duty. For both are necessary expressions of

An Indian Trinitarian Theology of *Missio Dei*

sought to move from an *ecclesiocentric* mission approach to a *trinitarian-centric* one, they did not imply "forsaking the church's mission, but rather a revisioning of that mission from a fresh biblical, missiological, and above all, eschatological point of view. This remains a priority task for the theology of Christian mission today."[198]

The aspect of trinitarian sending inherent in Jesus' commission to the disciples (John 20:21) formed the basis of the Willingen affirmation of the trinitarian ground of mission. Jesus' own ministry demonstrated the comprehensive nature of mission, which was to model as well as characterize the mission the disciples have been asked to undertake. This "involves both proclamation and service, both individual and communal renewal, both justification and justice, and both peace with God and peace on earth."[199] The secularized interpretations of the *missio Dei* came as a challenge to this comprehensive dimension of mission and consequently diminished the importance of the Church as an important participant in the mission of the Triune God.

CONCLUSION

The modern trinitarian renewal has led to an extensive exposition and reflection of this central doctrine of Christianity as demonstrated in the subsequent trinitarian development and the vast body of literature this discourse has produced. The important and perhaps the crucial dimension of this development has been the emphasis on the retrieval of the economic aspect of the doctrine of the Trinity. This was especially evident in the work of Karl Rahner, who played a key role in bringing this into focus. By calling attention to the neglect of the economic Trinity in the economy and history of salvation, Rahner sought to shift the focus to what Catherine LaCugna has demonstrated as concentration "on the mystery of *God with us, God*

---

our doctrines of God and man, our love for our neighbor and our obedience to Jesus Christ. The message of salvation implies also a message of judgment upon every form of alienation, oppression and discrimination, and we should not be afraid to denounce evil and injustice wherever they exist. When people receive Christ they are born again into his kingdom and must seek not only to exhibit but also to spread its righteousness in the midst of an unrighteous world. The salvation we claim should be transforming us in the totality of our personal and social responsibilities. Faith without works is dead" (Stott, *Making Christ Known*, 178).

198. Scherer, "Church, Kingdom, and *Missio Dei*," 85. See also Newbigin, *Trinitarian Faith and Today's Mission*, 24.

199. Engelsviken, "*Missio Dei*," 490.

for us."²⁰⁰ This emphasis has found resonance in trinitarian theologians of many confessional persuasions, who have sought to relate trinitarian doctrine to ecclesial, social, political, and ecological concerns.²⁰¹

One of the most important consequences of the modern trinitarian resurgence was the retrieval of a more theocentric and trinitarian understanding of mission. The recovery of mission as *missio Dei* (the mission of God) grounded in God's nature, a development began at Willingen, cannot be seen apart from the renewal of trinitarian theology. Given the sense of anthropocentrism that had dominated the understanding of mission in prior periods, the *missio Dei* concept provided a stronger theological foundation to mission. This meant a shift from an *ecclesiocentric* mission to a *trinitarian-centric* approach to mission.

Subsequent interpretations of the *missio Dei*, however, tended to marginalize the distinctive role of the Church in mission. The ecclesiological grounding of mission must be seen as important as the trinitarian grounding of mission in order to safeguard the role of the Church in mission. *Missio Dei* cannot be seen as God's mission unless it is God-centered and church-focused. This is a constant challenge that the Church encounters in the context of the global expansion of Christianity to non-Western lands. The following chapter will focus on the Indian context and will examine the development of mission theology in India within the larger framework of Indian Christian theology.

---

200. LaCugna, "Practical Trinity," 678.
201. See McDougall, "Return of Trinitarian Praxis?," 177–78.

2

Contours of Indian Christian Theology and Mission Discourse

INTRODUCTION

THE EMERGENCE OF INDIGENOUS theology in India manifests a fascinating confluence of Western and Indian influences. The Western influence in terms of education and secular ideology as well as the Christian mission launched by the West played a crucial role in the development of Indian Christian theology. The Western education and Christian mission together became instrumental in disseminating Christian principles among the educated Hindu elites during the nineteenth century. The response of the English educated Hindus to Christian faith set the stage for a Hindu-Christian dialogue which became decisive in the emergence of an indigenous Christian theology.

This chapter attempts to lay out the development of Indian Christian theology and mission thought in the religious, social, and cultural matrix of India. This discussion is deemed important as this study seeks to study the larger theme of trinitarian and the *missio Dei* theologies with reference to Indian Christian and mission theologies, and particularly the Indian trinitarian theology as represented in Brahmabandhab Upadhyay's work. The preceding chapter on trinitarian theology and the *missio Dei* was undertaken within this larger scheme. The present chapter will focus primarily on the evolving of an indigenous theology in engagement with Hinduism and subsequent theological and mission discourses in the thoughts of the pioneers and modern theologians as well as the contemporary liberation/

Contours of Indian Christian Theology and Mission Discourse

subaltern theologies. The scope of this chapter is confined to the discussion of the selected relevant themes of the representative thinkers among Indian theologians and missiologists. The emphasis is on the works of native Indian theologians and hence, the contributions of the Western missionary theologians and missiologists do not form part of this study.

HISTORICAL TRAJECTORY OF INDIAN CHRISTIANITY AND MISSION

The origin of Christianity in India has often been traced back to the earlier centuries of Christianity much before Europe was Christianized. The two sources to which the origin of Indian Christianity is attributed are the St. Thomas tradition—according to which Apostle Thomas brought the gospel to India in 52 AD—and traders and missionaries of the East-Syrian Church. The claim for the St. Thomas tradition is founded on the apocryphal writing of *Acts of Judas Thomas* (the Western tradition), believed to have been written in Syrian Edessan circle towards the close of the third century, and the fragmentary allusions found in the texts of the third and the subsequent centuries.[1] This Western tradition of *Acts of Judas Thomas* describes the apostle's ministry in North India and his martyrdom. While the historical accuracy and legitimacy of these writings and their references to the Indian apostolate of Thomas may be called into question, there are scholars who do not favor an outright rejection of historical legitimacy to the St. Thomas tradition.[2]

As against the Western tradition is the Indian tradition according to which St. Thomas came to South India in 52 AD. The apostle is believed to have converted Hindus of high castes, founded churches, and suffered martyrdom. This tradition draws its support from local records such as songs, certain written records including some Hindu accounts, oral traditions, and archaeological vestiges.[3] The earliest written sources of the Indian tradition come from the Portuguese in the sixteenth and seventeenth centuries who gathered the available sources and documented them.[4] Thus,

---

1. Mundadan, *History of Christianity in India*, 22–28; Firth, *Introduction to Indian Church History*, 8–17. See also Wright, *Apocryphal Acts of the Apostles*, 146–298; Klijn, *Acts of Thomas*; Garbe, "St. Thomas in India," 1–27; Ogilive, *Apostles of India*, 1–29.

2. See Mundadan, *History of Christianity in India*, 24; Frykenberg, *Christianity in India*, 93–102.

3. Mundadan, *History of Christianity in India*, 29–36.

4. Mundadan, *History of Christianity in India*, 36–66.

An Indian Trinitarian Theology of *Missio Dei*

conjectures have been made which are founded on various sources of traditions and allusions on Indian Christianity in the writings and documents outside of India to establish the presence of Christianity in (South) India and its continuity to the time of the arrival of the Portuguese.[5] The dearth of credible documented historical evidences has rendered the historicity of the apostolic origin of Christianity untenable. Nevertheless, one cannot certainly disregard a tradition which is deeply entrenched in the collective conscience of the Christian community in South India. Having made a comprehensive study of the Indian apostolate of Thomas, the Indian Catholic historian, Mundadan concludes:

> The investigation . . . into the western tradition and different aspects of the Indian tradition give me the impression that the central content stands out in clear relief, namely St Thomas the Apostle preached, died and was buried in South India. None of the arguments so far advanced seem to be strong enough to erode the validity of this central content. . . . The age-old consciousness of the community of St. Thomas Christians—that their origin as Christian is from the mission of St. Thomas the Apostle in India—stands sufficiently justified.[6]

Similarly, the former professor of History and South Asian Studies at Wisconsin University-Madison, Robert Frykenberg writes: "While, despite manifold, parallel, and venerable sources, there is not enough evidence to compel unqualified acceptance, neither are there sufficient grounds, due to the rich array of extremely complex and difficult strands of circumstantial evidence, to dismiss outright or disprove the historicity of this [St. Thomas] tradition."[7]

Historians further trace the development of Indian Christian communities believed to have been originated with the apostolate of St. Thomas until the coming of the Portuguese in the sixteenth century. This attempt points toward the relation between the Indian Christians and the East-Syrian Church of Persia. The original St. Thomas community, according to various sources, suffered decline over a period. The reinvigoration of this early Christianity is attributed to immigrant groups of East-Syrian Christians.

---

5. See Mundadan, *History of Christianity in India*, 67–115; Firth, *Introduction to Indian Church History*, 18–28.

6. Mundadan, *History of Christianity in India*, 64. See also Frykenberg, *Christianity in India*, 114–15.

7. Frykenberg, *Christianity in India*, 115.

Among these immigrants, two groups seem particularly important, the one led by Thomas of Cana, popularly called as "Cnai Thomman," in the fourth century, and the other is associated with two saints, Sapor and Prot in the ninth and the tenth centuries.[8] One cannot rule out intermix of social intercourse and intermarriages between the Syrian settlers and the St. Thomas Christians in South India. Perhaps the most important development—from the historical and ecclesiastical perspectives—of the relationship between the Indian Christians and the Syrian immigrants was the dependence of Indian Christianity on the East-Syrian Church and consequently the South Indian Christianity became virtually East-Syrian.[9]

Portuguese Christianity: Catholic Mission

Despite the long presence of Christianity in India from the third or fourth centuries, if not from the first century, there are no evidences of Christian mission. While the dependence of the Indian Christians on the Persian Church may have had its advantages, it prevented the Indian Christian community from developing a distinct theology and Christian vision of its own.[10] A new chapter opened with the arrival of the Portuguese in the sixteenth century and their introduction of Catholic Christianity in India. While trade and commerce remained the primary motive of the Portuguese, they also carried orders from the King and the Pope to propagate the Christian faith among India natives.[11] Thus, at the intersection of trade and religious fervor, began the Catholic mission movement in India.

Perhaps the most dominant paradigm of mission in India has been one of interpreting mission exclusively in terms of evangelization. This was, in fact, the mission paradigm represented in the mission movement begun by the Roman Catholic Church in the early sixteenth century which continued as the essential feature of both the Catholic and the Protestant theology of mission in India in the subsequent periods. This mission approach was very much evident in the missionary activity of the Jesuit pioneer, Francis

---

8. For details, see Mundadan, *History of Christianity in India*, 89–108; Firth, *Introduction to Indian Church History*, 28–33.

9. Mundadan, *History of Christianity in India*, 114–15.

10. See Mundadan, "Changing Task of Christian History," 35.

11. See Mundadan, *History of Christianity in India*, 240–42. Firth, *Introduction to Indian Church History*, 49–51.

An Indian Trinitarian Theology of *Missio Dei*

Xavier and later in the work of Robert De Nobili although their method of evangelization differed from each other considerably.[12]

The presupposition of the concept of mission as conquering was a fundamental aspect of the ideology of Western imperialism represented in a rather subtle manner in the Portuguese colonial expansion in India. One might see that within the close proximity between Roman Christianity and the Portuguese crown, the Christianization of India became an objective of imperial expansion at times with the use of force. Thus, the ecclesiastical and political coalition resulting, as it were, in an unholy alliance between Christianization and imperialism was to become detrimental to mission in India.[13] This not only alienated the natives from any leanings towards the gospel of Christ, but also discredited the Christian faith in the judgment of the non-Christian population. Christian mission, which was made subservient to political powers and to serve the objectives of imperial expansion, cannot be termed evangelization.

A significant departure from the imperialist stance on evangelization as well as an approach to mission, hitherto untested and unfamiliar, was to be found in the young Italian Jesuit, Robert De Nobili, who came to India in 1605. He took the local culture seriously in the communication of the gospel, and his work was perhaps the first attempt at indigenization as a tool for evangelization, particularly, of those from the upper strata of the Hindu society. De Nobili sought to identify with the Hindu culture in an attempt to present the Christian faith in its native cultural forms. He recognized that mastering Sanskrit, the language of the Hindu scriptures, as well as the local Tamil language was an important gateway into the thought world of Hinduism. Similarly, he felt the need for employing these languages to present the Christian doctrine which led to the composition of a number of works in Sanskrit and Tamil.[14] De Nobili was primarily a missionary, not a theologian, whose mission context became ground for an experiment in indigenization and dialogue. Drawing from the Hindu literature in Tamil and Sanskrit, he created an indigenous theological vocabulary in place of the Latin theological vocabulary. Nevertheless, De Nobili's experiments

---

12. Gladstone, "Mission and Evangelization in India," 74–75.

13. Boyd, *Introduction to Indian Christian Theology*, 11; Mundadan, *Paths of Indian Theology*, 5–6.

14. See Johnson, "Contextualization," 9–20.

Contours of Indian Christian Theology and Mission Discourse

were not expressions of an indigenous theology employing Hindu thought-forms and categories, but they were polemical in nature.[15]

Protestant Christianity: Danish Halle Mission

The presence of Protestant Christianity may be traced back to the seventeenth-century Dutch Reformed Church and its ministers whose ministry was primarily addressed to the Dutch in India.[16] The Protestant mission in India, in fact, began with the Danish Halle Mission in Tranquebar in Tamil Nadu with the arrival of Bartholomew Ziegenbalg and Heinrich Pluetschau in 1706. The Tranquebar mission represented the Pietist mission paradigm, which signaled a departure from "the superficiality of conversion that characterized much of contemporary Roman Catholic mission work."[17] Here evangelization was not aimed at group conversion, but at the individual who must undergo transformation through faith and the inner working of God.[18] Yet, the Tranquebar mission was not divorced of what Ziegenbalg called the "service of the body" (*Dienst des Leibes*). In keeping with the holistic view of mission in early Pietism, Ziegenbalg emphasized the interdependence of the spiritual and material needs of the community. This was reflected in the Tranquebar mission's works of charity and the establishment of schools.[19] Education formed an important part of the Tranquebar mission which was not merely intended to disseminate knowledge, but to train the convert in the Christian faith and present the gospel to the Hindus.[20]

Ziegenbalg was sympathetic towards Hinduism which was rarely seen in early Christian mission in India. In a letter written to his mission home base in Halle, Ziegenbalg writes, "I do not reject everything they teach, rather rejoice that for the heathen long ago a small light of the Gospel began to shine. . . . [One] will find here and there such teachings and passages in their writings which are not only according to human reason but also according to God's Word."[21] Ziegenbalg and colleagues were the earliest to

---

15. Boyd, *Introduction to Indian Christian Theology*, 13–14; Parappally, *Emerging Trends in Indian Christian Theology*, 4–5.
16. Hudson, *Protestant Origins in India*, 5–9.
17. Bosch, *Transforming Mission*, 253.
18. Hudson, *Protestant Origins in India*, 39–40.
19. Bosch, *Transforming Mission*, 254.
20. Neill, *History of Christianity in India*, 31.
21. Ziegenbalg quoted in Lehmann, *It Began at Tranquebar*, 31–32.

An Indian Trinitarian Theology of *Missio Dei*

discover the importance of Bible translation, a mission principle which has gained recognition among mission scholars today. He is credited with the first translation of the New Testament into Tamil, although an imperfect translation, which was later revised by John Philip Fabricius in 1750.[22] The contribution of the Tranquebar mission went beyond the missionary activities to cultural and religious encounters as well as the dissemination of the knowledge about the socio-religious and cultural contexts of South India to an international audience.

Protestant Christianity: Serampore Baptist Mission

The founding of the Baptist mission in Serampore, India by William Carey and his colleagues is regarded as a defining moment in modern mission history. With Carey's arrival in Calcutta in 1793 and of his associates William Ward and Joshua Marshman seven years later, the foundation was laid for a mission in the Danish settlement in Serampore near Calcutta. The Serampore mission was a multi-faceted one where Carey and associates launched out into a wide area of activities like Bible translation, education, journalism, social reform, and horticulture which perhaps hitherto had no precedence in mission, at least not in India.[23] With their ventures into social reform and social activities, the Serampore mission marked an important development in mission thinking in India. William Carey belonged to a group of people who under the influence of the Great Awakening in England were moved to compassion for the oppressed, the marginalized, and people who were exposed to degrading social conditions. Even prior to his mission undertaking in India, Carey protested against slavery and opposed the import of sugar produced by slaves in West Indies plantations.[24] In India, Carey and his associates launched their movement against female infanticide, *sati* (immolation of widow in husband's funeral pyre) and other social evils, and created public opinion against them. Speaking on the social aspect of the Serampore mission, the renowned Indian theologian M. M. Thomas calls it humanization which he believes was integral to Carey's mission.[25]

The major contributions of the Serampore missionaries, in terms of mission, are in the field of education and Bible translation, a mission

22. Jeyaraj, *Genealogy of the South Indian Deities*, 21.
23. Chatterjee, *William Carey and Serampore*, ix–xii.
24. Bosch, *Transforming Mission*, 281.
25. Thomas, *Salvation and Humanisation*, 11–12.

strategy already begun in the Tranquebar mission by Ziegenbalg and colleagues. Despite the imperfections, for several Indian languages Carey and his associates "established the basic vocabulary of Christian theology."[26] As a mission strategy, the translations of the Serampore trio set a trend, as it were, for the successive vernacular translations which became pivotal in Protestant mission in India.

The educational mission of the Serampore missionaries found its ultimate fruition in the establishment of Serampore College in 1818, which turned out to be a landmark in theological education in the Indian subcontinent. The college was intended to produce an educated class acquainted with Indian classical literature and Western science, as well as to prepare minsters and teachers for the Indian church. It was this vision which eventually led to the formation of a theology department in Serampore College which was empowered by the royal charter of the King of Denmark to confer theological degrees in 1827. Thus was formed the first "Christian university in embryo" in Asia.[27] Carey and associates demonstrated an ecumenical vision that characterized the theological education they launched. Theological education was pursued alongside a wide range of secular disciplines, thus creating an atmosphere of holistic learning.[28]

The Serampore missionaries themselves were not theologians, yet their mission and forays into education and social reform created a context which proved to be pivotal in the emergence of Christian theological inquiry. Carey and his associates were instrumental in launching a movement against social evils of the time which brought them into contact with Raja Ram Mohan Roy. The meeting between the missionaries and Roy further led to a relationship at a different level, to a debate on Christian faith. The theological engagements between Roy and Joshua Marshman later paved the way for a passionate discourse on Christian theology.[29] The beginning of the development of an indigenous Christian theology may be sought in this encounter in the context of Bengal Renaissance in which the Serampore missionaries played a very central role as much as did Roy. Thus, the Protestant mission in the nineteenth century may be said to have played an inadvertent role in the emergence of an indigenous theology in India.

---

26. Boyd, *Introduction to Indian Christian Theology*, 16.
27. See Firth, *Introduction to Indian Church History*, 153–54.
28. Daniel, "Ecumenical Pragmatism of the Serampore Mission," 106–7.
29. Chatterjee, *William Carey and Serampore*, 14–19.

An Indian Trinitarian Theology of *Missio Dei*

CHRISTIANITY AND HINDU RENAISSANCE

The seventeenth and eighteenth centuries witnessed the arrival of Europeans who were primarily driven by interest in commercial pursuits. This coincided with the arrival of European missionaries whose religious fervor often clashed with those of the business class. The increasing contact between India and Europe in the eighteenth century became a watershed in the history of British India in terms of politics, culture, and social change. The Indian aspiration for freedom and independence from the British rule was reflected in the Indian National Movement initiated in the second half of the nineteenth century. The nineteenth century also witnessed the resurgence of social and religious reform movements, and an intellectual awakening commonly known as the Bengal Renaissance. There was an intense desire to move away from the traditional beliefs, superstitions, and inertia that for long had created stagnation in the Indian society and hampered any kind of progress. The reawakening generated a new outlook towards a future society founded on reason, scientific advancement, social progress, freedom, and justice.[30] The impetus to this renaissance was provided by the East-West contact, the introduction of Western education, particularly the Christian ideals and values "which found their way through Christians from the West who came to India, as merchants, conquerors, missionaries, educationists and social workers . . . Western movements and ideologies, literature and philosophies."[31] It is important to note that the Bengali intelligentsia (*Bhadralok*) responded positively to these influences. Thus, various factors merged to form this historic reawakening, which signaled the transition of India from being a medieval society to one that would be modern and progressive.

---

30. Thomas, "Interaction of the Gospel and Culture in Bengal," 1:38.

31. Thomas, "Interaction of the Gospel and Culture in Bengal," 1:38. The beginning of Christianity in Bengal may be traced back to the arrival of the Portuguese in the sixteenth century and the subsequent missionary work by Catholic and Protestant missionaries. Although Christians were a negligible community in nineteenth-century Bengal, Christian values and ideals did have a significant influence on circumstances and events that led to Bengal Renaissance. Christian institutions and Christians, both European and native, became the carriers of Christian ideals and values to Bengal. It is important to note that although most of the Europeans were not professing Christians, nevertheless their outlook on life was shaped by the Western Christian civilization and culture. The morals and principles, which these Europeans were instrumental in bringing into the social and cultural life of Bengal, had their origin in the Christian faith and "in the liberal, progressive climate created by a Christian culture" (Thomas, "Interaction of the Gospel and Culture in Bengal," 1:38). See Fallon, "Christianity in Bengal," 448–59.

Contours of Indian Christian Theology and Mission Discourse

Hindu Theistic Movements and Christian Faith

One of the most important aspects of the Bengal Renaissance, which became catalytic in the emergence of Indian Christian theology, was the birth of Hindu theistic movements, *Brahmo Samaj* (also spelled *Brahma samāj*, literally, "Society of Brahma") and *Ārya Samaj* ("Society of Nobles") in the nineteenth century. These were socio-religious reform movements which sought to revive and reform the Hindu society and religion. The Western culture and education had left an impact on Hindu culture and to some extent on Hindu cult as well. There was an uncritical acceptance of the alien Western culture, and under its influence, the Hindu rituals, idol worship, and polytheistic elements were called into question. In this context, rejecting the practice of idolatry and polytheism in Hinduism, the Hindu reformers brought forward a theistic interpretation of religion.[32] The reformers also sought to counter the conversion of Hindus by Christian missionaries. These crises necessitated a revival of the Hindu creed in which the reformers claimed to see the personal dimension of the ultimate being, and asserted Hinduism as essentially theistic. Hence, the theistic movements sought for reform in the Hindu worship where there would be no room for idolatry, priest-craft, and temples. Emphasis was laid on simple rituals, congregational worship, and prayer. The reformers also opposed the social evils that had crept into the Hindu society such as child marriage, enforced widowhood, caste system, and untouchability.[33]

Interestingly, despite their disapproval of Christian conversion, the reform movements were evidently influenced by Christian values exerted through Christian education and mission. Prominent among the Hindu movements, from the perspective of the Christian faith, was the *Brahmo Samaj* founded in 1828 by Raja Ram Mohan Roy. *Brahmo Samaj* engendered perhaps the most significant responses to the Christian faith paving the way for a thoughtful and yet passionate Hindu-Christian dialogue touching the foundational doctrines of Christianity. In fact, Brahmoism of Roy and his successors and their theological engagements may be said to have formed a bridge for the development of an indigenous Christian theology.[34] We might see the emergence of an Indian Christian theology at this intersection of Hindu-Christian dialogue. The three key people regarded

---

32. Devanandan, *Christian Concern in Hinduism*, 42–44.
33. Devanandan, *Christian Concern in Hinduism*, 45.
34. Thomas, *Acknowledged Christ of the Indian Renaissance*, 100–101.

An Indian Trinitarian Theology of *Missio Dei*

as representing the Hindu responses to Christian theology are Raja Ram Mohan Roy, Keshub Chunder Sen, and Pratap Chander Mozoomdar.

Raja Ram Mohan Roy

Raja Ram Mohan Roy (1772–1883) was the foremost leader of the Hindu reform movements, who was drawn to the tenets of Islam, particularly its monotheistic belief and was exposed to the Unitarian theism of the West and Western liberal education. Under these influences, Roy realized the need for reforming his own Hindu society from superstitions and the prevailing social and religious customs and practices that hampered the potential of progress and advancement of Hindu society.[35] Something that profoundly influenced Roy in his fight for reform was the ethical teachings of Jesus which he called the "precepts of Jesus."

Roy developed his theological thoughts in interaction with Marshman, one of the Serampore missionaries, who sought to defend the orthodox doctrine of Christianity. Roy approached Christianity from a rationalist and monist stance, and regarded Christ as an ethical teacher and Christianity as an ethical religion. While he holds Christ in great esteem as a great teacher and a messenger of God, he denies the attribution of the title "Son of God" to Christ and his equality with God.[36] Rejecting the passion and the atoning death of Christ, Roy contends that Christ's saving work is accomplished through his instructions, the moral precepts.[37] Roy was more interested in the principles of Jesus rather than the person of Jesus, an approach to the Christian faith that was characteristic of many Hindus as found in Swami Vivekananda and Gandhi.[38] Roy rejects the personhood of the Holy Spirit who, he believes, is a holy influence and divine power.[39] Being a strong opponent of polytheism and idolatry in his own Hindu religion, Roy vehemently opposed the Christian doctrine of the Trinity. He regarded belief in the Trinity as reversing to a primitivism and verging towards polytheism.[40] Roy's critical analysis of the Christian faith is seen as an important theological engagement. Given his rational approach and

---

35. Thomas, "Interaction of the Gospel and Culture in Bengal," 2:50.

36. Roy, *Precepts of Jesus*, 155–74. For a brief analysis of the theological engagement between Marshman and Roy, see Kolencherry, *Universality of Modern Hinduism*, 77–84.

37. Roy, *Precepts of Jesus*, 201–3.

38. See Thomas, *Salvation and Humanisation*, 27–28.

39. Roy, *Precepts of Jesus*, 229–30.

40. Roy, *Precepts of Jesus*, 255–62.

selective use of the Christian Scripture and the more passionate posture of Marshman, one may not consider the dialogue rewarding. This apart, Hindu-Christian encounter signaled a direction in which the subsequent theological formulation would move.

Keshub Chunder Sen

A different approach to Christianity, particularly to the person of Christ, may be seen in Roy's successor, Keshub Chunder Sen (1838–1884). Moving away from the rationalist and monist stance of his predecessor, Sen made Christ central to his faith and experience. Sen regards Christ as the preexistent logos who was the agent of creation.[41] Christ's saving work is an example of moral influence which humanity can imitate and through which "fallen humanity rises sanctified and regenerated."[42] Christ, according to Sen, remains man and to whose nature God is superadded, and thus he is the God-Man. In Christ, "Humanity continues to be humanity, but Divinity is engrafted upon humanity."[43] In Christ, our human nature is perfected through its association with divinity and our humanity is exalted. Thus, Sen understands salvation in terms of exalted humanity through its association with divinity and this salvation is universal in scope.[44] It is becoming Christ, where every human being is made Christ, and Christ is the means to this end. It is "the spread of Divine Sonship, like a sweeping flood of light and life, carrying all mankind heavenward."[45] Strangely, one might notice a shift in Sen's views on Christ's saving work to a somewhat orthodox position. Sen refers to Christ as the "mediating link between man and God," "our mediator," and "the only way" to the Father.[46] However, despite his views expressed on Christ and his work, Sen attributes the work of salvation to the Holy Spirit and not to Christ. Christ may show the way, the *way* to overcome sin, but the *power* to overcome sin is given by the Holy Spirit.[47]

41. Sen, *Keshub Chunder Sen's Lectures in India*, 1:375–77, 2:10–12.
42. Sen, *Keshub Chunder Sen's Lectures in India*, 2:27.
43. Sen, *Keshub Chunder Sen's Lectures in India*, 2:18–19.
44. Sen, *Keshub Chunder Sen's Lectures in India*, 2:20.
45. Sen, *Keshub Chunder Sen's Lectures in India*, 2:15.
46. Sen, *Keshub Chunder Sen's Lectures in India*, 2:35–36.
47. Sen, *Keshub Chunder Sen's Lectures in India*, 2:40. The most significant contribution of Sen to Christian theological discourse is his doctrine of the Trinity, which we will be taken up in the next chapter.

An Indian Trinitarian Theology of *Missio Dei*

Sen's theological stance seems closer to the Christian faith in comparison to his predecessor Ram Mohan Roy. Despite the absence of a visible Christian commitment from the perspective of Christian orthodoxy and the eclectic nature of his theology, Keshub Chunder Sen remains a very crucial figure in the emergence of Indian Christian theology. Sen contributed to Christian theological formulation through his attempts to integrate Hindu philosophical and cultural insights with Christian theology which was pursued by successive Indian Christian theologians.[48]

Pratap Chander Mozoomdar

Pratap Chander Mozoomdar (1840–1905), a prominent disciple of Sen, employs the synthesis between the Christian and Hindu concepts of the Spirit as a framework in interpreting the Christian faith, particularly Christology. As a Brahmo, Mozoomdar repudiates a pantheism that destroys personality and identifies the universe with God. He discovers another kind of pantheism which recognizes "the spirit of a presiding Providence in all things."[49] There is a "Divine Spirit [that] permeates every pore of matter and of humanity, and yet is absolutely different from both."[50] Equating this Spirit with the Holy Spirit of the biblical revelation, Mozoomdar finds the revelation of the permeating Spirit in the incarnation of Christ. There have been numerous incarnations in diverse cultures and societies which were partial, local, and imperfect self-manifestations of God limited by time and nationality. Christ, according to Mozoomdar, comes as the central figure, an everlasting model, "a universal model, one who includes in himself all these various embodiments of God's self-manifestation . . . in whom all other incarnations [have been] completed."[51]

Mozoomdar identifies the Holy Spirit with Christ himself which is a recurring theme in Indian Christian theology, particularly found in Chenchiah and Chakkarai. The Holy Spirit, Mozoomdar believes, directed the life of Christ, and he was the Spirit made flesh. The risen Christ returns as a quickening spirit and as spiritual reality in the human hearts.[52] Mozoomdar's views on the Spirit bear close resemblance to those of his mentor, Sen. With his assertion in the uniqueness and the finality

---

48. See Parappally, *Emerging Trends in Indian Christian Theology*, 15–17.
49. Mozoomdar, *Oriental Christ*, 40–41.
50. Mozoomdar, *Oriental Christ*, 42.
51. Mozoomdar, *Spirit of God*, 239–40; cf. Mozoomdar, *Oriental Christ*, 89–90.
52. Mozoomdar, *Spirit of God*, 62, 259.

of the incarnation of Christ, Mozoomdar might seem to come closer to a Christian view of Christ.

PIONEERING APPROACHES TO CHRISTIAN THEOLOGY

The engagements of the Hindu renaissance leaders with the Christian faith provided an impetus to the already existing spirit of theological inquiry in the Indian church. The Christian theology that evolved out of the reading of the Hindu reformers was colored by their essential Hindu religious and philosophical presuppositions. Nevertheless, it was instrumental in awakening the Indian church to the necessity of the interpretation of the Christian faith which would be grounded in the Christian Scripture and tradition as well as relevant to the religious and cultural realities of India. This consciousness led to some significant pioneering efforts that have contributed towards a distinctive Indian theological discourse from the perspective of the Indian religious, philosophical, and cultural milieus. Interestingly, Christians who had attempted these pioneering efforts themselves were converts from the upper strata of the Hindu society and hence, their expression of the Christian faith was obviously influenced by their former religious faith, particularly the Sanskrit tradition. This section will seek to review some important theological formulations that have laid a foundation, as it were, for Indian Christian theology.

K. M. Banerjea and Vedic Theology

Krishna Mohan Banerjea (1813–1885) was a Hindu convert, ordained as an Anglican priest in 1839, and later became professor of theology at the Anglican seminary, Bishop's College, Calcutta. He was a Christian thinker, an apologist, and an outstanding Sanskrit scholar. His earlier writings were apologetic in nature and critical of Hinduism. His later writings, however, demonstrate a positive approach towards relationship between Hinduism and Christianity, and in fact, Banerjea pioneered a positive Christian stance towards Hinduism.[53]

In exploring the relationship between Christianity and Hinduism, Banerjea seeks to show the correspondence between the death of Christ and the sacrifice of *Prajāpati* (the Lord of creatures) who is both divine and human as described in the Vedas. The sacrifice of the Vedic ideal of the *Prajāpati*, maintains Banerjea, has never been fulfilled in any religion including Hinduism,

---

53. Philip, *Krishna Mohan Banerjea*, 81, 94.

other than in the person of the historical Christ, the true *Prajāpati* of the world.⁵⁴ "A fragment of a great scheme of salvation which was at first partially revealed and has since appeared in its integrity in the Person of Jesus Christ—the true *Prajāpati* of the world, and in His Church—the true Ark of salvation, by which we may escape from the waves of this sinful world."⁵⁵ Banerjea seems inclined to regard Christianity as the fulfillment of Hinduism. Hence, he sees the mission of the Church is to exhibit before all "the true Ark of salvation—that true 'vessel of sacrifice by which we may escape all sin.'"⁵⁶ Thus, from the Vedic doctrine of *Prajāpati* and its fulfillment in Christ, Banerjea surmises that Hindus ought to embrace the Christian faith and the Church. In the Vedic doctrine of *Prajāpati*, Banerjea finds the voice of the primitive ancestors of Hindus calling upon them "in the words of their Vedas to embark on the good ferrying boat for passing safely over the waves of sin. That Ark of Salvation can only mean the Church of Christ."⁵⁷ Banerjea saw Vedic religion as the original form of Hinduism and believed in a closer relation between the Vedic Hinduism and Christianity.⁵⁸ While being a great apologist, Banerjea saw dialogue as a means of Christian witness which begins from recognition of the other faith.

Nehemiah Goreh and Christian Orthodoxy

One of the important responses to Hinduism from Christian orthodoxy has come from Nehemiah Nilakantha Goreh (1825–1895) a Brahmin convert who was ordained to priesthood in the Anglican Church in 1870. He

---

54. Banerjea quoted in Philip, *Krishna Mohan Banerjea*, 195. The two propositions that Banerjea has enunciated in this regard are as follows: "That the fundamental principles of Christian doctrine in relation to the salvation of the world find a remarkable counterpart in the Vedic principles of primitive Hinduism in relation to the destruction of sin, and the redemption of the sinner by the efficacy of Sacrifice, itself a figure of *Prajāpati*, the Lord and Saviour of the Creation, who had given himself up as an offering for that purpose. . . . That the meaning of *Prajāpati*, an appellative, variously described as a *Purusha* begotten in the beginning, as *Viswakarma* the creator of all, singularly coincides with the meaning of the name and offices of the historical reality Jesus Christ, and that no other person than Jesus of Nazareth has ever appeared in the world claiming the character and position of the self-sacrificing *Prajāpati*, at the same time both mortal an immortal" (Philip, *Krishna Mohan Banerjea*, 181–82). See also Banerjea, *Two Essays*, 69–70.

55. Banerjea, "Relation between Christianity and Hinduism," 195.
56. Banerjea, "Relation between Christianity and Hinduism," 196–97.
57. Banerjea, "Relation between Christianity and Hinduism," 200.
58. Banerjea, "Relation between Christianity and Hinduism," 183–84, 200.

Contours of Indian Christian Theology and Mission Discourse

was well-read in the Hindu scriptures and was a reputed scholar of Hindu philosophy. Goreh's response to Hinduism was polemical and apologetic in nature. Having discovered the Christian doctrine of the *creatio ex nihilo*, Goreh sought to refute the Hindu concept of creation. The Hindu philosophical systems hold creation as being both eternal and having a material cause. Such a stance, according to Goreh, is unreasonable and it raises questions on the omnipotence and eternality of God. Over against such a view of creation, Goreh has found that the Christian doctrine of creation affirms the sovereignty of God who created everything by God's inscrutable might.[59] Challenging the Vedanta teaching on Brahman as *nirguṇa* (without attributes), Goreh contends that an attribute-less Brahman does not rise above nothingness, and "such a supreme Spirit . . . cannot be proved to exist."[60] Similarly, he rejects the Vedanta depiction of Brahman as "being, intelligence, and bliss" (*saccidānanda*). Brahman as intelligence "cognizes nothing, and [is] bliss without fruition of happiness" and therefore, the emancipated soul which attains realization of "Brahmanhood" cannot experience bliss.[61] Goreh posits true emancipation as freedom from sin obtained through forgiveness from God and true union with God is possible through Christ.[62]

Notwithstanding his rather antithetical view of Hinduism, Goreh was rooted in the Indian culture and tradition and genuinely believed that Christianity could be seen as a fulfillment of Hinduism and that God has prepared the Hindus to receive the Christian faith unlike any other people except the Jews.[63] Despite his strong refutation, Goreh believes there is divine light within Hinduism which could lead Hindus to the true religion of Christianity.[64] Goreh's theology has a strong missional motive and urge. As Balwant Paradkar has noted, his theology is a "Church-in-mission-theology."[65] Therefore, his polemical and apologetic tone often melts down

---

59. Gore, *Rational Refutation*, 36–41, 79–80.

60. Gore, *Rational Refutation*, 197.

61. Gore, *Rational Refutation*, 274.

62. Goreh, *Letter to the Brahmos*, 52–55; Goreh, *Proofs of the Divinity of Our Lord*, 36.

63. Boyd, *Introduction to Indian Christian Theology*, 54–56. Goreh, *Proofs of the Divinity of Our Lord*, 75.

64. Gore, *Rational Refutation of the Hindu Philosophical System*, 280.

65. Paradkar, *Theology of Nehemiah Goreh*, 23.

An Indian Trinitarian Theology of *Missio Dei*

to a gentle appeal to embrace the Christian faith and the Church, which he calls "the only keeper and infallible expounder of Christianity."[66]

Brahmabandhab Upadhyay and Indigenous Theology

Goreh's seemingly aggressive posture towards Hinduism was not shared by his young contemporary Brahmabandhab Upadhyay (1861–1907). In Upadhyay, we notice the pioneering efforts in interpreting the Christian faith employing categories of the Hindu philosophical system. Upadhyay was drawn to the Advaita philosophy of Shankara and he found it to be an important tool to articulate the Christian faith in order to express the gospel intelligibly in the religious and cultural context of India. Upadhyay felt it a necessity to formulate an indigenized theology in engagement with Hindu philosophy in order to build Christianity on Indian foundations.[67] Upadhyay appears to be taking a more serious view of Christian mission which is evident in his endeavor to build Christianity on Indian philosophical foundations. One such attempt is found in his exposition of the concept of *saccidānanda* in relation to the doctrine of the Trinity which we will deal with extensively in the next chapter.

Sadhu Sunder Singh and Christian Mysticism

Sadhu Sunder Singh (1889–1929), a convert from Sikhism, represents an altogether different approach to Christian faith, at least one that is not quite prominent in the Indian Christianity of his time. Sadhu, as Sunder Singh came to be called popularly, brought a new element, that of mystical and ecstatic experiences centered on the person of Christ, to Indian theological discourse. Sadhu could well be regarded as a practical theologian whose ideas of Christian faith and spirituality have been born out of his intense devotion to Christ, deep study of the New Testament, and his own mystical and ministerial experiences.[68] His spiritual experiences were largely characterized by a passionate love and devotion to the divine, a feature common to the Hindu *bhakti* tradition. Sadhu's mysticism has not attained much significance in the subsequent development of Indian Christian

66. Goreh, *Objections to Catholic Doctrine*, 91.

67. See Upadhyay, *Writings*, 1:228–29; 2:206.

68. There are incredible stories of Sadhu's spiritual encounter through visions, at times direct encounter with the divine and deep mystical experiences. See his book, *At the Master's Feet*. For a biography of Sadhu Sunder Singh, see Appasamy, *Sadhu Sunder Singh*.

theology. However, his mystical theology had a significant influence on A. J. Appasamy who himself had already been profoundly influenced by the *bhakti* tradition.

Sadhu's was not the sort of theology of the time being developed in engagement with Hindu philosophy. It was a theology of piety from the evangelical tradition and his mysticism was a practical one. Yet he was profoundly grounded in the Indian tradition and was convinced that "Indians desperately need the Water of Life, but they do not want it in European vessels!"[69] Being an itinerant preacher of the gospel and being fully identified with the life of the common people, Sadhu was far more convinced than anyone else about what it means to "offer the water of life in an Indian cup," what is today called "contextualization." He saw the need for an indigenized Christianity in its external form and appearance, and yet its fundamentals are to be kept intact. In its core, Christianity does not belong to the East or the West, but to humanity.[70] In that sense, Christianity belongs to Hinduism as well and is the fulfillment of Hinduism. "Hinduism," according to Sadhu, "has been digging channels. Christ is the water to flow through these channels."[71] Although he was not critical of Hinduism like Goreh, Sadhu rejected the Hindu *yoga* and especially *jnana marga* (path of knowledge) as means of salvation. Salvation comes from love which, for Sadhu, is to love the crucified and risen Christ.[72]

THE RETHINKING CHRISTIANITY

The Rethinking Group was a forum of Christian thinkers from South India who sought to reinterpret the Christian faith in engagement with India's religious, plural, and cultural contexts in an effort to develop an indigenous Christian theology. The prominent figures in this group were Appasamy, Chenchiah, and Chakkarai—known as the trio of South Indian theologians.

Aiyadurai Jesudasan Appasamy

A. J. Appasamy (1891–1975) was particularly drawn towards the *bhakti* tradition as an important framework to interpret the gospel in India. The characteristic feature of *bhakti* is its strong sense of loving adoration and

---

69. Comer, *Wisdom of the Sadhu*, 174.
70. Streeter and Appasamy, *Message of Sadhu Sunder Singh*, 181.
71. Sadhu quoted in Streeter and Appasamy, *Message of Sadhu Sunder Singh*, 181.
72. Boyd, *Introduction to Indian Christian Theology*, 107–8.

An Indian Trinitarian Theology of *Missio Dei*

ardent devotion to one's God. Relating the dimension of *bhakti* to the Christian faith, Appasamy suggests that Christian life may be regarded as a *bhakti marga* (path of devotion).[73] *Bhakti* as a school of Hindu thought was given a philosophical foundation by Rāmānuja, the proponent of *Vishishtadvaita* (qualified non-dualism).

Appasamy finds the mystic union of the devotee with the divine, a personal God as an essential hallmark of *bhakti* literature. This mysticism of the *bhakti* tradition, according to him, has resonance with mystic union of Christ with the Father, and Christian believers with Christ in the Fourth Gospel. The mysticism of John's gospel is quite significant in the Indian context as it safeguards against the tendency to identify the human soul with the divine.[74] Following Rāmānuja, Appasamy draws a parallel between the concept of Logos in John's gospel and the indwelling (immanent) God (*antaryāmin*) of Hinduism. In Rāmānuja's thought, God indwells the world as its soul: "God is the soul and the world is His body" and as the inner ruler, God controls the world.[75] Appasamy seeks to relate it with Christ, the eternal and immanent Logos who indwells the world and the human heart as the ubiquitous Lord. This is illustrated in the Fourth Gospel in Christ's union with the Father and the union of the Triune God with the believers. The immanent Logos is manifested in the incarnation of Christ in order that humanity will know him.[76] This incarnation of the Logos is the only and the complete incarnation (*purṇa avatāra*). For Appasamy, "there is no one except Jesus who could be regarded as an Incarnation of God."[77] Appasamy's affirmation of the uniqueness of Christ's incarnation virtually rules out the Hindu incarnations.

Appasamy was one of the earliest proponents of indigenization of Christian theological and ecclesiastical expression. He advocates that "the music, the architecture, the theology and the methods of government of the Indian Church must be really indigenous in its character."[78] While he is convinced of God's special and unique revelation in Christ, he believes that divine truth is deposited in all religious traditions including

---

73. See Appasamy, *Christianity as Bhakti Marga*.
74. Appasamy, *Christianity as Bhakti Marga*, 10–15.
75. Appasamy, *Gospel and India's Heritage*, 75.
76. Appasamy, *Gospel and India's Heritage*, 79; Appasamy, *Christianity as Bhakti Marga*, 41–42.
77. Appasamy, *Gospel and India's Heritage*, 259.
78. Appasamy, *Gospel and India's Heritage*, 14.

Hinduism as part of God's general revelation.[79] Therefore, Christian appropriation of India's spiritual heritage may be justified provided caution is applied against the adoption of religious and cultural elements that are contrary to the mind of Christ.[80] He believed that the "use of the heritage available in India will really make possible a richer and deeper spiritual life in the Indian Church ... [and] by doing so we shall make Christianity more attractive to the people of this land."[81] Appasamy, as a church leader, was deeply rooted in the Christian tradition and the Scripture. He held that the Church and its sacraments are important for the continuance of God's mission and the fulfillment of God's will in the world.[82] Yet he also believed that Christian openness to Indian spiritual heritage and the assimilation of the elements of Hindu spirituality are important in carrying out Christian mission in India.

Pandipeddi Chenchiah

Pandipeddi Chenchiah (1886–1959), a convert from the Hindu religion, was a distinguished lawyer and a Chief Justice in South India. According to him, "Indian Christian theology stands on three pillars—Hindu heritage, *pratyaksha* (direct) experience of Christ and ... the guidance of the Holy Spirit."[83] Chenchiah's theology is centered on the direct experience of Christ, the "raw fact of Christ" which he considers the only absolute.[84] To the question as to who is Christ, Chenchiah's response seems rather complex and at times ambiguous. He seeks to portray Christ as the *new creation*, the *new man*, the *God man*, the bridge between humanity and God. "Jesus is not God and is not Man, but is the Son of God and the Son of Man.... God is God. Man is Man. The twain have [sic] met in Jesus ... fused and mingled into one."[85] One needs to be clear that Chenchiah here does not refer to the metaphysical union of the Son with the Father or the perfect humanity and divinity of Christ. He seeks to show Christ as a new person, "a new creation" emerging from the union of God and human. In

---

79. Appasamy, *Gospel and India's Heritage*, 16.
80. Appasamy, *Gospel and India's Heritage*, 18.
81. Appasamy, *Gospel and India's Heritage*, 18.
82. Appasamy, *Gospel and India's Heritage*, 208.
83. Chenchiah, "Vedanta Philosophy and the Message of Christ," 18. Emphasis added.
84. Chenchiah, "Jesus and Non-Christian Faiths," 53.
85. Chenchiah, "Christian Message in a Non-Christian World," 27.

An Indian Trinitarian Theology of *Missio Dei*

Chenchiah's judgment, this Christ is "less than God" and yet he is more than human, the "God Man."[86]

Chenchiah's theology of Christ as the new creation is closely associated with the Holy Spirit, the cosmic energy. Salvation consists in humanity being made a new creation through union with Christ by power of the Holy Spirit, which Chenchiah calls the "*yoga of the Spirit.*"[87] This is a mystical union, a kind of *sāyujya* with Christ, "a transforming *sāyujya* in which the believer, though not 'identified' with Christ, becomes as it were 'a Christ' himself."[88] Chenchiah understands salvation in a social dimension. "Salvation is not translation into the kingdom of heaven after death but transportation of God into earth that He may find perfect expression in creation and history."[89] Salvation is not understood in the individualistic sense, but is associated with the Kingdom of God which is a "new world order to be evolved out of the present existence."[90] Chenchiah rejects the traditional teaching of the Church on salvation. In fact, the institution of the Church, the Christian tradition, and the formulated doctrines and creed hold no significance for

---

86. Chenchiah, "Jesus and Non-Christian Faiths," 60. In order to capture the meaning of Christ as the "new creation" and "God Man," it is important to observe Chenchiah's following passage: "It is not the relation of a religion to a religion or of a theology to a theology, but of a new creation to the old. If we may speak reverently, Jesus stands to man as man stands to the animal. Man is not the fulfillment or abrogation of the animal. He is not a perfected animal. He not only fulfills, but also transcends the lower creation. Jesus is not the 'Son'—Son of God or Son of Man—He is the product of God and man, not God-Man. The Spirit of God overshadowed Mary, and Jesus was born. He is a new creation—the Lord and Master of a new creative branch of cosmos. He is the Son of God because the Spirit of God entered him. He is the Son of Man because he was born out of the mother of man—the female. He transcends us as we transcend animals. Reason is our differentia, the Holy Spirit His. . . . Jesus is God's answer to man's ambition to become like God, to escape fate and destiny, to become master of life and death. This is an aspiration of all religions for which the answer can only be a new creation" (Chenchiah, "Jesus and Non-Christian Faiths," 60–61).

87. Chenchiah, "Our Theological Task VI," 67.

88. Boyd, *Introduction to Indian Christian Theology*, 152. *Sāyujya* is the fourth stage of spiritual progress in Hinduism where the devotee feels him/herself being identical with God.

89. Chenchiah, "Indian Christian Spiritual Discipline," 282. Frank Whaling's observation of Chenchiah's concept of salvation is pertinent here. He writes, "Chenchiah's stress . . . was switched from Jesus as the Saviour of the individual from sin, for a future in heaven, to Jesus as 'a term in the creative process' who is at work within the cosmic and historical process now, preparing a new future for man, [here on earth]" (Whaling, "Indian Christian Theology," 323).

90. Chenchiah, "Protest Against Barthianism," 93.

him.[91] Chenchiah seems to be drawn to a "religion-less," rather "Church-less" Christianity which is rooted in the Indian culture and tradition, and appealing to the religious conscience of the Hindu. Instead of an institutionalized church, Chenchiah proposes a Christian spiritual experiment after the model of the Hindu *ashram* (hermitage) where the power of the Holy Spirit will be captured as a dynamic divine energy which will "permeate the whole structure of Hinduism."[92] Chenchiah's thoughts appeared very radical and at variance with traditional Christianity. As a lay theologian not bound by the ecclesiastical structures, who already declared his antipathy towards the organized church and its creed, Chenchiah sought to move beyond his contemporaries in his theological views.

Vengal Chakkarai

Unlike Chenchiah, his contemporary and brother-in-law, Vengal Chakkarai (1880–1958) centered his theological thoughts on the incarnation and the cross, expounded in his two books, *Jesus the Avatar* and *The Cross and the Indian Thought*. For Chakkarai, the person of Christ ought to be the point of departure in Christian theological inquiry. We encounter the mysterious and the ineffable God in the revelation of Christ through whom we get a glimpse into the "unknown and infinite potencies" of the unmanifest God. "Whom we call God," according to Chakkarai, "stands behind Jesus, and it is Jesus who gives, as it were, colour, light and *rūpa* [form] to God."[93]

Chakkarai lays great emphasis on personal experience of the incarnated Christ (the *avatār* of God) through which one gains the knowledge of God.[94] The incarnation of Jesus is dynamic and perpetual unlike the Hindu *avatārs* which are transient and static. The resurrected Christ continues to be human, his humanity not being "sublimated into a kind of mystic divinity."[95] Chakkarai traces the continuity of Christ's incarnation in the Holy Spirit whom he identifies with the risen Christ. The Pentecost is seen as the fulfillment of the promises of Christ: "And remember, I am with you always, to the end of the age" (Matt 28:20); "I will not leave you orphaned;

---

91. Chenchiah, "Christian Message in a Non-Christian World," 8.

92. Chenchiah, "Church and the Indian Christian," 99–100. For a detailed exposition of Ashram, particularly Christian Ashram, see Chenchiah et al., *Asramas*.

93. Chakkarai, *Jesus the Avatar*, 165.

94. Boyd, *Introduction to Indian Christian Theology*, 168.

95. Chakkarai, *Jesus the Avatar*, 140.

I am coming to you" (John 14:18).⁹⁶ Since the Pentecost, the living Christ dwells in the Christian as the Holy Spirit (Gal 2:20), who is the "starting point" of our knowledge of Christ and God. Chakkarai does not see it as a negation of the historical Jesus, but an emphasis on the spiritual which is primary in the Indian tradition.⁹⁷

The work of the resurrected Christ as the Holy Spirit is understood in terms of mysticism which is embedded in the cross. The cross is most central to Chakkarai's theological thought. In the cross, sin is dealt with in its "darker and more sinister" form.⁹⁸ The cross is the fountainhead from which humanity receives healing and renewal, from which flows the power of the Spirit bringing spiritual restoration and transformation, and through the cross human communion with God is made possible.⁹⁹ Chakkarai finds resonance between the salvation through the cross of Christ and the emphasis on *bhakti marga* (path of devotion) in Hinduism. *Bhakti marga* is opposed to *karma marga* (path of works) and *jnanamarga* (path of knowledge) as legalistic ways of salvation¹⁰⁰ However, with its "intense and loving attachment to God" *bhakti marga* comes close to "the Pauline conception of faith . . . 'intense and loving attachment' to the crucified and risen Christ."¹⁰¹ Thus, according to Chakkarai, *bhakti marga* as a useful Hindu category to expound the Christian's union with God through the cross could be a *praeparatio evangelica*.

MODERN THEOLOGICAL AND MISSION DISCOURSE

The mid-twentieth and late twentieth century witnessed significant advances in Christian theological and mission discourse. Attempts have been made to interpret theology and mission in terms of dialogue, humanization, pluralism, and liberation. For the sake of brevity, we can only refer to the thoughts of the major figures that have bearing on the Indian Christian theology and mission.

---

96. Chakkarai, *Cross and Indian Thought*, 292; Chakkarai, *Jesus the Avatar*, 122.
97. Chakkarai, *Jesus the Avatar*, 122–23.
98. Boyd, *Introduction to Indian Christian Theology*, 176.
99. Boyd, *Introduction to Indian Christian Theology*, 176–77.
100. Boyd, *Introduction to Indian Christian Theology*, 178.
101. Boyd, *Introduction to Indian Christian Theology*, 178.

P. D. Devanandan

One of the key persons, contemporary to the Rethinking Group, was Paul David Devanandan (1901–1962). His major contribution to mission theology lies in the area of dialogue and nation building. Devanandan discovers within the renascent Hinduism, a renewal and newness contributed by the combined forces of secularism, Western liberal thought and education as well as Christianity.[102] This has led to a new understanding of humanity, a sense of personality, justice, relationship in community, and a new concept of history. This new anthropology emerging in the renascent Hinduism seemed to encounter the traditional worldview of Hindu metaphysics. Here Devanandan discerns a struggle within Hinduism in bringing about a synthesis between the classical Hindu theology and the new anthropology of Neo-Hinduism. This context, Devanandan believes, provides the opportunity for Christian dialogue and mission to proclaim the gospel of God incarnate in Christ. Devanandan would regard the Christian doctrine of creation and a personal God who has a purpose and destiny for humankind as important in this Christian-Hindu dialogue. In the Christian theology of creation, human beings are not merely the creatures of God, but they are also the children of God. There is a mutuality of relationship between God and humankind.[103]

Devanandan draws his biblical premise for dialogue from the reconciliation between the Jew and the Gentile effected through the death of Christ. Barriers that separate humanity, boundaries created by religions, have been broken down in Christ, and the way is open for a common humanity of people of all faith and no faith. The influence of the gospel on non-Christian renascent religions, particularly in Hinduism, is visible in the ferment in their religious thinking and values. According to Devanandan, "it is apparent that the fact of Christ has made an obvious difference, and that it continues to make a difference in the living and thinking of men of all faith."[104] The Christian impact on Hindu renaissance and a recognition of "the inner working of the Spirit of God" in the renaissance and renewal of contemporary Hinduism, for Devanandan, set the context

---

102. See Devanandan, *Preparation for Dialogue*, 37–41. For an introduction on P. D. Devanandan, see Lacy, "Legacy of Paul David Devanandan," 18–21.

103. Devanandan, *Preparation for Dialogue*, 38–40. Thomas and Thomas, *Towards an Indian Christian Theology*, 212.

104. Devanandan, *I Will Lift up Mine Eyes unto the Hills*, 118; Morton, "Humanism of Paul D. Devanandan," 10.

An Indian Trinitarian Theology of *Missio Dei*

for meaningful interreligious dialogue.[105] Thus, dialogue is an important aspect of Christian mission in the changed context of religious resurgence in the world, particularly the renaissance of Hinduism.

Mission, according to Devanandan, is the mission of God and it is fundamental to the being of the Church. The Church is "God's design . . . the community of forgiven sinners who have been entrusted with a mission. It is this mission which gives the Church its main reason to exist . . . this mission is the Mission of God in Christ reconciling the world to Himself."[106] Devanandan maintains that God's redemptive work in Christ has both social and cosmic character to it. The premise for social mission of the Church is founded on the scriptural affirmation and confession of Christ as the agent, the beginning, and the end of creation. The Christ event is central to God's revelation and human reconciliation to God, and in him human history finds its meaning and fulfillment.[107] God in Christ has created a new humanity, a new creation, and the church is called to bear witness to this new creation in Christ. This task, according to Devanandan, is accomplished through the Church's "active participation in the struggle for a new society and through a life of spiritual dialogue with the religious and secular faiths on the meaning and basis of being human."[108] The social mission of the Church is an integral part of its total life and mission. This mission is constituted of three key essentials, worship, evangelism, and service. While worship is the offering of ourselves to God, evangelism is our witness to the saving revelation of Christ through the proclamation of the gospel, and in service, we assume the servant role of Christ. Our service ought to be "the continued flowing out into the world" of God's love in Christ, and this Christian witness must point to the revelation of God in Christ.[109] One

---

105. Devanandan, *Preparation for Dialogue*, 177. See Morton, "Humanism of Paul D. Devanandan," 10. Devanandan's associate and successor M. M. Thomas has put Devanandan's biblical premise distinctly. He writes, "Just as the Cross and the Divine Forgiveness mediated by it destroyed the Jew-Gentile religious hostility, so also today the Cross is able to destroy the hostility between Christianity, Hinduism and Secularism and build a spiritual basis for a community of persons transcending religion and ideology" (Thomas and Thomas, *Towards an Indian Christian Theology*, 212–13).

106. Devanandan, *Christian Concern in Hinduism*, 116–17. See also Devanandan, *Christian Concern in Hinduism*, 120–21.

107. Devanandan, *Christian Participation in Nation-Building*, 290.

108. Thomas and Thomas, *Towards an Indian Christian Theology*, 212.

109. Devanandan, *Christian Participation in Nation-Building*, 291.

might notice in Devanandan, a constant struggle to bring together the social dimension and the evangelistic concern of the Christian mission.

M. M. Thomas

Devanandan's close associate and successor, Madathilparampil Mammen Thomas (1916–1996), further developed the theology of mission and dialogue. Thomas located the framework for his theological reflection in the person of Christ. God's act in the Christ event is decisive and central to Thomas's understanding of theology and mission. "God sent His Son into the world that the world through Him might be saved (John 3:17). That in the life, death and resurrection of Jesus of Nazareth God has acted to save the world is the core of the Christian gospel."[110] Thus, gospel, for Thomas, "is what God has done for the salvation of humankind through the life, death on the cross, resurrection, and glorification of Jesus of Nazareth."[111] Mission, for him, is "the communication of this message of salvation through Jesus Christ to the end that men may respond in faith and be saved" and it is essentially the "mission of salvation."[112] This dimension of mission, for Thomas, was essential and the cutting edge of Christian mission.

However, Thomas did not confine mission only to this concept, what he called the ultimate human destiny, the mission of salvation, but believed that mission must also be understood in terms of humanization, the historic human destiny—the social and moral transformation of human society.[113] Thomas does not see the mission of salvation and humanization as identical, but as integrally related to each other. "Salvation remains eschatological, but the historical responsibility within the eschatological framework cannot but include the task of humanization of the world in secular history."[114] He believes that the ultimate human destiny in the eschaton must be realized, albeit partially, within the historic human destiny. This partial realization signals the presence of the Kingdom of the resurrection life in the here and now.[115] Thomas views humanization as the entry point in gaining our knowledge of the ultimate human destiny within the economy of God. He discovers an interconnectedness of the eternal and historical destinies,

110. Thomas, *Salvation and Humanisation*, 2.
111. Thomas, *To the Ends of the Earth*, 35.
112. Thomas, *Salvation and Humanisation*, 2.
113. Thomas, *Salvation and Humanisation*, 2–4.
114. Thomas, *Salvation and Humanisation*, 8.
115. Thomas, *Salvation and Humanisation*, 8–9

An Indian Trinitarian Theology of *Missio Dei*

"the reality of the historical and the human in the eternal, and the presence of the eternal in the historical and the human."[116] Hence, the task of our mission is to demonstrate that "salvation is the spiritual inwardness of true humanisation, and that humanisation is inherent in the message of salvation in Christ."[117] Salvation in Christ offers a richer and fuller humanity for all, a new humanity. Christ as the bearer of this new humanity implies that "the final destiny of [human beings] is ultimately an incorporation into Christ's glorified humanity."[118] Thus, for Thomas salvation could be defined as "humanisation in a total and eschatological sense."[119]

According to Thomas, the issue of salvation and humanization is also characteristic of contemporary religious renaissance, which became fundamental in the renascent Neo-Hinduism as well as secular movements in India. Humanization, Thomas maintains, "provides the most relevant point of entry for any Christian dialogue with these movements on Salvation in Christ at spiritual and theological depth."[120] Thomas discovers within the renascent Hinduism, especially in Neo-Hindu thought and Indian nationalism, an acknowledgment of and response to Christ which create an important premise for a dialogue between Christianity and Hinduism.[121] His contention is that Indian Christian theology does not emerge only from within the church's own reflection. The Church

---

116. Thomas, *Salvation and Humanisation*, 10.

117 Thomas, *Salvation and Humanisation*, 10.

118. Thomas, *Salvation and Humanisation*, 18. See also Thomas, *Salvation and Humanisation*, 14.

119. Thomas, *Salvation and Humanisation*, 18. See also Thomas, *Salvation and Humanisation*, 14.

120. Thomas, *Salvation and Humanisation*, 20. See also Kuruvila, *Word Became Flesh*, 155. Thomas sees humanization as deriving from God's humanity in Christ, which justifies human struggle for humanization. Thus, Thomas's humanization may be termed as Christocentric anthropology. In response to Peter Beyerhaus's criticism of humanization, Thomas writes, "The ultimate framework of reference for Christian thought is neither God nor man in the abstract, neither the metaphysics of God nor the science of man taken in isolation, but Jesus Christ who is God-man rather God-for-man or to use Karl Barth's expression, the humanity of God. Therefore, properly speaking, Christian missionary thinking cannot be either theology or anthropology except as either of them is related to Christology. On the same reasoning, if it is Christ-centred, anthropology could become truly Christian in its framework. The distinction in humanism is between closed self-sufficiency and openness to the judgment and redemption of Christ in its spiritual inwardness" (Thomas, *Salvation and Humanisation*, 7). See also Beyerhaus, "Mission and Humanization," 11–24.

121. See Thomas, *Acknowledged Christ of the Indian Renaissance*, xiii–xiv.

must also seek for theological insights in the thoughts and reflections of the Neo-Hinduism on Christ found in the dialogical context created in the Indian renaissance. Therefore, Thomas believes "the Indian Church and the Indian nation have both their theological history and its evaluation is an obligation laid upon every new generation."[122]

Raymond Panikkar

Parallel to M. M. Thomas's *The Acknowledged Christ of the Indian Renaissance*, Raymond Panikkar (1918–2012) took Christian-Hindu dialogue to a different plane in his *Unknown Christ of Hinduism*. Panikkar seeks to demonstrate Christ as being already present in all religions and the presence of Christ makes all religions salvific. This universal salvation offered through Christ includes all peoples and religions. Hence, Christ, according to Panikkar, "is not *only* the historical redeemer, but *also* the unique Son of God . . . the only ontological—temporal and eternal—link between God and the World."[123] Panikkar's primary focus is on Hinduism where he feels the presence of Christ is not recognized, and hence, he sees Christ as being hidden and unknown in Hinduism. This hidden Christ, Panikkar contends, can be the meeting point of Hinduism and Christianity.[124] Recognizing the salvific and hidden presence of Christ in Hinduism, according to Panikkar, the task of Christian mission is to unveil the unknown Christ of Hinduism.[125]

Continuing the exploration of the relation between Christianity and Hinduism, Panikkar further seeks to relate the Christian doctrine of the Trinity with Hindu spirituality in a distinctive manner. Moving away from the typical interpretation of the Trinity in terms of being, knowledge, and love (*saccidānanda*) followed by other Indian theologians, Panikkar seeks to relate action, love, and knowledge as found in the three major Hindu paths of salvation, *karma marga*, *bhakti marga*, and *jnana marga* with the spirituality of the Christian Trinity.[126] Accordingly, *karma marga* is related to the Father, the transcendent one who is silent and ineffable, qualities that characterize the concept of the divine in all religions. Obedience to

---

122. Thomas, *Acknowledged Christ of the Indian Renaissance*, 319.

123. Panikkar, *Unknown Christ of Hinduism*, 83.

124. Panikkar, *Unknown Christ of Hinduism*, 50–57.

125. Boyd, *Introduction to Indian Christian Theology*, 222–23. See also Panikkar, *Unknown Christ of Hinduism*, 168–69.

126. See Panikkar, *Trinity and World Religions*.

the law of this absolute and ineffable God is the appropriate response.[127] *Bhakti marga*, the personalist dimension of spirituality corresponds to the Son, "the God with whom one can speak, establish dialogue, enter into communication."[128] Here "the way of devotion and love, *bhaktimarga*, is the normal blossoming of the personalist dimension of spirituality."[129] *Jnana marga*, the path of non-dualism, is related to the Holy Spirit, the immanent God, the *atman* who is also *Brahman*. Here spirituality is one of knowledge, abandonment and union, and "yielding totally to God."[130]

Stanley J. Samartha

Going beyond M. M. Thomas's *Acknowledged Christ* and Panikkar's *Unknown Christ*, Stanley Jedidiah Samartha (1920–2001) postulates the Hindu recognition of the *Unbound Christ*. Christ, according to Samartha, is already present in Hinduism and it is amply evident in the diverse Hindu responses to Christ, although "the manner of the response and its characteristics" may not correspond to the traditional understanding of the Church.[131] In appraising these Hindu responses, Samartha seeks to formulate a Christology for the Indian context from the framework of Advaita. The Hindu responses have attempted to interpret the life and work of Christ primarily in the Advaita categories. Therefore, Samartha maintains that any formulation of Christology in the Indian context "must in some way come to terms with Advaita, not just in its classical form but also in its modern interpretations."[132] He believes that it is not in terms of the Semitic or the Greek philosophical thought forms that the Indian church must communicate its faith in Christ in India, but in terms of the Advaita system of thought expounded by Shankara.[133]

---

127. Panikkar, *Trinity and World Religions*, 16, 44–45.

128. Panikkar, *Trinity and World Religions*, 51.

129. Panikkar, *Trinity and World Religions*, 22.

130. Panikkar, *Trinity and World Religions*, 38–39, 62.

131. Samartha, *Hindu Response to the Unbound Christ*, 4. Samartha has selected the following representatives of modern Hinduism who responded to Christ: Raj Ram Mohan Roy, Shri Ramakrishna, Swami Vivekananda, Swami Akhilananda, Mahatma Gandhi, and S. Radhakrishnan.

132. Samartha, *Hindu Response to the Unbound Christ*, 119–20. For Samartha's reasons for preferring Advaita to *Bhakti* categories and *Vishishtadvaita* of Rāmānuja, see also Samartha, *Hindu Response to the Unbound Christ*, 162–66.

133. Samartha, *Hindu Response to the Unbound Christ*, 167.

Contours of Indian Christian Theology and Mission Discourse

The need for a revised Christology, for Samartha, stems from the context of religious pluralism which is missing in the Western Christologies. Christology that does not address the cultural and religious pluralism of Asia, particularly of India, can be detrimental to the mission of the Church.[134] While the substance of Christology remains the person of Christ, it must seriously take into account the dominant presence of non-Christian religions, "with their culture and civilization, scriptures, institutions, philosophy, ethics, social structures, and art."[135] Revised Christology does not imply diminishing the person of Christ or the weakening of the Christian faith, but it questions the exclusive claims of Christianity. It calls for Christian recognition of the commitment of non-Christians to their religious traditions, beliefs, and scriptures, and recognition of the validity of other faiths.[136] Christian recognition is essential in building bridges across others faiths. An important area to which Samartha points is interreligious dialogue which requires Christians's commitment to their own faith as well as recognition of and openness towards neighbors of other faiths.[137] He sees dialogue in a multi-religious context as inevitable which must be carried out with integrity to build relationship between religious communities and promote an attitude of mutual respect and love. Hence, in interreligious dialogue, there is no room for either syncretism or mission.[138]

Samartha does not see mission as part of interreligious dialogue. "Mission is God's continuing activity through the Spirit to mend the brokenness

---

134. Samartha, *One Christ—Many Religions*, 93–94. See also Samartha, *One Christ—Many Religions*, x.

135. Samartha, *One Christ—Many Religions*, 93. What Samartha advocates is for "a larger ecumenical framework in which Christian theology would remain distinctively *Christian* theology but at the same time respond to different needs of people in different situations without betraying Christian commitment to God in Christ" (Samartha, *One Christ—Many Religions*, 94).

136. Samartha, *One Christ—Many Religions*, 98–99. Revised Christology, according to Samartha, does not imply that this is to "be done by diminishing Christ or by diluting the substance of the Christian faith. It is not a matter of restructuring the Christian faith in order to accommodate neighbors of other faiths, but of critical reflection on the God-human encounter in Jesus Christ in a situation where new perceptions of religious pluralism cannot be ignored anymore" (Samartha, *One Christ—Many Religions*, 98). Further, in a multi-religious context, the function of Christology "is not to claim uniqueness for Christ by proving that others are wrong or false, but to confess, explain, and help Christians live in obedience to the truth manifested to them in Jesus Christ" (Samartha, *One Christ—Many Religions*, 104).

137. Samartha, *Courage for Dialogue*, 98.

138. Samartha, *Courage for Dialogue*, 100–101.

An Indian Trinitarian Theology of *Missio Dei*

of creation, to overcome the fragmentation of humanity, and to heal the rift between humanity, nature, and God."[139] The growing recognition of religious pluralism has created a new context for mission which, in Samartha's view, calls for a new understanding and a restatement of Christian mission. Here mission is not only seen as participating *in* God's continuing mission, but participating (cooperating) *with* the followers of other faiths for the common good of humanity. While granting the distinct identity of Christian mission as being grounded in the person of Christ and carried out in the power of the Holy Spirit, one cannot deny the missions of non-Christian religions.[140] Samartha is convinced that the person of Christ and God's saving work in Christ are foundational to Christian mission. The motivation for Christian mission, the ethical and social concerns, and the concern for freedom, justice, and humanization stem from what God has done in the Christ event. However, Samartha insists that in a pluralist society, this mission must be carried out in cooperation with the people of other faiths because they also demonstrate the same commitment for justice and human liberation.[141] The challenge for the Church is to be rooted in its commitment to Christ and Christian mission as well as being open to the mission of other faiths.[142] Despite his radical approach to mission, Samartha seeks to place Christ central to any understating of mission.

Sebastian Kappen

A different approach to Indian Christian theology from that of Thomas, Panikkar, and Samartha was pursued by their contemporary, Sebastian Kappen (1924–1993). Kappen moved away from doing theology from the Brahmanic-Sanskrit tradition which has been predominantly characteristic of Indian Christian theology. His approach to theology was from the

---

139. Samartha, *One Christ—Many Religions*, 149.

140. Samartha, *One Christ—Many Religions*, 150.

141. Samartha, *One Christ—Many Religions*, 151–52.

142. Samartha, *One Christ—Many Religions*, 152. In the following passage, Samartha captures this struggle: "A one-way proclamation of the name of Jesus without any sensitivity to other faiths alienates Christians from their neighbors and becomes an obstacle to cooperation with them. A one-sided emphasis on struggles for social justice without making clear that for Christians the source and goal of this struggle are in Jesus Christ, obscures Christian witness and fails to recognize that without the mercy and judgment of God, all human efforts are in danger of being infected with human pride and self-righteousness" (Samartha, *One Christ—Many Religions*, 152).

perspective of liberation theology colored by Marxian influence on his thoughts.

The liberation elements, according to Kappen, found in the dissent and revolt of Buddhism and *Bhakti* movement in India against the Brahmanical hegemony and dominance in the religious, cultural, and social spheres of life, anticipated the concerns of Jesus who encountered the repressive forces unleashed by the foreign cultural invasion of the Greeks and the political invasion of the Romans supported by the ruling and religious elites of the Jewish society.[143] The Jesus movement, Kappen maintains, was a counter-culture and a prophetic movement centered on the reign of God that stood against the cultural, social, political, and religious dominance of the ruling class and the elites.[144] Therefore, leaving the Catholic emphasis on inculturation—which sought to clothe Christianity in India in the costume of the Brahmanic-Sanskrit upper caste tradition for relevance—Kappen advocates "the socio-religious movements of dissent, originating from the repressed culture of the downtrodden and the marginalized," as the point of insertion of Jesus and the elements of his counter culture movement.[145]

Taking his cue from these and similar movements in India, Kappen envisages the possibility of an Asian, particularly an Indian theology of liberation emerging from the symbiosis of the Jesus tradition and "the radical currents in the Indian religious tradition and with the positive insights of Marxism.... Its breeding ground will not be closed Christian communities but *basileic communities* engaged in the struggle for a fuller humanity."[146] The objective of Christian mission is to work towards the emergence of a new humanity and it involves working for freedom for all and engaging in the "struggle against the economic, social, political, ideological and other forces which enslave men."[147] This is the task, Kappen maintains, that Jesus committed to his disciples and it is both relevant and urgent in the contemporary mission of the Church. When the Church does not take its stand against the forces of evil and darkness, it demonstrates nothing but its infidelity to Christ.

---

143. Kappen, *Towards a Holistic Cultural Paradigm*, 45–50; Kappen, *Jesus and Culture*, 9, 126; Kappen, *Jesus and Society*, 121–22.

144. See Kappen, *Jesus and Culture*, 21–22.

145. Muricken, "S. Kappen," 17–18.

146. Kappen, *Jesus and Culture*, 127.

147. Kappen, *Jesus and Society*, 140.

An Indian Trinitarian Theology of *Missio Dei*

SUBALTERN/LIBERATION THEOLOGIES

The preceding discussions demonstrate the various attempts to relate Christian theology with the dominant Hindu philosophical thoughts in an attempt to interpret the Christian faith and to identify the Indian church's mission and its distinct identity in the religiously plural context in India. While this remains an ongoing pursuit, the later part of the twentieth century witnessed the emergence of subaltern/liberation theologies that seek to relate the Christian faith with the struggles of weaker sections of the Indian society, the marginalized groups such as the Dalits and the Tribals. One of the most significant developments in the horizon of Christian theological discourse in India in recent times has been the emergence of the two distinctive liberation theologies, Dalit theology in the 1980s and Tribal theology in the 1990s.

Dalit Theology

The Dalits, believed to be one of the earliest inhabitants of India, according to the Indian census 2011, constitute 16.2 percent of the Indian population. Their history has been one of age-old oppression, exploitation, and subjugation at the hands of the social structure sanctioned by the Hindu caste system. One of the most significant developments towards Dalit emancipation was the Dalit mass movement to Christianity in the nineteenth century. The mass conversion to Christianity is regarded as having initiated the modern Dalit movement.[148] The rise of Dalit theology may be seen as part of the modern Dalit movement. As a counter theology, Dalit theology attempts to break with the traditional Indian Christian theologizing from the elitist perspective of Brahminic tradition, which for the Dalits represents the oppressive socio-religious structure.[149]

The classical Indian Christian theology has not taken into account the Dalit's experience of suffering or given expression to it, despite the fact that Dalits constitute the majority in the Indian church. It has not dealt with issues of socioeconomic and political realities of the Indian society such as the caste system and the economic exploitation and political deprivation of Dalits. Dalit Christian theology is Dalits's own attempt to relate their Christian faith to their experience of longstanding pain and suffering inflicted by the socio-religious structure of India. Therefore, it "will narrate

---

148. Webster, *Dalit Christians*, 71. See Danam, "Indian Church," 270.
149. See Nirmal, "Toward a Christian Dalit Theology," 29.

the story of their pathos and their protest against the socio-economic injustices they have been subjected to throughout history."[150] This concern about Dalit theology as well as the dominance of theological formulation from the elitist perspective of caste Hinduism continues to be an issue in Indian theological discourse.

Dalit theology brings the Christian gospel into engagement with the Indian context largely controlled by the system of social stratification, called the caste system.[151] This not only brings to focus the struggles of Dalits in India, but also underlines the necessity of theologizing from the perspective of the Dalits. Thus, it seeks to formulate a theology in India that will "affirm the oppressed, particularly the Dalits as the subjects of theology and undertake theological task from the perspective of the Dalits."[152] The need for Dalit theology stems from the realities of the perpetual struggle of Dalits and the denial of justice and freedom in a religious caste-ridden social institution. Theological articulation from the context of Dalit struggle and their experience of suffering and pain is seen as a pathway towards Dalit liberation.

Tribal Theology

Parallel to the development of Dalit theology is another significant attempt at theologizing from the context of the Tribal people of India who are 8.2 percent of the population of India. The Tribal communities of India, similar to the Dalits, have always been at the receiving end of the hegemony of the dominant and elite caste groups in India. Christianity came as a transforming force and became liberative to a significant part of Indian Tribals, especially in the Northeast India. However, Tribals continue to face political, social, cultural, and economic alienation. While Christianity, for the Tribals, was transformative in terms of education and social progress, one cannot overlook its role in the cultural alienation of the Tribals leading to a crisis of Tribal identity.[153] Tribal theology comes as a critical reflection of Christianity as well as an attempt to reinterpret the Christian faith and the Scripture from the cultural context and worldview of the Tribals.

Tribal theology attempts to develop a theology founded on tribal worldview that does not dichotomize between the spiritual and material.

150. Nirmal, "Toward a Christian Dalit Theology," 31.
151. Devasahayam, "Doing Dalit Theology," 272.
152. Devasahayam, "Doing Dalit Theology," 275.
153. Thanzauva, "Issues in Tribal Theology," 18.

An Indian Trinitarian Theology of *Missio Dei*

This worldview is built around a holistic approach to reality, where the Supreme Being, the creation, and all of life—human life, nature, land, and animals—are seen as being interrelated, and humans and all creations live in harmony with each other. One of the most significant issues which has bearing on developing a Tribal theology is the centrality of land to the tribal life. The Tribal articulation of theology takes as its subject the relationship of human and creation/land unlike the contemporary liberation theologies, including Dalit theology, which are more anthropocentric where humans and their struggle become the subject matter of theologizing.[154]

Tribal theology also seeks to rediscover the gospel values evident in the Tribal culture and worldview. These values include egalitarianism, sense of community rather than individualism, principle of consensus rather than majoritarian dominance, concept of sharing and mutuality rather than greed, democratic ideals, and stewardship of nature.[155] A rediscovery of these ideals inherent in the Tribal culture can contribute to evolving an ideology for the liberation of the subalterns in India as well as to a more humane and responsible way of life in modern society which is domineering, individualistic, and consumeristic.

Tribal and Dalit Mission Discourse

Subaltern theologies envisage a mission paradigm that will address the continuing struggles of Dalits and Tribals for justice and freedom. Mission approaches to the Dalits and Tribals identify their experience of suffering and alienation with God's suffering in Christ. The Tribal theologian and Lutheran bishop, Nirmal Minz, sees Christ as "being crushed, mutilated, and crucified" in the experience of the Tribals.[156] According to Indian Catholic missiologist, Lazar Stanislaus, in the experience of the Dalits, Christ is a slave (Phil 2:7) and a Dalit like them who was rejected as an outcaste (Luke 4:18).[157] Identifying the experience of the Tribals and Dalits with Jesus provides a theological paradigm for their liberation. Jesus' association with the marginalized and the outcastes of the Jewish society, his confrontation with the evil forces in the religious and political system, and his ultimate victory in the resurrection provide a new meaning and direction to Christian

---

154. Longchar, "Need for Doing Tribal Theology," 6–16. Thanzauva, *Theology of Community*, 186–213; 214–34.

155. Thomas, "Indian Tribal Culture," 76–77. See Minz, *Rise Up, My People*," 115–17.

156. Minz, "Mission in the Context of Diversity," 18–19

157. Stanislaus, "Dalits and the Mission of the Church," 197.

mission among the subalterns.[158] Therefore, faith in Christ must be expressed historically in the Church's commitment to the liberation of the subaltern communities from their continuing suffering and pain.[159]

There is a growing recognition that political and economic empowerment is very crucial for the liberation of Dalits and Tribals. Political power remains at the root of achieving social or economic transformation. This assumes importance in the present Indian political scenario where the Dalit communities are emerging as a decisive political force. Many Indian theologians and missiologists are inclined to believe that the Church has to rediscover and perhaps redefine its mission in such an environment.[160] This points to the necessity of a "political dimension of the mission of the Church ... [that] involves enlightenment, empowerment and enabling the subalterns through conscientization, motivation and mobilization."[161] The realization of the reign of God and the kingdom values of freedom, justice, and righteousness form the objective of the political dimension of Christian mission.[162] However, given the rising evils of communalization, criminalization, and corruption that plague contemporary Indian politics, political empowerment of the subaltern communities as a mission endeavor seems an enormous challenge.

The resurgence of the ideology of Hindutva and its emphasis on Hindu nationalism as a means of creating a Hindu nation-state pose another serious challenge to Christian mission and the subaltern communities. There is a well-orchestrated attempt to persuade and entice the Dalits and Tribals, including those who accepted Christianity, "to renounce their cultural and religious differences and embrace the all-encompassing Indian identity in its Hindu visage. . . . There is a systematic effort to educate them at the grassroots level of their religio-cultural space within Hinduism."[163] Speaking on the isolation of Indian Tribals from the mainstream of national life, missiologist, Roger Hedlund, draws attention to the attempts to assimilate them into the Hindu fold as a caste through Sanskritization.

---

158. Stanislaus, "Dalits and the Mission of the Church," 197–99.

159. Kavunkal, "Developing an Indian Missiology," 181.

160. See Stanislaus, "Dalits and the Mission of the Church," 203–4; Danam, "Indian Church," 277; Gorantla and Thumma, "Dalit Christians in the Third Millennium," 157–59.

161. Gorantla and Thumma, "Dalit Christians in the Third Millennium," 158.

162. Gorantla and Thumma, "Dalit Christians in the Third Millennium," 158.

163. Clarke, "Hindutva," 205.

An Indian Trinitarian Theology of *Missio Dei*

Assimilation destroys the tribal entity, makes the Tribals new low castes within Hinduism, and thus their perpetual subjugation is ensured. In this context, Hedlund regards Christianization of Tribals "as a viable alternative which preserves tribal culture and identity."[164] He believes that mobilization of tribal social movements is necessary as a critique of the oppressive caste structures and act as a liberative force. He regards these developments as "the stuff from which a truly Indian tribal missiology is to be constructed."[165] There is growing recognition among the subaltern communities of the need for their liberation from the oppressive caste structures as well as the consciousness of their rights and privileges as Indian citizens. On the other hand, there is the resurgent and militant movement of the Hindutva forces. These opposing forces provide opportunities as well as challenges for Christian mission.

CONCLUSION

Modern scholars have, at times, exhibited tendencies to recognize as "theology" only those systems of thought that display the complexity and methodological rigor of a *Church Dogmatics* or *Summa Theologica*. Judged by this standard, the Indian church has not formulated any system of thought that could be considered theology. This way of understanding theology gave rise to an often-stated criticism that Indian Christians have not produced a decent heresy, let alone theology![166] However, if one were to regard theology as arising from the encounter of the gospel with the living situations of people, their religious and cultural traditions, then there are remarkable indigenous theological formulations in India as demonstrated in this chapter.

The development of an Indian indigenous theology is a classic example of the necessity for contextual theologies in the face of the growth of Christianity as a global movement. The expansion of Christianity into the non-Western world has necessitated the articulation of indigenous theologies which are birthed in the conversation between theology and mission. What eminent historian and missiologist, Andrew Walls, has said about this interconnectedness of mission and theology holds good for Indian Christian theology: "the stimulus or creative force in making theology is Christian mission. Indeed, it is Christian mission that most often creates

---

164. Hedlund, "Glimpses of India Today," 124.
165. Hedlund, "Glimpses of India Today," 124.
166. Thomas, "Foreword," vi.

the need for fresh theological activity."[167] As demonstrated in the preceding overview, Indian indigenous theology emerged in the context of Christian mission, and the mission of the Church in the religiously plural context has continued to be the burden of theological discourse in India. Theological reflections in India continue to be undertaken with the objective of the mission of the Church in the most diverse and plural situations in India. One of the pioneering Indian theologians, who undertook such a daring task, as indicated earlier in this review, was Brahmabandhab Upadhyay, whose trinitarian theology forms the subject matter of the following chapter. Upadhyay was perhaps the first Indian theologian to recognize the importance of the indigenization of the gospel in India. His call for Christian dialogue with Indian philosophy, particularly the Advaita Vedanta in presenting the gospel in Indian religious and cultural thought forms, will be examined in the following chapter.

167. Walls, "Foreword," xv.

3

The Trinitarian Theology of Brahmabandhab Upadhyay

INTRODUCTION

ACCENTUATING THE IMPORTANCE OF the cultural translatability of the Christian faith, Andrew Walls has stated: "Christian faith must go on being translated, must continuously enter into vernacular culture and interact with it, or it withers and fades."[1] The cross-cultural transmission continues to play a pivotal role in the expansion and survival of Christianity. One of the most challenging religious and cultural contexts that Christianity has encountered in its cross-cultural expansion is found in India. This chapter addresses a pioneering endeavor of Christian theological engagement with the Indian religious tradition through one of the central doctrines of the Christian faith, the Trinity. The doctrine of the Trinity, interestingly, occupied a significant place in the Indian religious discourse even prior to the emergence of Indian Christian theology.[2] In the subsequent development of Christian theology in India, Trinity came to be related to the Advaita Vedanta of Shankara in an effort aimed at indigenizing the Christian faith. The person who developed this project and thus brought the Christian Trinity to the forefront of Indian theological discourse was Brahmabandhab Upadhyay. This effort was born out of his conviction that Christian faith would take root in India only if it disburdens itself of the foreign clothing and ground itself in native tradition

1. Walls, *Cross-Cultural Process in Christian History*, 29.
2. See Sen, *Keshub Chunder Sen's Lectures in India*, 2:1–48.

The Trinitarian Theology of Brahmabandhab Upadhyay

and culture. This chapter seeks to examine Upadhyay's use of the Advaita Vedanta concept of *saccidānanda* in restating the Trinity as an attempt to build a foundation for Christianity in India. Towards that end, we will explore in detail various aspects of this discourse and the missional underpinnings of this exercise in indigenization.

BIOGRAPHICAL SKETCH OF BRAHMABANDHAB UPADHYAY

The previous chapter briefly examined the political, cultural, and social movements of the nineteenth-century India. Among those who were part of the Indian Freedom Movement and Bengal Renaissance, there were some whose contribution and place have not been adequately recognized. One such figure was Brahmabandhab Upadhyay who, in the words of his biographer, Julius Lipner, "made a significant contribution to the shaping of the new India whose identity began to emerge from the first half of the nineteenth century."[3] Lipner further quotes a contemporary of Upadhyay on his role in the Indian National Movement as follows: "Vivekananda lit the sacrificial flame of revolution, Brahmabandhab in fueling it, safeguarded and fanned the sacrifice."[4]

Brahmabandhab Upadhyay was born Bhavani Charan Bandyopadhyay Banerji in an orthodox Brahmin family of Bengal on 11 February 1861. Bhavani lost his mother, Radhakumari, before he was a year old and he was raised up by his grandmother Chandramani who had a great influence on him. Under the care of Chandramani, a deeply religious and a strong personality, Bhavani grew up in knowledge and love for tradition and culture of rural Bengal. Bhavani came from a family which already had ties with Christianity primarily through his uncle, Kalicharan Banerji, who became a Christian in 1864 through the ministry of the Scottish missionary, Alexander Duff, while studying in the latter's Free Church Institution in Calcutta. Kalicharan, while being a Christian, was a patriot actively involved in the freedom movement. The fact that the Banerji family was tolerant towards the Christian faith and that Kalicharan regularly visited the family certainly influenced young Bhavani, who would subsequently follow his uncle's faith and his sense of patriotism.[5] Lipner refers to the remarkable influence of Kalicharan on Bhavani which was to be very decisive later in his life as a

3. Lipner, *Brahmabandhab Upadhyay*, xv.
4. Lipner, *Brahmabandhab Upadhyay*, xv.
5. Lipner, *Brahmabandhab Upadhyay*, 33–34, 37.

An Indian Trinitarian Theology of *Missio Dei*

Christian. According to Lipner, "by becoming a Christian without being abrasively unHindu, Kalicaran [sic] had broken an important psychological barrier vis-à-vis his family. If he hadn't exactly legitimized conversion to the Christian faith, he had at least made the prospect conceivable. Perhaps a seed had been sown in the impressionable Bhabani's mind that was to come to fruition years later."[6] This example of Kalicharan was deeply ingrained in Bhavani's heart that he would, in the future, consider himself a Hindu-Christian, Hindu by culture and Christian by faith. He asserted his cultural bond with his country and identified himself fully with his homeland.

Nineteenth-century Bengal witnessed an interface between Indian traditionalism of the older order and the new and nascent modernity unleashed by the western influences. The Banerji family was not unaffected by this impact of Westernization and English education. Bhavani's father, Debicharan Banerji, himself a police inspector under the British, was among those educated Bengalis who were called the *bhadralok* (i.e., the "cultured folk").[7] Bhavani received his schooling during this period of transition initiated by reform movements and Western education. After his learning in the local village school, he continued further education in English medium schools and colleges. The English education modeled after the British system exposed Bhavani, like his contemporaries, to Western liberal ideas and more importantly instilled in him a strong sense of nationalism.

As an adolescent, Bhavani had shown incredible strides and commitment both in westernized education and traditional learning, especially in Sanskrit. Lipner observes that unlike the teenagers of his age and time, Upadhyay exhibited extraordinary devotion and dedication to the learning of his own Hindu tradition so swiftly along with the excellence he had already demonstrated in his westernized education.[8] Along with this passion for learning, he imbibed a spirit of nationalism which flamed a revolutionary ardor in young Bhavani.

A remarkable religious inclination that occurred in Bhavani, quite uncommon for an early teenager, was his attraction to Christ. This began even prior to the age of 13 during his school days at the General Assembly Institution of the Scottish General Missionary Board. However, it was his association with the charismatic Keshub Chunder Sen and his *Brahmo Samaj* that drew Bhavani further towards the person of Christ. Sen's intellectual

---

6. Lipner, *Brahmabandhab Upadhyay*, 38.
7. Lipner, "Introduction," Upadhyay, *Writings*, 1:xv.
8. Lipner, *Brahmabandhab Upadhyay*, 41.

acumen, vibrant personality, puritan ethic, his synthesis of the Christian and Hindu elements, and perhaps more importantly, his ardent devotion to Christ appealed to Bhavani. He gave himself to the various religious and social involvements with Sen's *Samaj* and maintained a close association with Sen until his death in 1884. Bhavani maintained a strong relation with Sen's successor Pratap Chandra Mozoomdar and had great admiration for him. Mozoomdar's affection for Christ only strengthened Bhavani's already strong devotion to Christ and his study of the Christian Scriptures.[9]

Bhavani went beyond his mentors, Sen and Mozoomdar, in his affection for Christ. He became more convinced that Christ was more than a human, and took his claim of being sinless seriously. Bhavani acknowledged Jesus as the fulfillment of the spiritual aspirations and hope of Hinduism. Although this declaration from a Brahmo did not go well with the *Brahmo Samaj*, Bhavani stood firm in his conviction. Finally, he made a personal commitment to Christ under the guidance of the CMS missionary, Joseph Redman, and the Anglican priest, R. Heaton in May 1890. He was baptized by Rev. Heaton on February 26, 1891, but did not feel it necessary to join any church. However, after serious thought, Bhavani later joined the Roman Catholic Church for historical and theological reasons.[10] In 1894, he adopted the baptismal name, "Theophilus," and translated it into Bengali as "Brahmabandhab," the friend of Brahman, and added to it the second part of the family surname "Bandyopadhyay" (*Bandya* means "praised" and

---

9. See Lipner, *Brahmabandhab Upadhyay*, 65–70. Mozoomdar's *Oriental Christ* is considered a significant work on Christ by any Hindu reformer.

10. Animananda, *Blade*, 36, 44. Lipner, "Introduction," Upadhyay, *Writings*, 1:xxxii. As Lipner notes: "It would have offended [Upadhyay's] patriotic sentiments to have joined the religion of his political masters." On the theological front, Upadhyay was attracted to "the *kind* of theological approach the Catholic Church officially fostered towards non-Christian faiths." In the Catholic religion, represented especially in Thomas Aquinas, he found more recognition of natural theology which became an important framework for his theological formulations (Lipner, "Introduction," 1:xxxii–xxxiii). In the nineteenth-century intellectual ferment of Bengal, Christ became a "magnetic person" to which the Hindu intelligentsia, including the Hindu reformers responded in various ways. For instance, while Raja Ram Mohan Roy was drawn to Christ as a great ethical teacher, Christ was the center of Keshub Chunder Sen's religious experience. Similarly, Pratap Chandra Mozoomdar and several others were deeply attracted to the person of Christ. Yet their response to Christ was characterized by ambivalence and marked by "an insoluble conflict between their respect for Christ and attachment to their national tradition and social practices." It was Upadhyay who resolved "the dichotomy between Hinduism and Christianity" and thus, "successfully reconciled Christ with Hinduism" (Fonseca, "Prophet Disowned," 188).

An Indian Trinitarian Theology of *Missio Dei*

Upadhyay is "teacher," literally, "sub-teacher").[11] Henceforth, Bhavani came to be popularly known as Brahmabandhab Upadhyay. Although, he had an uneasy relationship with the church, Upadhyay continued to remain a Catholic until his death at the age of 46 in 1907.

THEOLOGICAL THOUGHT OF BRAHMABANDHAB UPADHYAY

The entire theological enterprise of Upadhyay centered on his deep conviction about the need for indigenous Christianity. The Danish Theologian, Kaj Baago, calls Upadhyay "the great pioneer of indigenization."[12] Upadhyay found that the Christian faith brought to India from the West had come in the Greco-Roman scholastic clothing and hence unintelligible to the Indian mind. In order to make the Christian gospel relevant to the Indian context, it was essential that the Christian faith must be interpreted in the Indian philosophical and cultural categories. Upadhyay, therefore, attempted three different foundations for an indigenous expression of Christianity in India. First, he began with a strong commitment to natural theology where he was convinced that every culture had a native, primitive theism, which could be tapped. Here Upadhyay extensively developed human reason as a potential foundation, which is all part of the natural theology or general revelation foundation. The second and the most important foundation was his reinterpretation of Advaita Vedanta within the context of a Thomistic worldview, where Upadhyay essentially took Aristotle out (Thomas Aquinas's project) and inserted Shankara, the celebrated eighth-century Indian philosopher and exponent of the Advaita Vedanta school of philosophy. The third foundation was developed in Upadhyay's more anti-British, nationalistic phase where he sought to build upon a foundation of Indian culture. Here he used the tools of social science and became more optimistic about redirecting popular Hindu religious forms into more generic cultural forms.[13]

---

11. Upadhyay, *Writings*, 2:449. Several years after his baptism, Upadhyay explained the change of his name in the periodical, *Sophia*. He says he has adopted the life of a mendicant as well as a new name after the pattern of Indian tradition. He writes, "I have abandoned the first portion of my family surname ["Bandyopadhyay"], because I am a disciple of Jesus Christ, the Man of Sorrows, the Despised Man" (Upadhyay, *Writings*, 2:449).

12. Baago, "Indian Indigenous Theology," 221.

13. A detailed discussion on these three attempts of Upadhyay is found in Tennent, *Building Christianity on Indian Foundations*, 147–207, 208–99, 300–54.

The Trinitarian Theology of Brahmabandhab Upadhyay

Upadhyay became prominent for his second foundation. An important step in this direction was his attempt to restate the Christian doctrine of the Trinity using the framework of the Advaita Vedanta concept of *saccidānanda*. His attempt here was to express the gospel, which is universal and global in scope, in India's religious and cultural context in an intelligible manner. In this sense, he sought to bring Christian theology and mission together. "In the process," says Tennent, "Upadhyay was decades ahead of his time in his insight into the dynamic relationship between good theology and good missiology"[14] Although missional objective was the underlying drive behind Upadhyay's attempts at indigenization, none of his three approaches was oriented towards the *missio Dei* theology as such.

Upadhyay believed that Christianity is for all ages and for all nations and hence it has a universal appeal. But the Indian Christianity, as he saw it, was in a dismal state: "There it stands in a corner, an exotic, stinted [i.e., stunted] plant, with poor foliage, showing little or no promise of blossom."[15] Upadhyay believed in both the necessity and possibility of building Christianity on Hindu philosophical foundations, which he found to be an important task if Christianity were to grow in India. As indicated above, Upadhyay sensed that the European clothing of the Christian faith prevented Indians from "perceiving its universal nature." Hindus could not "see the sublimity and sanctity of our divine religion because of its hard coating of Europeanism."[16] He felt that the Christian faith presented in European scholastic apparel was unintelligible to Hindus. "The Hindu mind is extremely subtle and penetrative, but is opposed to the Graeco-Scholastic method of thinking."[17] In order for the Christian faith to take root in Indian soil, it must be presented in Hindu thought forms. In this task, Upadhyay explored the viability of employing Vedanta philosophy in interpreting the Christian faith in India just as Greek philosophy was employed for Christianity in the West:

> We must fall back upon the Vedantic method in formulating the Catholic religion to our countrymen. In fact the Vedanta must be made to do the same service to Catholic faith in India as was done by the Greek philosophy in Europe. The assimilation of the Vedantic philosophy by the Church should not be opposed on the

---

14. Tennent, *Building Christianity on Indian Foundations*, viii.
15. Upadhyay, *Writings*, 2:220.
16. Upadhyay, *Writings*, 2:206.
17. Upadhyay, *Writings*, 2:207.

ground of its containing certain errors. . . . Catholic philosophy is so sweet, so transcendent, but it repels our countrymen because of its alien dress. . . . The European clothes of the Catholic religion should be removed as early as possible. It must put on the Hindu garment to be acceptable to the Hindus.[18]

In another article, published two years later Upadhyay raises the same concern that India would never accept Christianity unless it was freed from its Western garb. In order for Hindus to comprehend the Christian faith, Upadhyay felt, it should be articulated from the Vedantic perspective.[19] "Vedanta," according to Upadhyay, "rightly interpreted and brought into line with modern thought, will make the natural truths of Theism and the supernatural dogmas of Christianity more explicit and consonant with reason than was done by the scholastic philosophy."[20] He felt that the reinvigoration of Christianity in India could come from Vedanta: "Vedantic philosophy will rejuvenate Christianity, show forth newer harmonies and co-ordinations binding its different parts into one integral whole, and formulate it in a way adaptable to the growing intellect of man without adding to or subtracting from its doctrines even an iota."[21]

Upadhyay explored the feasibility of employing Hindu philosophy in interpreting the Christian faith in India. He believed that it is in Hinduism that "true light shone forth so brilliantly . . . [and] has human philosophy soared so high except, perhaps, in ancient Greece."[22] In this context, he was especially drawn to Thomas Aquinas's bold application of Aristotelian philosophy as "a rational basis for the mysterious edifice of the Christian religion to stand upon." Without overlooking the limitations of Hindu philosophy, he continues: "Christianity has again, after a long period, come in contact with a philosophy (the Advaita philosophy of Shankara) which . . . still unquestionably soars higher than her western sister." Therefore, Upadhyay believes that "attempts should be made to win over Hindu philosophy to the service of Christianity as Greek philosophy was won over in the middle ages [sic]."[23] The Indian Christianity has not reached

18. Upadhyay, *Writings*, 2:207. See also, Animananda, *Blade*, 74.
19. Upadhyay, *Writings*, 1:143.
20. Upadhyay, *Writings*, 1:228.
21. Upadhyay, *Writings*, 1:229.
22. Upadhyay, *Writings*, 1:5.
23. Upadhyay, *Writings*, 1:17–19. Upadhyay held that the Vedanta system was superior to the Aristotelian-Thomistic synthesis and believed in the possibility of

The Trinitarian Theology of Brahmabandhab Upadhyay

its full development, and the humid Indian soil offers the most conducive environment for its growth and expansion. From this Indian foundation, Upadhyay anticipated the emergence of a new Christianity, where the "Hindu mind and heart, coming under the dominion of the One, Holy, Apostolic and Catholic Church, will sing a *new* canticle which will fill the earth with sweetness from end to end."[24]

Upadhyay believed Christianity to be the true revelation of God and as a complete religion, which did not require any deletion from or addition to it. However, he felt it necessary, in the Indian context, to seek the help of Indian philosophy, in order to "strengthen revelation by preserving its unity . . . through the process of reason."[25] He found the Advaita Vedanta philosophy expounded by Shankara to be an appropriate aid in supplying new clothing to Christianity "without affecting in the least the essential Christian tenets. It will, in its broader aspect, serve as a natural, metaphysical basis for the one unchangeable, supernatural, universal religion," namely, Christianity.[26] In this attempt, Upadhyay sought to combine the Thomistic concept of God as pure being with the absolute Brahman of the Vedanta. God of the Vedanta is the *nirguṇa* Brahman, the impersonal, the absolute and unrelated being, divorced of all relations. Holding on to this concept would mean accepting the "'attributelessness' of the Godhead [which] makes it impossible to predicate anything to God."[27] How would this Vedanta idea of God be compatible with the Christian idea of a personal and loving God who seeks to relate with humanity? Without abandoning the *nirguṇa* Brahman concept, Upadhyay seeks to resolve the problem with the Christian doctrine of Trinity in terms of *saccidānanda*.

Vedantic-Thomistic synthesis in the Indian context perhaps after the model of former in the West. He sought to construct "more or less exact correspondences between Vedantic ideas and Thomistic ones so that Vedanta in some respects may be seen as a form of crypto-(neo) Thomism and Shankara as St. Thomas in disguise." (Vettanky, "Patriot, Pioneer," 662). See also Vetticatil, "Brahmabandhav Upadhyaya," 323–24.

24. Upadhyay, *Writings*, 1:19.

25. Upadhyay, *Writings*, 1:30.

26. Upadhyay, *Writings*, 1:33. See also Upadhyay, *Writings*, 1:19.

27. Boyd, *Introduction to Indian Christian Theology*, 72. By using the term, "unrelated" (*asanga*) Upadhyay seems to be saying what has been understood historically in traditional theology as the aseity (absolute independence or self-existence) of God. Hence, in the subsequent discussion in this chapter the noun form of "unrelated" is used as "unrelatedness" as a neologism.

An Indian Trinitarian Theology of *Missio Dei*

TRINITARIAN THEOLOGY OF BRAHMABANDHAB UPADHYAY

Upadhyay's application of the Vedanta doctrines of *saccidānanda* and *maya* in explaining the Christian doctrines of the Trinity and creation respectively is regarded as a major contribution to Indian Christian theology, and perhaps to the theology of religions at a broader level. Since this chapter deals only with *saccidānanda* and Trinity, Upadhyay's teaching of creation as *maya* does not fall within the purview of the present discussion. In gaining a better understanding of Upadhyay's use of *saccidānanda* in terms of the Christian Trinity, it is important to examine his views on the Advaita doctrine of *nirguṇa* and *saguṇa* Brahman, and the sources of *saccidānanda* from the Hindu texts. Hence, the subsequent section will attempt to distinguish between the *nirguṇa/saguṇa* and unrelated/personal distinction in Brahman, as well as trace the sources from which Upadhyay has drawn the doctrine of *saccidānanda* before elucidating his trinitarian theology.

Nirguṇa *and* Saguṇa *Distinction in Brahman*

Vedanta teaches that Brahman is independent, absolute, and unrelated being (*asanga*) who transcends human comprehension.[28] The only way Brahman can be described is in apophatic manner, in negative terms as spoken of in the *Brhadaranyaka Upanishad*: "not this, not this [*neti, neti*] for there is nothing higher than this [Brahman]."[29] He is the *nirguṇa* Brahman—who alone is real and all else is unreal—"without any quality or distinction," the "undifferentiated being," and the "pure unqualified unconsciousness."[30] Upadhyay concurs with this Vedanta position on God as evident from his own statement here: "God, the Absolute is asanga . . . *nirguṇa*, unrelated, absolutely independent of anything that He is not."[31] The absoluteness and the

---

28. The Sanskrit term "asanga" has been used to mean "aseity" (Latin "aseitas"), a concept used in western philosophy and theology to signify the absolute independence of God's self-existence and complete self-sufficiency. One might use "asanga" for "aseity" as long as one does not use it in a way which makes the incarnation impossible. "Asanga" is about being unattached and unrelated. If this means that God does not "need" God's creation for God's colloquy, then it is good Trinitarian theology. If it is used to reinforce a Greek idea that God is immutable and unmoved by the human condition and cannot enter into the world with vulnerability and—yes—attachment, then it is not a good connection.

29. *Brhadaranyaka Upanishad* (Radhakrishnan, *Principal Upaniṣads*, 194).

30. Deutsch and Buitenen, *Source Book of Advaita Vedanta*, 308.

31. Upadhyay quoted in Animananda, *Blade*, 155. Emphasis added.

unrelatedness of God raise questions about God's relationship to creation and humanity. Two renowned thinkers of the Vedanta school, Rāmānuja and Shankara have advocated two divergent solutions to this predicament. Brahman, for Rāmānuja, is the ultimate reality, "the cause of the world," and the "ocean of noble qualities."[32] Emphasizing his conviction of Brahman's relation to the world, Rāmānuja formulated a theology of embodiment, according to which Brahman "ensouls the world by constituting the soul of the world, and that all entities constitute the body of Brahman."[33] In this regard, Rāmānuja interprets the Upanishadic dictum, *tat tvam asi*, as meaning that Brahman "is the self of which the world is the body."[34] While Brahman is the ultimate and absolute being, he is related to creation.

The cornerstone of Shankara's philosophy is the doctrine of the aseity of Brahman, the absolute independence, the self-existence, the impersonality, and the unrelatedness of Brahman to the world.[35] Shankara is firmly grounded in his conviction of the independence and the unrelatedness of Brahman that he is accused of sacrificing "the reality of the world, the knowability of God from the world [and] . . . the knowability of God from mere reason."[36] Interestingly, contrary to Shankara's unbending conviction about the absolute and impersonal Brahman, the Upanishads evince a propensity towards theism and personal nature of Brahman.[37] Shankara seeks to resolve this dichotomy by postulating the two aspects of Brahman. Differentiating these two aspects, Shankara maintains that one is "possessed of the limiting adjunct constituted by the diversities of the universe which is a modification

---

32. Krishnamacharya and Narasimha Ayyangar, *Vedāntasāra of Bhagavad Rāmānuja*, 19, 20, 24, 44.

33. Rāmānuja, *Vedārthasamgraha*, 125. See also *Vedāntasāra of Bhagavad Rāmānuja*, 11.

34. Barua, "God's Body at Work," 13.

35. Johanns, *To Christ Through the Vedanta*, 1:7–11. Shankara's whole philosophical enterprise is founded on his conviction of Brahman as the highest, transcendental, and the ultimate reality, the Parabrahman. The most crucial issue at stake is the personhood of Parabrahman, an aspect vehemently denied by the great majority of Shankarite scholars. Bradley Malkovsky, in a very significant study on the personhood of Shankara's Parabrahman, examines arguments and interpretations advanced for and against this contentious topic. See Malkovsky, "Personhood of Śaṁkara's 'Para Brahman.'"

36. Johanns, *To Christ Through the Vedanta*, 1:11.

37. *Svetasvatara Upanishad* displays theistic tendencies where the Absolute Brahman identified with Rudra where the emphasis is given on personal God (*Īśvara*). See *Svetasvatara Upanishad* 1:9, 12; *Chandogya Upanishad* 3:14:2, 7:24:1; *Brhadaranyaka Upanishad*, 4:5:15. Cf. Tennent, *Building Christianity on Indian Foundations*, 121–22.

An Indian Trinitarian Theology of *Missio Dei*

of name and form, and the other devoid of all conditioning factors and opposed to the earlier."[38] For Shankara, both the facets constitute two different points of view of the one and the only ultimate reality, the Brahman. The former represents the *saguṇa* Brahman (*Īśvara*), the qualified Brahman with distinctions and characteristics, who falls within the realm of nescience and is the object of meditative worship. The latter refers to the Absolute Brahman, the *nirguṇa* Brahman, devoid of all qualities and relations, which is the true aspect of Brahman as upheld by the scriptures.[39]

Upadhyay, being committed to God as *asanga*, found Rāmānuja's views of Brahman's embodiment in the world not only jettisoning the independence and the absoluteness of God, but also tends towards pantheism. Therefore, rejecting Vishishtadvaita (modified non-dualism or qualified monism) of Rāmānuja, Upadhyay sought to reconcile Thomas Aquinas's concept of God with Shankara's Advaita. However, given the Christian teaching of God's personal and relational nature, harmonizing Shankara's *nirguṇa/saguṇa* distinction with Thomism is rendered rather problematic. In resolving this impasse, Upadhyay calls for differentiating between that which is ontologically necessary (*paramārthika*) and that which

---

38. *Brahma-Sūtra-Bhāṣya of Sri Śaṅkarācārya*, 1:1:12, 62. Deutsch and Buitenen, *Source Book of Advaita Vedanta*, 160. Tennent, *Building Christianity on Indian Foundations*, 123.

39. *Brahma-Sūtra-Bhāṣya*, 1:1:12; 3:2:14, 62, 611. Deutsch and Buitenen, *Source Book of Advaita Vedanta*, 197. The *saguṇa* Brahman with qualities and attributes is regarded as *Īśvara*, God as related to the world. The following two observations in this regard are very pertinent: "The qualified Brahman, if personified, becomes the God or *Īśvara* of Advaita" (Hiriyanna, *Essentials of Indian Philosophy*, 164). Malkovsky enumerates the Advaitins's view of *Īśvara* as follows: "What makes *Īśvara* personal is its possession of consciousness and freedom but, even more important, its governing relatedness to the world. It is this character of being essentially related to the universe that makes *Īśvara* the lower or inferior brahman, that which Advaitins often translate as 'God.'" Concluding his discussion on the arguments of the impersonalists (Advaitins) about the personhood of Parabrahman, Malkovsky remarks that Advaita does not rule out the personal concept of God. In fact, according to the Advaitins, "the path to the impersonal . . . leads first through the personal." Therefore, as the "highest manifestation of the personal" God, *Īśvara* is the object of worship, yet "*Īśvara*'s status is mirage-like" and illusory, and is subject to sublation. (Malkovsky, "Personhood of Śaṁkara's Para Brahman," 550). Malkovsky's own contention is "that to ascribe personhood to Śaṁkara's para brahman not only is legitimate exegetically," but there are "compelling philosophical reasons" to do so. For details on Malkovsky's arguments in favor of personal Parabrahman, see Malkovsky, "Personhood of Śaṁkara's Para Brahman," 552–62. For Brahman and Personal God, see also Raju, *Structural Depths of Indian Thought*, 394–95.

The Trinitarian Theology of Brahmabandhab Upadhyay

is contingent (*vyavahārika*) to the being of God.[40] Taking the argument further, Upadhyay claims that what *nirguṇa* implies is that "the attributes which relate the Infinite to the finite are not necessary to his being."[41] In illustrating this point, Upadhyay says that "creator-hood is not an intrinsic attribute of the divine Nature."[42]

There are two things, namely *nirguṇa/saguṇa* distinction and relational/personal aspect of Brahman that call for more clarity. Upadhyay's thoughts on these two aspects are found in a three-part critique of M. Thibaut's views on Vedanta written under his pseudonym, Narhari Das. For the sake of the continuity of the discussion, we begin with the *nirguṇa/saguṇa* in the third part of Upadhyay's critique. He attempts to make a distinction between *nirguṇa* and *saguṇa* aspect where he maintains that *saguṇa* is a superimposition on *nirguṇa* and a superabundance which are not necessary to the being of Brahman. He says, "The *nirguṇa* aspect of Brahman consists in the state of being self-centred. . . . The *saguṇa* aspect consists in Creator-hood. It is a free superimposition and not essential to the being of the Absolute. It is a superabundance whose presence is the equivalent to its absence so far as the fullness of Brahman is concerned."[43]

Secondly, in the first part of his critique, Upadhyay categorically denies the impersonality of Brahman: "Nothing can be more unjust than to translate 'nirgunam' as 'impersonal.'"[44] Upadhyay's argument runs as follows: A person can be thought of only in terms of relation, freedom, and self-consciousness. God is a self-conscious and free being who is unrelated. Nevertheless, the unrelatedness of Brahman does not imply that Brahman is an impersonal being. Upadhyay suggests that Brahman may be called "supra-personal," but he should never be regarded non-personal.[45] Being free, Brahman is "free to enter into relationship . . . through a contingent superimposition of his essence" yet there is nothing in Brahman's "pure nature impelling him to be related."[46] The coexistence of the unrelatedness

---

40. Tennent, *Building Christianity on Indian Foundations*, 218–19.

41. Upadhyay, *Writings*, 1:138.

42. Upadhyay, *Writings*, 1:138. See also Tennent, *Building Christianity on Indian Foundations*, 219; cf. Upadhyay, *Writings*, 1:130; Aleaz, "Trinity as Sat-Chit-Ananda," 84–85.

43. Upadhyay, *Writings*, 2:305.

44. Upadhyay, *Writings*, 2:294.

45. Upadhyay, *Writings*, 2:295.

46. Upadhyay, *Writings*, 2:295.

An Indian Trinitarian Theology of *Missio Dei*

and personal dimension of Brahman is critical for expressing compatibility between Vedanta and the Catholic theology.

Saccidānanda *as a Way Forward*

Upadhyay discovered that the more plausible way ahead in reconciling the Advaita Vedanta's impersonal and absolute Brahman with the personal God of the Catholic thought lies in the Upanishadic concept of *saccidānanda* and the Christian doctrine of the Trinity. The God of the Upanishads is "a Personal Being, who knows all, who watches over us with a Father's eye—a Being who is the plenitude of being; consciousness, pure and luminous; and Bliss Supreme: *sat, chit, ānanda*."[47] In Shankara's Advaita philosophy, while God is *nirguṇa* Brahman, God is also *Sat-cit-ānanda* (positive being-intelligence-bliss). Upadhyay finds a striking resemblance between this Vedanta concept and the Christian Trinity.[48] He seeks to resolve the problem of the *unrelatedness* of God by appealing to "the nature of *Brahman* as *Cit*, Thought, and in the fact that though God is 'unrelated without' he may yet be 'related within.'"[49] Upadhyay makes it clearer in the following passages:

> Brahman, the supreme Being *per se*, is *nirguna*. . . . He is *sat*—existing by himself; he is *cit*—self-knowledge himself without any external intervention; he is *ananda*—supremely happy in his self-colloquy. But looked at from the standpoint of relation, he is *saguna*, he is *Iswara*, creator of heaven and earth, possessing attributes relating him to created nature. Then he is not only being (*sat*) but Power; he makes other beings to endure. His self-knowledge (*cit*) is then manifested as mind, knowing the universe and making designs for its preservation and perfection. On the relative plane his bliss (*ananda*) shines as Love and Holiness.[50]

> External relationship indeed implies limitation; but not so internal relationship. The Infinite, Self-sufficient Being is related within Himself. He is not necessitated to enter into relationship with any objective unit external to Himself. The Subjective Self of God sees and contemplates the Objective Self of God and in this single eternal act are his knowledge and love fully satisfied.[51]

---

47. Upadhyay quoted in Tennent, *Building Christianity on Indian Foundations*, 222.

48. Upadhyay, *Writings*, 1:20–23, 2:395. Aleaz, *Christian Thought Through Advaita Vedanta*, 11–13. See also Lobo, "Tripersonalising the Parabrahman," 165.

49. Boyd, *Introduction to Indian Christian Theology*, 73.

50. Upadhyay, *Writings*, 1:130.

51. Upadhyay quoted in Tennent, *Building Christianity on Indian Foundations*, 223.

The Trinitarian Theology of Brahmabandhab Upadhyay

How does one resolve the complexity of the external and internal relationship within the divine? According to Upadhyay, it is not possible through human reason, but one has to appeal to Christian revelation in comprehending this mystery. He held that the real meaning of Brahman could be understood only through a Christian trinitarian exposition of *saccidānanda*.[52] Accordingly, taking God to be Triune in accordance with the Vedanta concept of *saccidānanda* and the Christian Trinity would offer the possibility of presenting God as personal who is "related within himself (*ad intra*), and not necessarily outside himself (*ad extra*)."[53] Such an attempt, while affirming the personal and relational nature of the divine, does not negate the unrelatedness of Brahman. Before delineating Upadhyay's articulation of *saccidānanda* as Trinity, it is appropriate to examine the Hindu philosophical sources of the concept.

SACCIDĀNANDA IN HINDU PHILOSOPHY

The fundamental concept of Advaita Vedanta is that Brahman is the ultimate and supreme reality (the only reality, and the world is illusory) beyond any human description and comprehension. Brahman is not different from the innermost human spirit and soul, which is the Atman. "Thus the Cardinal

---

52. Christian Trinity, according to Upadhyay, is a supernatural mystery which is about the "inner life of God, the doctrines of Incarnation, Atonement and Resurrection." It can never be revealed by human reason, but by God or God's "infallible messengers" (Upadhyay, *Writings*, 1:51). However, Upadhyay is prepared to accept glimpses of the inner relationship of the Trinity in the Hindu scriptures. He cites the example of *Hiranyagarbha*, "the first-begotten, begotten of eternal wisdom" in the Rig Veda Hymn *Ka* (Rig Veda 10:121). He is portrayed as "the giver of his own self" in sacrifice. According to the later pantheistic philosophy, *Hiranyagarbha* is "an emanation of the supreme Being . . . the first product of the illusory self-limitation of Brahman." Upadhyay says, according to contemporary Hinduism, "Hiranyagarbha is the personal God, the Creator of all things visible and invisible, but subject to the common fate of being absorbed in Brahman." More interestingly, "the first-begotten is said to have been sacrificed by the gods and *rishis* (Rig Veda 10:90) . . . [and] this sacrifice was the first religious act and by the virtue of this act the creation with all its creatures and the Vedas came to exist." Upadhyay apparently believes that this is an enlightenment on the inner life of God perhaps in a corrupt form outside of the biblical revelation. He wonders if this insight is an erred human speculation or a privilege given to the saints to have "fore-glimpse of the inner life of God having its entire satisfaction in a co-eternal interior generation?" He is inclined to believe that "in the Vedas are found a very sublime conception of one supreme Being, the idea of divine generation somewhat resembling the Christian doctrine of divine Sonship, and an account of the sacrifice of the first-begotten of God the virtue of which supreme act is far-reaching" (Upadhyay, *Writings*, 1:152–53). See Lipner, *Brahmabandhab Upadhyay*, 181–82.

53. Lobo, "Tripersonalising the Parabrahman," 165.

An Indian Trinitarian Theology of *Missio Dei*

principle of the *Advaita* is that *Brahman-Atman*, the Ultimate Reality is only One (*ekam eva*) and non-dual (*advitiyam*) and the world of multiplicity is illusory (*nana iva*)."[54] While Brahman is "the eternal principle as realized in the world as a whole," Atman is "the inmost essence of one's own self." Brahman as the universal principle and Atman as the human essence are regarded as "ultimately the same."[55] This identification of Brahman and Atman is expressed in the well-known sayings in the Upanishads, *Tat tvam asi* (That thou art) and *Aham Brahmāsmi* (I am Brahman). The classical formulation of the Vedanta concept *saccidānanda* expresses the ultimate reality Brahman-Atman and its spiritual and unitary character.[56] Perhaps the clearest compound form of the term *saccidānanda* in the Hindu texts is found in the opening of the *Vedantsara*: "I take refuge in the Self, the Indivisible, the Existence-Knowledge-Bliss [*sat-cit-ānanda*] Absolute."[57]

Since, the term *saccidānanda* is used by scholars in various forms, a brief explanation of the usage of the term is in order. *Saccidānanda* is a compound noun of three Sanskrit words, *sat*, *cit*, and *ānanda*, which respectively mean Being or Truth, Intelligence or Consciousness, and Bliss. The compound form of these words is variously used as *saccidānanda*, *satcitānanda*, *satchitānanda*, and *satchitānandam*. Orthographically, a closer transliteration of the three Sanskrit words separately could be as follows: *sat, chit, ānanda*. When the first two words are joined together, they sound *sach-chit*, and along with the final word *ānanda*, they sound *sachchidānanda*. Together, *ch-ch* in *sach-chit* sound *cc*, and hence, the compound word is accented as *saccidānanda*, a usage that has become quite prevalent in scholarly writings. Upadhyay draws the concept of *saccidānanda* from two different Hindu sources, namely, the Upanishads and the writings of Shankara.

Saccidānanda in the Upanishads

The compound form of *saccidānanda* is absent in the early Upanishads, yet its equivalent formulations can be found which describe Brahman as *Sat* (Being), *Satyam* (Truth, Real), *Jnānam* or *Vijnānam* (Knowledge),

---

54. Thannippara, "Saccidananda, Isvara, Avatara," 94.

55. Hiriyanna, *Essentials of Indian Philosophy*, 21. See Thannippara, "Saccidananda, Isvara, Avatara," 93.

56. Hiriyanna, *Essentials of Indian Philosophy*, 21–22. For a brief exposition of the Advaita Vedanta concept of saccidānanda, see Brück, *Unity of Reality*, 25–30.

57. Nikhilananda, *Vedantasara of Sadananda*, 1.

The Trinitarian Theology of Brahmabandhab Upadhyay

and *Ānantam* or *Ānanda* (Bliss). The phrase, "*satyam jñānam anantam brahma . . . brahmanā vipascitā*" ("*Brahman* as the real, as knowledge and as the infinite . . . Brahman, the intelligent*") used in the *Taittiriya Upanishad*, one of the earlier Upanishads, is perhaps the one, which bears close resemblance to *saccidānanda* in the later Upanishads.[58] According to *Brhadaranyaka Upanishad*, "Brahman who is knowledge, bliss (*vijñānam ānandam brahma*) is the final goal of him who offers gifts as well as of him who stands firm and knows (*Brahman*)."[59] *Brhadaranyaka Upanishad* also speaks of Brahman as "*anantam apāram vijñāna-ghana*" (the "great being, infinite, limitless, [which] consists of nothing but knowledge").[60] A clearer and direct reference to Brahman as *saccidānanda* is found in the later Upanishads. In *Nrisimha Poorva Tapaniya Upanishad*, Brahman is being, intelligence, and bliss: "Therefore this song is the supreme Brahman, which consists of being, intelligence and bliss; he who knows it as such becomes immortal here itself."[61] Direct references to *saccidānanda* is also found in *Mandalabrahmana-Upanishad* and *Tejobindu-Upanishad*.[62] The following passage in *Tejobindu-Upanishad* is very significant: "I am of the nature of the Parabrahman. I am the supreme bliss. I am solely of the nature of divine wisdom."[63]

SACCIDĀNANDA IN THE WRITINGS OF SHANKARA

The compound form of *saccidānanda* is absent in Shankara's writings as well. Nevertheless, Shankara discusses, albeit in a dispersed manner, the concepts of *Sat* (*Satyam*—Truth), *Cit* (*Jñānam* - Knowledge) and *Ānanda* in his commentaries on the *Upanishads* and *Brahma Sutras*.[64] *Sat*, according

---

58. See *Taittiriya Upanishad* 2.1.1 (Radhakrishnan, *Principal Upanishads*, 541–42); Thannippara, "Saccidananda, Isvara, Avatara," 77–83. One must bear in mind the difference between *anantam* and *ānandam* or *ānanda*. While the former refers to Brahman as "infinite," the latter signifies Brahman as "bliss." *Anantam ānanda* would mean "infinite delight."

59. *Brhadaranyaka Upanishad* 3.9.28 (Radhakrishnan, *Principal Upanishads*, 244–45).

60 *Brhadaranyaka Upanishad* 2.4.12 (Radhakrishnan, *Principal Upanishads*, 200). See also *Brhadaranyaka Upanishad* 1.6.3; 2.1.20; 4.5.13.

61. *Nrisimha Poorva Tapaniya Upanishad* quoted in Dhavamony, *Hindu-Christian-Dialogue*, 69.

62. See Dhavamony, *Hindu-Christian-Dialogue*, 69–70.

63. *Tejobindu-Upanishad* quoted in Dhavamony, *Hindu-Christian-Dialogue*, 69.

64. Thannippara, "Saccidānanda, Isvara, Avatara," 95. Raju, *Structural Depths of*

An Indian Trinitarian Theology of *Missio Dei*

to Shankara, refers to Brahman, "which is extremely subtle, undefinable, all-pervading . . . taintless, indivisible, pure consciousness."[65] *Sat* also signifies the reality of Brahman as the only one that exists and apart from Itself nothing exists.[66] In his commentary on the *Brahma Sutra*, Shankara speaks of Brahman as the "supreme Self" as the "One full of Bliss."[67] Similarly, the following observation of Shankara is noteworthy: "That the supreme Brahman is eternal consciousness by Its very nature is mentioned in such Vedic texts as 'Knowledge, Bliss, Brahman' . . . 'Brahman is Truth, Knowledge, Infinite' . . . 'and pure Intelligence alone.'"[68] Upanishads and Shankara form the basis for Upadhyay's restatement of the Christian doctrine of the Trinity in relation to the Advaita concept of *saccidānanda*. However, it was Keshub Chunder Sen who was the first one to bring to the fore the concept of *saccidānanda* and attempted to relate it with Trinity.

Saccidānanda and Keshub Chunder Sen

The emergence of Indian Christian theology can be traced back to the historical context of Bengal renaissance birthed at the convergence of the Eastern and Western thought in the nineteenth century. We have noted in the second chapter the immediate impetus to Indian theological development provided by Hindu engagement with the Christian faith led by people like Raja Ram Mohan Roy, Keshub Chunder Sen, and others. The dialogue between Christianity and Hinduism initiated by Ram Mohan Roy played a very significant role in the emergence of Indian Christian theology. Roy, who was influenced by Sufi philosophy, Vedantic monism, and Unitarianism, rejected the Christian doctrine of the Trinity. He considered only God as the sole object of worship, the Son as the mediator through whom worship is offered to God, and the Holy Spirit as the holy influence through

---

Indian Thought, 392–93.

65. *Chandogya Upanishad and Sri Sankara's Commentary*, 87.

66. *Chandogya Upanishad*, 89.

67. *Brahma-Sūtra-Bhāṣya*, 1.1.12.

68. *Brahma-Sūtra-Bhāṣya*, 2.3.18. It is important, in this context, to take note of the observation of Pierre Johanns, according to whom, Shankara's definitions of Brahma as *Tat tvam asi* and *saccidānanda* are equivalent. Comparing both the definitions, Johanns writes, "*Sat* is identical with *tat* in the former definition, *cit* with *tvam*, and *ānanda* with the *asi*. The definition of God *sac-cid-ānanda* puts forth the objective aspect of God, whereas the *tat-tvam-asi* exposes the subjective aspect; in reality the two definitions are equivalent" (Johanns, *To Christ Through the Vedanta*, 1:186. Emphasis added).

The Trinitarian Theology of Brahmabandhab Upadhyay

whom spiritual blessings are dispensed to humanity.[69] Unlike his predecessor, Roy, Keshub Chunder Sen had great appreciation for the doctrine of Trinity. Going beyond Roy, Sen accepted the doctrine of the Trinity albeit in a Unitarian sense. In his letter to Max Muller, Sen describes his stance on Christian Trinity and Christ thus:

> My position is that of a Uni-Trinitarian. . . . I set my face completely against the popular doctrine of Christianity. Yet I recognise divinity in some form in Christ, in the sense in which the Son partakes of the Father's divine nature. We in India look upon the son as the father born again. . . . Hence the Hindu, while regarding the father and the son as distinct and separate persons, connects them in thought by some kind of identity.[70]

Sen's lecture, *That Marvelous Mystery—The Trinity*, is a very passionate and a perceptive piece of writing. Sen was the first Indian thinker to explore a correspondence between the Christian doctrine of the Trinity and the Vedanta concept of Brahman as *saccidānanda*. A succinct description of his trinitarian view is given here in his own words:

> Gentlemen, look at this clear triangular figure with the eye of faith, and study its deep mathematics. The apex is the very God Jehovah, the Supreme Brahma of the Vedas. Alone, in His own eternal glory, He dwells. From Him comes down the Son in a direct line, an emanation from Divinity. Thus God descends and touches one end of the base of humanity, then running all along the base permeates the world, and then by the power of the Holy Ghost drags up degenerated humanity to Himself. Divinity coming down to humanity is the Son; Divinity carrying up humanity to heaven is the Holy Ghost. This is the whole philosophy of salvation.[71]

Further explaining the Trinity within the *saccidānanda* framework, Sen draws a parallel between the Christian Trinity and *saccidānanda* which may be placed as follows as Robin Boyd attempts to show for the sake of clarity:[72]

---

69. Roy, *Precepts of Jesus*, 229–30.

70. Cited in Parekh, *Brahmarshi Keshub Chunder Sen*, 149. This is a modalistic view of the Trinity much closer to Sabellianism than the mature orthodox faith.

71. Sen, *Keshub Chunder Sen's Lectures in India*, 2:16. See Boyd, *Introduction to Indian Christian Theology*, 34–35. Whaling, "Trinity and the Structure of Religious Life," 362–63.

72. Sen, *Keshub Chunder Sen's Lectures in India*, 2:16–17. "God coming down and going up—this is creation, this is salvation. In this plain figure of three lines you have

An Indian Trinitarian Theology of *Missio Dei*

THE FATHER	THE SON	THE HOLY SPIRIT
The Creator	The Exemplar	The Sanctifier
I am	I love	I save
The Still God	The Journeying God	The Returning God
Force	Wisdom	Holiness
The True	The Good	The Beautiful
Sat (Truth)	*Cit* (Intelligence)	*Ānanda* (Joy)

Sen believes this parallel demonstrates a remarkable resemblance between Christian Trinity and *saccidānanda*. He observes that "the Trinity of Christian theology corresponds strikingly with the *Sachchidānanda* of Hinduism. You have three conditions, three manifestations of Divinity. Yet there is one God, one Substance, amid three phenomena. Not three Gods, but one God. . . . But remember the true Trinity is not three Persons, but three functions of the same Person."[73]

While Sen sought a certain similarity between the Christian Trinity and *saccidānanda*, his understanding of the Trinity is quite removed from the classical Christian doctrine of the Trinity. Sen does not accept the personal distinctions within the Trinity, and his view seems to lean towards modalism. More importantly, the radicalness of Sen's view of the Trinity is obvious in his assigning a subordinate place to the Son. While the Father is worshipped, the Son is honored. Similarly, Sen transfers the saving role of the Son to the Holy Spirit who inspires and saves humanity.[74] According to Sen, the "identity of the Father and the Holy Ghost few will question, but the position of the Son is a subject of controversy."[75] Christ, for Sen, is a "God-man" and not a "man-God." Christ is a man and "God is superadded to his nature. Humanity continues to be humanity, but Divinity is engrafted

---

the solution of a vast problem. The Father, the Son, the Holy Ghost; the Creator, the Exemplar, and the Sanctifier; I am, I love, I save; the Still God, the Journeying God, the Returning God; Force, Wisdom, Holiness; the True, the Good, the Beautiful; *Sat, Chit, Anananda*: 'Truth, Intelligence and Joy.' Has not the Holy Ghost been described as the 'Comforter'? Truly He is the heart's joy. Thus the Trinity of Christian theology corresponds strikingly with the Sachchidānanda of Hinduism" (Boyd, *Introduction to Indian Christian Theology*, 34. Emphasis added).

73. Sen, *Keshub Chunder Sen's Lectures in India*, 2:17–18.

74. Sen, *Keshub Chunder Sen's Lectures in India*, 2:43. See also Pape, "Keshub Chunder Sen's Doctrine of Christ," 68; May, "Trinity and Saccidānanda," 94–95.

75. Sen, *Keshub Chunder Sen's Lectures in India*, 2:18.

The Trinitarian Theology of Brahmabandhab Upadhyay

upon (Christ's) humanity."[76] This is a simple and pure humanity where Divinity dwells. Sen goes as far as calling Christ a "creature."[77] The inferior space of Christ in Sen's interpretation of the Christian doctrine evinces not only an inadequate Christology but also a binitarian tendency rather than a full-orbed trinitarianism of Christian orthodoxy.

Saccidānanda *and the Trinity*

Sen's views were not initially well-received. One of those who refuted Sen and the *Brahmo Samaj's* version of theism was Nehemiah Goreh. He felt that Sen and other Brahmos took only parts of the Bible to suit their taste without accepting it in its totality. He found them advocating "the ethics of Christianity while substituting a vague theism for the full Christian orthodoxy."[78] Goreh contends that Brahman devoid of qualities (*nirguṇa*) is reduced to nothing, and as such, the existence of Brahman is not known to be possible.[79] Brahman as *saccidānanda* is "only nominally intelligence and bliss. He is intelligence that cognizes nothing, and bliss without fruition of happiness. What hope is there, that the soul would be happy, if it came to such a state as this?"[80]

Brahmabandhab Upadhyay took a different approach from that of Goreh. While Sen's views may be unorthodox, nevertheless, Upadhyay felt they could be carried on with more theological skill in order to make the Christian faith more relevant to the Indian context.[81] Therefore, Upadhyay sought to build on *saccidānanda* in order to provide a distinctive interpretation of the Christian doctrine of Trinity from the perspective of this Vedanta concept of God. This attempt of Upadhyay is considered an original contribution to theology. In the words of Lipner, "Upadhyay's originality lay in his attempt to show that the *sat*, *cit* and *ānanda* of classical Vedanta as a description of ultimate reality corresponded more or less exactly to the understanding of the nature of God of Catholic *natural* theology, that is, neo-Thomistic reasoning about the essence of the divine being."[82]

---

76. Sen, *Keshub Chunder Sen's Lectures in India*, 2:18–19.

77. Sen, *Keshub Chunder Sen's Lectures in India*, 2:21.

78. Boyd, *India and the Latin Captivity of the Church*, 22–23; Boyd, *Introduction to Indian Christian Theology*, 44.

79. Goreh, *Rational Refutation*, 219–21.

80. Goreh, *Rational Refutation*, 274.

81. Boyd, *India and the Latin Captivity of the Church*, 24.

82. Lipner, *Brahmabandhab Upadhyay*, 191.

An Indian Trinitarian Theology of *Missio Dei*

Upadhyay's *saccidānanda* concept of God is demonstrated in his magnificent Sanskrit hymn to the Triune God entitled *Vande Saccidānandam* (Adoration to the Triune God). Any attempt at analyzing Upadhyay's restatement of Trinity in terms of *saccidānanda* would be incomplete without examining his trinitarian hymn. This song, originally written in Sanskrit, is a pioneering attempt at indigenization. Although there are a couple of translations of this hymn, for the sake of originality, I quote below Upadhyay's own English rendering of the hymn in a slightly annotated form:[83]

A CANTICLE: Translated by Brahmabandhab Upadhyay

Refrain:
I adore:
The *Sat* (Being), *Cit* (Intelligence) and *Ānanda* (Bliss):
The highest goal, which is despised by the worldly,
Which is desired by the devotees.

Stanza 1:
The supreme, ancient, higher than the highest,
Full, indivisible, transcendent and immanent.
One having triple interior relationship, holy,
Unrelated, self-conscious, hard to realise (the mystery).

Stanza 2:
The Father, Begetter, the highest Lord, unbegotten,
The rootless principle of the tree of existence
The cause of the universe, one who creates intelligently,
The preserver of the world.

Stanza 3:
The increate, infinite Logos or Word, supremely great.
The Image of the Father,
One whose form is intelligence,
The giver of the highest freedom.

Stanza 4:
One who proceeds from the union of *Sat* and *Cit*,
The blessed Spirit (breath), intense bliss.

---

83. Upadhyay, *Writings*, 1:126–27. Lipner has an annotated version of this hymn in Lipner, *Brahmabandhab Upadhyay*, 201. George Gispert-Sauch has given a stricter translation of the hymn in Gispert-Sauch, "Sanskrit Hymns," 75–76.

The Trinitarian Theology of Brahmabandhab Upadhyay

The sanctifier, one whose movements are swift,
One who speaks of the Word, the life-giver.

This hymn by Upadhyay is a very significant and original contribution to Indian Christian theology. It is regarded as an enduring contribution to Indian theology and the Indian church. Gispert-Sauch calls it "a gem of Christian hymnology, and probably the best example of a deep adaptation of the Christian faith to the cultural patterns of Indian religious thought."[84] In the composition of this song, Upadhyay was not attempting any radical indigenous reconstruction of the Christian doctrine, but so ingeniously expresses the Christian doctrine of the Trinity in the Hindu categories and thought-forms and thus made "a Sanskritic articulation of Catholic doctrine."[85] Upadhyay himself confirms this in his introduction to the hymn: "The canticle sings of the Father-God (*Parabrahman*), the Logos-God (*Sabda-Brahman*) and the Spirit-God (*Svasita-Brahman*), One in Three, Three in One."[86] The hymn gives expression to Upadhyay's deep sense of belief in the Triune God and his offer of worship to that Trinity indicated by *Vande* (which means "I worship") which is the only verb used in the entire hymn. Although we will not attempt an exposition of this hymn, we will explore the theological thoughts behind Upadhyay's use of the Hindu categories used in the hymn. In the following section, we will examine Upadhyay's *saccidānanda* concept in relation to three persons of the Trinity, and analyze the *saccidānanda* hymn as it relates to the Father, the Son, and the Holy Spirit.

Parabrahman as Sat in Relation to God the Father

Upadhyay contends that the Vedanta teaching of Brahman as *saccidānanda* concurs with the Catholic philosophers, the Neo-Thomists, who "arrive by reasoning at the knowledge of God who is eternal, one, purely positive, intelligent and supremely happy."[87] Unfolding this, Upadhyay begins with the absolute necessity of an eternal existence, "an uncaused, eternal being"

---

84. Gispert-Sauch, "Sanskrit Hymns," 60. For a detailed commentary on the hymn, see Gispert-Sauch, "Sanskrit Hymns," 68–74.

85. Lipner, *Brahmabandhab Upadhyay*, 201.

86. Upadhyay, *Writings*, 1:126.

87. Upadhyay, *Writings*, 1:20. Elsewhere, Upadhyay describes the nature of this being as "existence by itself (*sat*), eternal, immutable and infinite . . . absolute existence is necessarily intelligence (*cit*) and bliss (*ānanda*)" (Upadhyay, *Writings*, 1:131). He brings a detailed analysis of this in an article entitled "Being."

An Indian Trinitarian Theology of *Missio Dei*

which is indispensable for accounting all existence in the world. This eternal being must be self-existent, self-sufficient, and "it has no need of being related to any other being for the purpose of its existence."[88] Drawing on the Upanishad (*Aitareya Upanishad* 1.1) assertion, Upadhyay identifies it as *Parabrahman*, the "only One Eternal Being who is the cause of all other beings," the First Cause.[89] *Parabrahman* is *Sat* (being), the eternal, the self-existent Being, the Supreme Being of the Vedanta. *Sat* is the primary and the principal being, the necessary being, the absolute and the immutable being, who "exists in and for itself."[90] The existence of this being, *Sat*, explains the existence of all other beings. One cannot conceive of any being without conceiving of "an eternal self-existent being. . . . If there exists no being from eternity but the perfect blank of nothingness, then there can never be any existence—unless *nothing* gives birth to *something*. But we see there *are* beings, therefore there must be an eternal Being. This eternal being is *Sat*."[91] The phenomenal universe and everything owe its existence to the *Sat*. In this context, it is worth noting Upadhyay's rejection of Descartes's *Cogito ergo sum* (I think, therefore I am). He considers Descartes's "passage from thought to reality" as a dangerous proposal. Instead, Upadhyay proposes, "*Ens est ergo cogito*—Being is, therefore I think." For him, "Being is the ultimate foundation of all certitude, the foundation of thinking. Thought is based upon the identity of *being* with its contents."[92]

Upadhyay's thoughts on God as *Sat* must be understood in view of his Vedantic understanding of Brahman as being *asanga* and *nirguṇa*. The absoluteness and the unrelatedness of Brahman are strongly entrenched in Upadhyay's thoughts on *Sat*. For instance, as *Sat*, God is self-existent and eternal being who cannot but be immutable and infinite. Immutability necessarily implies the independence and eternal state of the actuality of God. Immutability of being, says Upadhyay, does not mean "mere permanence of its essence." "A being whose essence and existence coalesce, that is, whose

---

88. Upadhyay, *Writings*, 1:20–21.

89. Upadhyay, *Writings*, 1:21. Upadhyay has drawn the use of Parabrahman from Shankara for whom the supreme reality is Parabrahman, the "higher Brahman" who is distinguished from the "lower Brahman," as *aparabrahman* (Īśvara). "This distinction between a higher and lower brahman is one of the hall-marks of Śaṁkara's advaita-vāda" (Malkovsky, "Personhood of Śaṁkara's Para Brahman," 545).

90. Lipner, *Brahmabandhab Upadhyay*, 191.

91. Upadhyay, *Writings*, 1:127–28.

92. Upadhyay, *Writings*, 1:130–31; Tennent, *Building Christianity on Indian Foundations*, 233.

The Trinitarian Theology of Brahmabandhab Upadhyay

essence is an unmodifiable existence, whose duration cannot be divided into stages of a by-gone potentiality and a future actuality, is immutable."[93] *Parabrahman* is also infinite. Infinity is fullness, completeness, abundance, and plenitude of the eternal being. "Plenitude is the necessary content of existence *per se* and plenitude is infinitude."[94] Furthermore, infinity necessarily entails the unity of the ultimate reality and hence, there cannot be more than one infinity. Multiple infinities cause distinctions within the Godhead where one lacks what the other has, and thus reducing the former to "want and destroying its infinity.... Hence infinity is unity; a self-existent being cannot but be one."[95] In Upadhyay's quite judicious treatment of the immutability and infinity of the Supreme Being, one cannot fail to detect his conviction of God's *asanga* and *nirguṇa* character. It is also important to observe the Thomistic language that characterizes Upadhyay's expression of *asanga* and *nirguṇa* aspect.

How does Upadhyay relate *Parabrahman* as *Sat* with God the Father of the Christian Trinity? He seeks to identify *Sat* with the Father in the adoration (*vande*) of the Father in his trinitarian hymn. *Sat* in the first stanza of the hymn is a reference to the "Father" in the second stanza. The Sanskrit words used for the Father are quite significant. The opening of the stanza is with the most common Sanskrit word for father, *pitṛ*. The significant word used along with *pitṛ* is *savitṛ*—translated as "Begetter," "Impeller"—which in the Rig-Veda refers to the Sun (rather the Sun-god). Gispert-Sauch, in his exposition of the hymn, feels *savitṛ* could symbolize "the Father's creative role and of his being the source of all power and energy."[96] *Savitṛ* (begetter) is also called "unbegotten," the uncaused one who brought all creation into being and Itself being uncaused. In using *savitṛ*, Upadhyay certainly had in mind not only the idea of Brahman as "the great Unborn (*aja*)," but also the expression of the early Christians creeds where the Father is known as the "not begotten."[97] The Father being rootless—Boyd has it "seedless Seed" and Gispert-Sauch calls it "Unsown Seed"—suggests the Father's eternal and self-existence, who is the Seed (*bījam*), and yet remains seedless (*abījam*). The Father as the cause (*kāraṇam*) of the whole creation is the intelligent and personal creator. It recalls Thomas Aquinas's "Intelligent, Personal, First

---

93. Upadhyay, *Writings*, 1:134; Lipner, *Brahmabandhab Upadhyay*, 192.
94. Upadhyay, *Writings*, 1:135.
95. Upadhyay, *Writings*, 1:136.
96. Gispert-Sauch, "Sanskrit Hymns," 71–72.
97. Tennent, *Building Christianity on Indian Foundations*, 251.

An Indian Trinitarian Theology of *Missio Dei*

Cause," which Upadhyay, being a committed Catholic, fully endorses in his writings on creation. This idea is contrary to Samkhya philosophy which rejects the cause of the universe as being personal or intelligent. For Upadhyay, the cause of creation is not the unintelligent *prakriti* of the Samkhya system, but the Father, the "one who creates intelligently," and therefore, creation is an "intelligent (*ikṣaṇa*), [and] a personal act."[98] The personal and intelligent dimension is further affirmed by the use of *Govinda*, which literally means shepherd or cowherd. Gispert-Sauch sees it as a bold use in a Christian song since it is an appellation often employed for Krishna in the Hindu mythology.[99] Given Upadhyay's own translation of *Govinda* as "preserver of the world," it could perhaps be seen in line with the shepherd imagery of God in both the Old and New Testaments. Hence, *Govinda*, for Upadhyay, has a broader meaning where the hymn portrays the Father as the creator and preserver of the world. This also underscores another point, namely, how much Upadhyay draws from popular Hinduism rather than only Advaitic thoughts. For instance, literally speaking, Father is the cow herder (*Govinda*) of the universe, the creator and preserver of the world.

Parabrahman as *Cit* in Relation to God the Son

Upadhyay has sought to demonstrate that *Parabrahman* as *Sat* is the eternal and self-existent principle, which is the ground of all other existence. *Parabrahman* is also *Cit* (intelligence), and it is through intelligence that

---

98. Tennent, *Building Christianity on Indian Foundations*, 252; Gispert-Sauch, "Sanskrit Hymns," 70–71. Upadhyay, *Writings*, 1:23, 222–23. In Samkhya philosophy, creation takes place through the union of *purusha* and *prakriti*, interpreted by Gaudapāda as the union of Spirit and Nature. (Gaudapāda is believed to be the teacher of Shankara's teacher Govinda, whom Shankara calls *paramaguru*, teacher's teacher). Samkhya Kārika 21 says, "(The union) of the Spirit (with the Nature) is for contemplation (of the Nature); (the union) of the Nature (with the Spirit) is for liberation. The union of both (i.e., the Spirit and the Nature) is like that of a lame man with a blind man. The creation is brought about by that (union)" (*Samkhya Kārika*, 32). This union of the Spirit with Nature is similar to the association of a lame man and a blind man, who mutually help each other find their way ahead. While the blind carries the lame, the latter directs the steps of the blind man in their journey. The resemblance is that the Spirit has the power of contemplation (sight) like the lame man, and the Nature, like the blind, has the faculty of action (walking). At the end of journey, the object of both the men is accomplished, and they part ways. Similarly, "the Nature also ceases to act after bringing about the release of the Spirit; and the Spirit becomes isolated after contemplating the Nature." Out of this union of the Spirit and Nature, "the creation is brought about" (*Samkhya Kārika*, 33). See also, Majumdar, "Doctrine of Evolution in the Sankhya Philosophy," 51.

99. Gispert-Sauch, "Sanskrit Hymns," 72.

The Trinitarian Theology of Brahmabandhab Upadhyay

the eternal being relates to that which yet does not exist in actuality. Upadhyay takes his cue from the Spanish Catholic priest and philosopher Jaime Balmes, according to whom, "the intelligence alone can relate to that which does not exist; for it can *think the non existent* [sic]."[100] Causality must have its ground in intelligence, and it is through intelligence that the eternal cause relates to the possible cause. Herein lies, for Upadhyay, the importance of the Vedanta claim of *Parabrahman* as *Cit*. Upadhyay delineates it with the help of the declaration in the *Aitareya Upanishad* as follows:

> [Vedanta] affirms with admirable brevity the fact of God's intelligence. *Sa ikshata lokan nu srija iti* [Ait. Up 1.1] (He beheld: shall I create the *lokas* [world]?). He beheld before creating. What did he behold? The great Sankara says that he beheld the universe not as yet actualised. He beheld the origin, the preservation and the destruction of the universe; He beheld all these before He had created it.[101]

The world, prior to its creation, existed eternally in its archetypal (ideal) form in the divine intelligence, and this truth was revealed to the Vedantic saints. Brahman beheld the world before creating it. "Nothing was created that was not beheld, for he created only *lokas* [the world]."[102] Thus, God related to the universe in its nonexistent state through the *Cit*.

Although Upadhyay wanted to develop the above thoughts that he wrote in the monthly *Sophia* (January 1898), he did not continue it for reasons unknown to us. He did expand his thoughts on the relational aspect of *Cit* more profoundly in several articles written between 1899 and 1901 in

---

100. James (Jaime) Luciano Balmes (1810–1848) was an ecclesiastic, political writer, and philosopher. According to Balmes, "The absolute beginning of anything is not possible unless we conceive causality as having its root in the intellect." He says it is a necessity that the Self-existent is able to relate to (think) the non-existent. "If something has begun, something must have existed from all eternity, and that which began was known by that which existed. Not admitting intelligence [in the] beginning is absurd" (Balmes quoted in Upadhyay, *Writings*, 1:22). Elucidating Upadhyay's restatement of *saccidānanda*, the Indian theologian K. P. Aleaz attributes Balmes's views, cited above, to Upadhyay. This error may have occurred because of the fact that Upadhyay seldom acknowledges the external sources. However, he does leave evidences to indicate passages and ideas that are not his as found in the present article. Due to this oversight of Aleaz, the influence of Balmes's thoughts on Upadhyay goes unnoticed for readers who do not have access to Upadhyay's original works. See Aleaz, "Trinity as Sat-Chit-Ananda," 86.

101. Upadhyay, *Writings*, 1:23. Emphasis added. Cf. *Aitareya Upanishad* 1.1.1 (Radhakrishnan, *Principal Upanishads*, 513).

102. Upadhyay, *Writings*, 1:23.

An Indian Trinitarian Theology of *Missio Dei*

Sophia Monthly, *Sophia Weekly*, and *Twentieth Century*. His major concern here was the ontological distinction within the Godhead which he sought to expound in an Advaitic framework.

Brahman, understood as *Cit* ("intelligence" "knowledge" and "consciousness"), is a relational being, because "a being cannot exist without being related. . . . An unrelated being, a unity without multiplicity, is as repugnant to all knowledge as the simultaneous existence and non-existence of an entity."[103] It is also essential that the self-existent must act. Relation and action are indispensable features of the self-existent. "But what does it act upon and how does it act?"[104] Apart from the self-existent one, there is no separate being which receives its influence. Admitting more than one self-existent being is self-destructive for the self-existent being. For Upadhyay, the solution to this dilemma is to be found within the being of the self-existent itself. "The act of the self-existent Being is primarily confined within Itself."[105] This raises another question: "How can a being act upon itself?"[106] In answer to this question, Upadhyay seeks to bring in the idea of *Cit*. He states that "the self-existent Being acts upon itself by intelligence. Its act is self-knowledge. For it to be is to know. It is related within the term of its own being as subject and object. It is not a sterile unity without multiplicity. The result of its self-act is an eternal distinction between its knowing self and known self without any division in the substance."[107]

Appealing to the Upanishad, Upadhyay writes further: "The knowing God is mirrored as the known God in the ocean of *Cit*. And by knowing himself he knows all possible varieties of particular beings contained in his universality."[108]

Now the important question that concerns Upadhyay is how does one distinguish between the knowing self and the known self, the knowing Infinite and the known Infinite. We have seen that *Cit*, according to the above discussion, is the intelligence, the consciousness, the knowledge of God. Upadhyay sees it is necessary to distinguish *Cit*, the intelligence of God, from *Sat*, the Subject "because a being cannot stand in *relation*

---

103. Upadhyay, *Writings*, 1:136.
104. Upadhyay, *Writings*, 1:136.
105. Upadhyay, *Writings*, 1:136.
106. Upadhyay, *Writings*, 1:136.
107. Upadhyay, *Writings*, 1:136–37.
108. Upadhyay, *Writings*, 1:128.

The Trinitarian Theology of Brahmabandhab Upadhyay

to its *identical* self."[109] Yet, outside of himself, God cannot seek for any *necessary* relations—a thought seems to have been drawn from Thomas Aquinas's immanent actions and transient actions—because the infinite God is "the All and includes all."[110] Then, what does distinguish between God the subject and God the object? Human reason is able to recognize that the eternal being is necessarily intelligent, but it fails to comprehend the distinction within the inner life of God. Upadhyay believes that since reason cannot explain it, its answer must be sought in the revelation of Christ. He writes, "Revelation teaches us . . . that the differentiating note in divine knowledge is the response of intelligence. God begets in thought his infinite Self-Image and reposes on it with infinite delight while the begotten Self acknowledges responsively his eternal thought-generation."[111] Thus, "God comprehends Himself by one act of eternal knowledge. The knowing Self is the Father, the known Self or the Self begotten by His knowledge is the Son."[112] Here Upadhyay does not see any division in the divine substance between the Father and the Son, "no break of integrity, but only a relation of reciprocity."[113] This is the relationship that *Sat* and *Cit* reveal. God's revelation in Christ only confirms that God can be thought of as *saccidānanda*. This revelation is Christ's declaration that "God is *self-related* by means of *internal* distinctions that do not cast even a shadow of division upon the unity of his Substance."[114] Upadhyay states this relation conclusively in the following two passages:

> The infinite, eternal God who cognizes his own Self reproduced in thought, is the Father; and the same God who is the begotten Image of divinity, who acknowledges the Father in reason, is the Logos, the Son. This is the mystery of the timeless Word-colloquy which sweetens the divine bosom and fills it with joy ineffable.[115]

---

109. Upadhyay, *Writings*, 1:189.

110. Tennent, *Building Christianity*, 234; Upadhyay, *Writings*, 189. "God knows himself through himself. To show this, Aquinas recalls the difference between operations that remain in the operator (immanent actions) and those which pass into an external effect (transient actions)" (Elders, *Philosophical Theology*, 225).

111. Upadhyay, *Writings*, 1:189, 137. See also Tennent, *Building Christianity*, 234.

112. Upadhyay, *Writings*, 2:397. See also Tennent, *Building Christianity*, 226–28.

113. Upadhyay, *Writings*, 1:189. See also Aleaz, *Christian Thought*, 15.

114. Upadhyay, *Writings*, 1:193.

115. Upadhyay, *Writings*, 1:189.

An Indian Trinitarian Theology of *Missio Dei*

> There can be no operation in the being of the Absolute which is not of simple, unalloyed intelligence. Then it is knowledge and nothing but knowledge which can distinguish the knowing Self or God from his known Self. Jesus Christ has told us that there is a response of knowledge in the Godhead. God knows his own Self begotten in Thought and is known in return by that begotten Self. It is this correspondence of knowing and being known, of cognition and re-cognition, which generates the relative distinction of subject and subject in the Absolute. This unique revelation gives us a glimpse of the inner life of the supreme Being. God reproduces in knowledge a co-responding, acknowledging Self-image, and from his colloquy of reason proceeds his spirit of Love which sweetens the divine Bosom with boundless delight. . . . Jesus Christ claims to have laid open the mystery of divine Life that man may apprehend it in faith and walk by its light to the final goal of beholding God as he is, living in communion of self-relation within himself.[116]

Christ as *Cit* resolves the problem that Upadhyay encountered with *nirguṇa* Brahman, who was thought to be unrelated and unknowable. Through Christ's revelation, humanity is able to peek into the life of God and walk towards its divine destiny.

The two important thoughts that underlie, perhaps in an ambiguous manner, in the above interpretation find expression in his hymn on the Trinity. They are represented in the hymn by two important Sanskrit phrases, *anāhataśabdam* and *pitṛ-svarūpa*. *Anāhata śabda*, is used for the second person of the Trinity in the third stanza of the hymn. It is not without significance that Upadhyay translates *anāhata śabda* as "increate," which factually means, "never having been created" or "existing without having been created." Lipner and Gispert-Sauch translate *anāhata śabda* literally as "Word unsounded" and "Word . . . unheard" respectively. *Anāhata śabda* (non-struck sound) is sound "produced without striking two things together," "the divine unstruck [sic] sound," the "unbeaten" sound.[117] As the mystical sound, in the Hindu thought *anāhata śabda* is identified as the sacred *OM* sound, "the sum and substance of the whole of reality."[118] Identifying the Son with *anāhata śabda* as the transcendent, cosmic, and non-struck sound evidently expresses the eternality (cf. begotten) of the second person

---

116. Upadhyay, *Writings*, 1:193–94.

117. Garg, *Encyclopaedia of the Hindu World*, 2:406. Flood, *Introduction to Hinduism*, 145.

118. Gispert-Sauch, "Sanskrit Hymns," 72. See *Mandukya Upanishad* 1 (Radhakrishnan, *Principal Upanishads*, 695).

The Trinitarian Theology of Brahmabandhab Upadhyay

of the Trinity. The fact that the *anāhata śabda* is not an abstract concept is established in the description of the Son (Logos, Word) being *ananta* (infinite). The eternality and the infinity of the Son are further affirmed by the use of *prasuta* (begotten) *purusha* (person). It must be noted in this regard that the eternal generation and infinity of God the Son have been vital points in Upadhyay's discourse on *saccidānanda* and the Trinity.

Perhaps the most significant part of the stanza that has direct bearing on Upadhyay's interpretation of *saccidānanda* is the consubstantiality of the Son with the Father expressed by the compound term *pitṛ-svarūpa* (Father-image).[119] *Svarūpa* itself is a compound form of *sva* (one's own) and *rupa* (form or image). It could also mean, "actual" or "essential nature," and "essence."[120] Thus, *pitṛ-svarūpa* could mean "the image of the Father" and "the essence (cf. substance) of the Father." This is reflective of Upadhyay's conviction of the classical trinitarian doctrine of *homoousios*. *Pitṛ-svarūpa* is followed by *cinmaya-rupa*. Since *cin* in *cinmaya* refers to *cit*, the compound word could be translated as "image full of consciousness." Therefore, the two compound terms, *pitṛsvarūpa cinmayarūpa* do refer to the Son, the image of the Father "whose essence is made of Consciousness" (intelligence).[121]

PARABRAHMAN AS ĀNANDA IN RELATION TO THE HOLY SPIRIT

Brahman is not only the ground of all existence (*Sat*) and is intelligence and relational (*Cit*), but he is also *Ānanda* (bliss). *Ānanda* is "the complacent repose of a being upon its own self or its like."[122] It signifies that God is self-satisfied and content within himself and thus, *Ānanda* completes the Tri-unity of the Godhead.

Upadhyay's concept of *Ānanda* reveals three emphases which are very central to his theology of the Spirit. First, *Ānanda* is the necessary content of the absolute and Supreme Being, Brahman. The infinity of the ultimate reality entails that it finds repose within its own self and not in anything external and finite. It is in *Ānanda*, according to Upadhyay, that the First cause finds repose. Therefore, *Ānanda* shows that the infinite being "is self-sufficient, self-satisfied and not dependent upon relations which are not

---

119. Gispert-Sauch, "Sanskrit Hymns," 73. Tennent, *Building Christianity*, 253.

120. See Grimes, *Concise Dictionary of Indian Philosophy*, 308.

121. Gispert-Sauch, "Sanskrit Hymns," 73.

122. Upadhyay, *Writings*, 1:137. In the subsequent discussion of Upadhyay's view on the bliss as the Holy Spirit, generally I follow Tennent's pattern of discourse on the Holy Spirit as *ānanda*. See Tennent, *Building Christianity*, 242–44.

An Indian Trinitarian Theology of *Missio Dei*

co-terminous [*sic*] with his substance."[123] Any being which is "obliged to form alliance with something other than its own self cannot be essentially happy."[124] Further, the completeness and perfection of the eternal being necessitate that it reposes in its own self. Or else, it becomes deficient, and "a deficient infinity is a contradiction." Hence, it is important to "attribute bliss to infinite intelligence." Upadhyay concludes that "the necessary contents of being are *sat* (self-existence), *cit* (intelligence) and *ananda* (bliss)."[125] The following statement of Upadhyay, which he wrote in continuation of the *Sat-Cit* relationship, is important in this regard:

> The eternal, intellectual act of divine generation and the correspondence which binds the Father and his Logos Image in the Spirit of Love completes the life of God and makes it self-sufficient. Revelation has given us a fore-glimpse of the inner life of God and has declared how his knowledge and love are fully satisfied by the colloquy of God with God in Spirit.[126]

The depth of the divine bliss is found in a profound way in Upadhyay's use of *śubha-śvasitānanda-ghanam* in the second of the fourth stanza of the hymn. The Holy Spirit is *śubhaśvasita*. In a moral sense, *śubh* means good, righteous, virtuous, and honest; it could also mean beautiful, pure, bright, or splendid. While *śvasita* could mean breathed, possessed of breath or life, vivified, revived, the meaning of breath or Spirit seems more appropriate in the hymn.[127] *Ānandaghana* means, "consisting of pure joy," and it conveys the sense of purity, "pure bliss unmixed with anything else," and thus can be taken as referring to the holiness of the Spirit, hence the *Holy Spirit*. Yet it has the sense of the joy being so intense—hence Upadhyay's use of "intense bliss."[128] His translation of "intense bliss" seems to convey a meaning more than purity. It could be taken to mean the

---

123. Upadhyay, *Writings*, 1:145. Tennent, *Building Christianity*, 243.

124. Upadhyay, *Writings*, 1:27.

125. Upadhyay, *Writings*, 1:138.

126. Upadhyay, *Writings*, 1:189.

127. For the meaning of *śubha* and *śvasita*, see Monier-Williams, *Sanskrit-English Dictionary*, 1083, 1105–6.

128. Monier-Williams, *Sanskrit-English Dictionary*, 140, 376; Gispert-Sauch, "Sanskrit Hymns," 73. *Ānanda* is bliss and *ghana* is intense and hence "intense bliss." Monier-Williams gives a variety of meaning to *ghana* such as "compact, solid, material, hard, firm, dense . . . full of . . . densely filled with" (Gispert-Sauch, "Sanskrit Hymns," 376).

The Trinitarian Theology of Brahmabandhab Upadhyay

supreme bliss in which the infinite finds repose and it is more in keeping with his own interpretation of *saccidānanda*.

Second, for Upadhyay, *Ānanda* is not a quality within *saccidānanda*, rather a personal distinction within the Godhead. We have already noted the personal dimension of *Sat* and *Cit* in his description. *Sat*, *Cit*, and *Ānanda* are eternal personal distinctions in the Godhead, and they are "not inconsistent with the unity of God."[129] Maintaining the Vedanta expression of Brahman being "one and many" at the same time as a universal truth, Upadhyay believes the distinctions within the divine being cannot be given up. He writes, "*sat, chit,* and *ānandam* cannot be made to give up their distinctions though they are one in Brahman"[130] His idea of the Spirit's personhood is grounded in both the Scripture and Christian tradition, and it is also quite evident in his hymn. His association of *saccidānanda* with the filioque theology of double procession of the Spirit, proceeding from the *Sat* and *Cit*, is consistent with the Western tradition, although as Gispert-Sauch points out it does not have resonance with the Indian tradition.

Third, *Ānanda* reveals the relational and personal nature of God. Upadhyay rejects the view that God is unknowable and unapproachable.[131] This does not deny the fact that God is self-sufficient, self-satisfied, and independent. Locating the relational nature of God in *Ānanda*, he says that creation is an outflow of *Ānanda*. Quoting the Vedanta in support of this, he writes: "In the *Vedanta* it is written: 'To know that the supreme being is bliss (*ānanda*) and that the creation of the world (*loka*) is an outflow of that bliss, is the culmination of divine science (*vidya*).'"[132] As explained earlier in our discussion on *Parabrahman* as *Cit*, God beheld the world before God created it. God here relates to the world through the act of beholding before its actualization in creation. God does not bring anything into actuality if God is "not related to it in any way."[133] God who beholds (relates to) creation in its ideal form delights in it and this delight, this complacency "leads to the transfer of the ideal into the actual. If the finite ideas had repelled the

---

129. Tennent, *Building Christianity*, 243.

130. Upadhyay, *Writings*, 1:42. Tennent, *Building Christianity*, 243. For "many gods and one Brahman," see *Brhadaranyaka Upanishad* 3.9.1–9 (Radhakrishnan, *Principal Upanishads*, 234–37).

131. See Animananda, *Blade*, 101; Tennent, *Building Christianity*, 244.

132. Upadhyay, *Writings*, 1:221.

133. Upadhyay, *Writings*, 1:221–22.

divine will, there would have been no actual fructification. Fecundity is the result of the complacent repose of a being upon its like. Creation, then, is the outflow of bliss (*ananda*) which sweetens the divine bosom."[134] Yet, creation is not a divine necessity. God has not made creation out of necessity, but out of the supreme divine bliss (superabundance). In the same vein, he says that God is merciful and loving, yet these acts of God are not out of necessity. For Upadhyay, "God's act of mercy is a mystery" and so is God's creation. "The why of creation and of mercy is a mystery."[135]

An apparent implication to the personal nature of the Spirit may be found in the final line of the hymn. Upadhyay has encapsulated three important ministries of the Holy Spirit in the three Sanskrit phrases, *pāvanajavana-vāṇīvadana-jīvanadam*. *Pāvana* is purifying, sanctifying and purificatory. It also refers to the purifying agencies of wind and fire, which signifies the Spirit in the Scripture.[136] The Spirit is *javana* (quick, swift), a quality connected to the wind. *Vāṇī* is voice or speech and *vadana* is the act of speaking. *Jīvana* is vivifying, giving life, enlivening, and thus *jīvanadam* is the one who gives life, the Spirit. The Spirit as the sanctifier (*pāvana*) with swift movements, and as the one who bears witness to the Son, points to the biblical witness about the Spirit. *Pāvana* is connected to both fire and wind which in Sanskrit sense are both purifiers. These are great images of the Holy Spirit worth noting.

BRAHMABANDHAB UPADHYAY'S CONTRIBUTION: AN APPRAISAL

Upadhyay has demonstrated a comprehensive knowledge of the Advaita Vedanta philosophical tradition, which became foundational for his subsequent theological development. In Advaita Vedanta expounded by Shankara, he discovered the prospects of moving away from the established traditional approaches and notions of Western theologizing to an indigenized method of theological expression in India. His call to fall back on the Vedanta for interpreting Christian theology in India could also be seen as a corrective to the dominance that Western theology has exercised on Indian Christian theological discourse. He felt that in a similar way the theological interpretation was seeped through the Eurocentric filter, the articulation of Christian

---

134. Upadhyay, *Writings*, 222.
135. Upadhyay, *Writings*, 1:223–24.
136. Gispert-Sauch, "Sanskrit Hymns," 73.

The Trinitarian Theology of Brahmabandhab Upadhyay

faith in India should be filtered through the Sanskrit tradition.[137] Restating the Christian faith in the Vedanta framework could render it intelligible to Hindu India and make it more at home with the Indian sensibilities. In this attempt, he was not merely "seeking to adapt or synthesize western language into the Indian context," rather he endeavored to lay "a whole new philosophical base" in order to expound Christian theology which would be founded on Indian cultural and religious realities.[138] His articulation of the Trinity in *saccidānanda* frame of reference is a very significant and daring attempt in this direction. It should not just be seen as an achievement in Indian Christian theology, but needs to be recognized as a significant contribution to theological discourse in the global landscape.

As an astute student of Catholic theology represented by Thomas Aquinas, Upadhyay had gained a very clear grasp of the classical doctrine of the Trinity. He remains the first Indian Christian theologian to articulate the doctrine of the Trinity using this Vedanta category of *saccidānanda*. His trinitarian formulation is based on the Christian tradition and can be seen as a corrective to the modalistic interpretation of his teacher Keshub Chunder Sen. While Upadhyay admired his teacher, he clearly distanced himself from Sen's *saccidānanda* interpretation. It must be pointed out in this context that Robin Boyd apparently misunderstood the thoughts of Upadhyay about Sen's views on Christ, when he says, the former "believed that Sen had been truly Christ-centered."[139] This observation is contrary to Upadhyay's own position on Christ. Upadhyay himself writes that Sen denied the eternality and the co-equality of the Son with the Father. He calls Sen, "the mighty opponent of the [classical] doctrine of the Trinity" and "the Indian Arius."[140] One would not expect Upadhyay who subscribes to an orthodox position on the Trinity to call Sen Christo-centric in any Catholic/Christian sense. Upadhyay's interpretation of Trinity in terms of *saccidānanda* never weakened his faith in this most crucial doctrine of the Christian faith as witnessed in his trinitarian hymn, *Vande Saccidānandam*.

The hymn on the Trinity is hailed as a pioneering beginning at a time when the Catholic hierarchy was apprehensive about the approach to contextualization that Upadhyay was advocating. Given the ecclesiastical ambiance of the time, bringing such a key doctrine as the Trinity in

---

137. See Lipner, "Brahmabandhab Upadhyay," 167.
138. Tennent, *Building Christianity*, 358–59.
139. Boyd, *Introduction to Indian Christian Theology*, 67.
140. Upadhyay, *Writings*, 2:368.

An Indian Trinitarian Theology of *Missio Dei*

dialogue with a non-Christian language with deep Hindu cultural roots and terminologies represented a daring attempt. According to Lipner, "In Upadhyay's day and circumstances, this was a marked and influential achievement."[141] It is a remarkable poetic exposition, as it were, of the Christian doctrine of the Trinity in Hindu philosophical categories. K. P. Aleaz thinks the hymn does not have much theological significance.[142] While one would agree with Aleaz's view that the hymn should not be interpreted in isolation of other writings of Upadhyay on *saccidānanda*, one cannot fail to notice the theological underpinning of the hymn. The hymn can be seen as reaffirmation of the trinitarian theology in Sanskrit language. The Sanskrit terms do have a Hindu resonance; even so, they communicate the Christian trinitarian doctrine in profoundly significant ways. The hymn remains a remarkable achievement in Indian Christian theology in particular and in trinitarian theology in general.

Upadhyay launched out his entire scheme of formulating the Christian faith in Indian philosophical categories of thought with an obvious missional focus. The central objective of his endeavor was to make Christianity authentically Indian rooted in the foundations of native culture and traditions in order that the Christian faith would be intelligible to the Hindus. In Upadhyay's view, what holds key to this mission of the church in India is "the Vedantic method [of] formulating the Catholic religion to our countrymen" and "preaching the Holy faith in the Vedantic language."[143] *Saccidānanda* was an important effort directed to this end and its true meaning is understood in the Christian doctrine of the Trinity. It invites people to know God who is revealed as the *Sat, Cit,* and *Ānanda* (Being, Intelligence, and Bliss) in the Christian Trinity. Upadhyay would call it, "investing Christianity with a Hindu garb."[144] Certainly, for him, this is not to "insinuate any change or compromise in matters of dogmatic faith, for to me dogma is the bulwark of truth."[145] While preserving the purity of Christian dogma, Upadhyay called for employing the Hindu thought in

---

141. Lipner, *Brahmabandhab Upadhyay*, 203.

142. See Aleaz, "Theological Writings of Brahmabandhav Upadhyaya," 63–64.

143. Upadhyay, *Writings*, 2:207. See also Upadhyay, "Conversion of India," 2:175–78; "Casthalic Matha," 2:207–9. Upadhyay has combined the two Sanskrit words, "ka" (time) and "sthala" (land) into the adjective compound, "kasthalika" (pertaining to all times and lands) and applied it to the Catholic faith. He derives "Casthalic" from "kasthalika." "Matha" is monastery. See Upadhyay, "Casthalic Matha," 2:205.

144. Upadhyay, *Writings*, 2:224.

145. Upadhyay, *Writings*, 2:223.

The Trinitarian Theology of Brahmabandhab Upadhyay

formulating Christian faith for the sake of mission. Yet, he finds his plea remained unheeded and he laments that Christian "contempt for Hindu philosophy has repelled all intelligent inquiry and led to the monumental failure of Christian missions in India."[146] A serious impediment to Christian mission in India is the Western fabric of the Christian faith, and Upadhyay is convinced that Indian Christianity would grow only on indigenous soil watered by Indian tradition and culture. Upadhyay's use of *saccidānanda* was a pioneering effort in contextualizing the gospel. Such efforts of contextualization continue to hold importance in the context of the expansion of Christianity in the non-Western world.

The preceding appraisal reveals the overarching concern of Upadhyay to build Christianity on Indian foundations. In order to realize this vision, he believed, it was imperative to formulate a distinctive and authentic indigenous Christian theology. Some scholars, however, believe that an effort to formulate the gospel through the Sanskrit tradition overlooks the presence of significant sections of the population, particularly the Dalits and Tribals, who are, strictly speaking, not part of Hinduism. In fact, there has been an increasing disenchantment among the Dalits, Tribals, and other similar communities with Hinduism, and especially Hinduism as represented by Brahminicalism (domination by the Brahmins). The last few decades have witnessed greater awareness among these communities about the fact that they are not part of the Hindu religion. They are seeking a new self-identity, and many of them reassert their Dalit and Tribal identities as being different from Hinduism. On the theological front, the consequence of this new development, as discussed in the second chapter, has led to the emergence of subaltern theologies like Dalit theology and Tribal theology in the second half of the last century. In this context, one may ask, what is the relevance of Upadhyay's formulation of an indigenous theology from the Hindu tradition?

The Indian subaltern communities's rejection of the Sanskrit tradition as a paradigm for developing an indigenous expression of the Christian stems from the latter's association with Brahminicalism. The subaltern groups have viewed Sanskrit tradition as theology from the upper side which is hegemonic and oppressive to Dalits, Tribals, and other such communities in India. However, while one cannot overlook the hegemonic and oppressive structures of Brahminicalism, one cannot also negate the liberation elements and strands of dissent against Brahminicalism identified

146. Upadhyay, *Writings*, 2:224.

within the Sanskrit language and tradition. Notwithstanding its association with Brahmanicalism, the pioneers of Indian Christian theology including Upadhyay found Sanskrit tradition, given its influence in shaping the pan-Indian worldview, could be instrumental in restating the Christian faith in India.[147] It is important to dissociate the Sanskrit language and tradition from Brahminicalism and rediscover its usefulness as a pan-Indian worldview, and recapture its strands of liberation and its historical continuity with movements of dissent, such as Buddhism in articulating subaltern theologies as well as strengthening the subaltern movements for freedom and justice. These issues will be explored further in detail in the final chapter of this study.

CONCLUSION

Brahmabandhab Upadhyay was a multifaceted figure, an erudite and perceptive thinker, "Christian and Hindu, holy man and savant, prophet and revolutionary nationalist."[148] He was a "disowned prophet," whose prophetic utterances and radical propositions for theologizing in India grounded on Indian culture and religious traditions was not recognized by his own generation.[149] Yet, Upadhyay occupies a very significant place in the history of Indian nationalism, the Indian church, and Indian Christian theology. His place is that of a pioneer who dared to break new grounds for Christian theology and mission in India, and challenged the church for serious engagement with the Indian culture and religious traditions. He was one of the earliest Indian Christians to have developed a positive attitude towards Hinduism, and the first to have entered into serious and meaningful interaction with Hindu philosophy. He was also perhaps the first Christian to recognize the necessity for indigenization as an essential part of Christian mission. He found the church of his time clothed in Western costume, and her theology in a Greco-scholastic framework which appeared alien to the Hindu mind. Hence, Upadhyay set out to interpret the Christian faith through the Advaita Vedanta philosophy of Shankara in an attempt to indigenize the Christian gospel. His "life and writings represent a clarion call for Indian Christians to be authentically Indian in their search to root Christianity in Indian soil."[150] Upadhyay believed that the appropriation

147. Tennent, "Contextualizing the Sanskritic Tradition," 343–45.
148. Lipner, *Brahmabandhab Upadhyay*, xv.
149. Fonseca, "Prophet Disowned," 177–94.
150. Tennent, *Building Christianity*, 380.

of the Advaita Vedanta in articulating the gospel as demonstrated in the restatement of the doctrine of the Trinity from *saccidānanda* perspective would provide a way forward in this direction. In the following chapter, the trinitarian theology of Augustine and the concept of the *missio Dei* will be examined, with a view to bringing it in relation to the trinitarian thought of Upadhyay that has been expounded in the present chapter.

4

St. Augustine and Trinitarian *Missio Dei* Theology

INTRODUCTION

IN THE PRECEDING CHAPTER, we have examined one of the important attempts to expound the Christian doctrine of the Trinity in terms of the Hindu philosophical category of *saccidānanda*. This daring attempt at indigenization was undertaken with an objective of building Christianity on Indian foundations. As an important part of bringing this Indian theologizing into conversation with the doctrine of the Trinity in the larger Christian tradition represented by St. Augustine, an attempt is made to locate the roots of the concept of the *missio Dei* in his trinitarian writings. The *missio Dei* is a relatively new concept that has become quite prominent in recent missiological discourses. Its origin is often positioned in the International Missionary Conference at Willingen in 1952 where the source of mission came to be situated in the nature of the Triune God. Nevertheless, the idea of the *missio Dei* originated in the trinitarian theology of Augustine, particularly in his monumental work on the Trinity, *De Trinitate* in defense of the doctrine against the Arians.

Augustine was not a mission theologian, nor was it his intention to launch a discussion on mission in the sense it is pursued today. He deems mission as the sending of the Son and the Holy Spirit by the Father in the economy of salvation which demonstrates how each person of the Trinity is distinct, and yet they are inseparable in their being and operations. This divine mission is grounded in the trinitarian being of God. Mission takes

St. Augustine and Trinitarian Missio Dei Theology

place in the outward movement, the sending (*missio*) of the Son and the Holy Spirit from the Father into the world, and it happens only in their manifestations in the incarnation and at Pentecost. This mission of God, Augustine believes, is a pivotal event in the divine economy of salvation which is revelatory in which mission itself is a revelation of the Triune God, and reconciliatory, in which humanity is reconciled to God through the sacrifice of the Son. The following discussion seeks to expound this divine mission from Augustine's trinitarian thought.

AN OVERVIEW OF AUGUSTINE'S TRINITARIAN THOUGHT

Augustine's exposition of trinitarian doctrine has been influential in shaping Western trinitarian discourse for over fifteen centuries. Augustine has been credited with providing the Western Church what is called a "Latin paradigm" of the trinitarian doctrine and its mature exposition.[1] His trinitarian theology emerges in a milieu where the reverberations generated by the Nicene Creed continued unabated in polemic engagements.[2] Having been firmly grounded in the Nicene tradition of trinitarian doctrine and the Scripture, Augustine, in his *De Trinitate*, took on the opponents of the Nicene doctrine, and sought to establish the scriptural foundations of the doctrine of the Trinity, particularly, the deity and consubstantiality of the Son. Simultaneously, to the pagan philosophers of his time, Augustine demonstrated the necessity of God's self-revelation that comes only through the divine mediation expressed in the incarnation of the Son of God himself, through which the divided humanity would be united to the only one God.[3] This chapter is primarily concerned about the concept of the *missio Dei* in Augustine's trinitarian theology and does not attempt a comprehensive exposition on his trinitarian doctrine.[4] What follows is

---

1. See Ayres, "Augustine on the Trinity," 123; Kelly, *Early Christian Doctrines*, 271.

2. Books 1–4 of *De Trinitate* may be seen as Augustine's attempts to demonstrate to the opponents of the Nicene faith from the Scripture, the deity of the Son and the Holy Spirit and their equality with the Father. See Augustine, *De Trinitate*, Books 1–4. Henceforth, citations from *De Trinitate* are given in the following format: Augustine, *De Trinitate* 2.9 (103); "2.9" refers to the book and paragraph and "(103)" refers to the page number. See also Barnes, "Exegesis and Polemic," 43–60; Bucur, "Theophanies and Vision of God," 74.

3. Clark, "*De Trinitate*," 91. Augustine, *De Trinitate* 5–7; 4.2–12 (153–66). See also Muller, "Dynamic of Augustine's *De Trinitate*," 71–72.

4. For a comprehensive treatment of Augustine's trinitarian theology, see the following recent works: Ayres, *Augustine and the Trinity*; Gioia, *Theological Epistemology*.

An Indian Trinitarian Theology of *Missio Dei*

a review of the important aspects of Augustine's doctrine of the Trinity in order that it may serve as an entry point into the major discussion on his trinitarian mission of God.

Augustine's emphasis on the unity of God is regarded as one of the most fundamental aspects of his trinitarian thought. It is generally held that in Augustine, the divine nature (*ousia*) is made the highest ontological principle as opposed to the person (*hypostasis*) as in the Eastern tradition which emphasized the *monarchia* of the Father.[5] Therefore, Augustine is believed to be taking the unity of the divine nature as the point of departure of his trinitarian theology. Hence, Augustine's modern critics have accused him of overstressing the unity of God under the influence of the Platonic and the Neo-platonic metaphysics, elevating the immanent Trinity and sacrificing the economic theology of the Trinity. This traditional notion has been contested in modern Augustinian scholarship.[6] Augustine's emphasis on the unity of God comes from the inseparable operations of the Triune persons, a principle which did not originate with Augustine. In fact, Augustine inherited it from his predecessors in the Nicene tradition, especially his mentor Ambrose and Hilary of Poitiers.[7] Interestingly, the Eastern Fathers did teach the doctrine of inseparability, and prominent among them are Athanasius, Basil the Great, Gregory of Nyssa, and Gregory of Nazianzus.[8] In this respect, Dennis Jowers comments, "Anti-Augustinian theologians can by no means, therefore, legitimately appeal

---

5. See LaCugna, *God for Us*, 101; Fortman, *Triune God*, 140.

6. It is not within the scope of this chapter to undertake a discussion of the debate on the unity of God in Augustine's theology. For a critique of Augustine's unity of God and the neglect of the economic Trinity, see Gunton, *Promise of Trinitarian Theology*, 30–55; LaCugna, *God for Us*, 81–104. For an alternate reading of Augustine's account of the trinitarian unity, countering the accusation that the unity of God is Augustine's point of departure of his trinitarian doctrine, see Ayres, "Remember that You Are Catholic"; "Fundamental Grammar of Augustine's Trinitarian Theology," 59–69; Barnes, "Augustine in Contemporary Trinitarian Theology," 237–50; Ormerod, *Trinity*, 33–53; Jowers, "Divine Unity and the Economy of Salvation," 68–84.

7. Ayres, "Remember That You Are Catholic," 80; Ambrose, *On the Holy Spirit*, 1.12.131; 2.10.101; Hilary of Poitiers, *On the Trinity*, 7.17–18. Ayres includes in this group the anti-Homoian theologians such as Gregory of Elvira, Phoebadius of Agen, Eusebius of Vercelli, and Rufinus who emphasized inseparability. See Ayres, "Fundamental Grammar," 55–56, 73.

8. See Athanasius, *Letters Concerning the Holy Spirit*, 1.19, 28, 31; 3.5; Basil, *On the Holy Spirit*, (NPNF2/8:10.24–26 [16–17]; 16.37–40 [23–26]); *Letter* (NPNF2/8:189.6–7 [230–31]); Gregory of Nyssa, *On the Holy Trinity*; *On "Not Three Gods"* (NPNF2/5:326–36); Gregory of Nazianzus, *Fifth Theological Oration* (NPNF2/7:318–28).

to the great Fathers of the East to bolster their critique of this aspect of Augustine's doctrine of the Trinity."[9]

Inseparability implies the one divine essence (substance) and will of the Triune persons where every operation/action of the one person of the Godhead applies to all the three persons equally.[10] The Father, the Son, and the Holy Spirit are distinct persons without being separate individual beings in the human sense. Being distinct persons, the Father, the Son, and the Holy Spirit do not make three Gods, but one God who is a Trinity. The "Trinity is one God . . . one eternity, one power, one majesty . . . [and] one almighty."[11] Thus, whatever is predicated with reference to the divine nature is expressed in the singular. Accordingly, while each person is God, each is good, each is almighty, each is infinite, increate, omnipotent, and eternal, there are *not* three Gods, or three good ones, or three almighty ones, or three infinite ones, and so on, but only one God, the Triune God, who is almighty, infinite, increate, omnipotent, eternal, and so on.[12] In their inseparability, no person is alone, but each person is always in each other in a perichoretic unity. Although Augustine does not use the term *perichoresis*, the idea may be seen as being ingrained in his use of trinitarian inseparability. He sought to maintain the Cappadocian Fathers's "relational principles grounded in the notion of *perichoresis*."[13]

As noted above, Augustine's critics have accused him of elevating the unity of God, undermining the plurality of the Trinity, and thus tending towards modalism. One of the trenchant critics was Colin Gunton, the late professor of Christian Doctrine at King's College, London. Gunton attributes what he believes to be a weakening of the distinctions of the persons in Augustine's trinitarian theology to the supposed influence of Neo-Platonism as well as the latter's chief concern to repudiate Arianism which questioned divinity of Christ.[14] There are evidences, however, within Augustine's trinitarian writings that question the validity of Gunton's claim. Two passages would suffice to substantiate trinitarian plurality and

---

9. Jowers, "Divine Unity and the Economy of Salvation," 71.

10. See Augustine, *Homilies on the Gospel of John* 20.13 (NPNF1/7:137). *De Trinitate* 1.7 (70–71); 1.25 (88–89); 2.3 (98–99); 5.9 (196–97); 8.1 (241–42); *Sermon* 2.2.

11. Augustine, *Homilies on the Gospel of John* 39.3–4; *De Trinitate* 7.11 (232).

12. Augustine, *De Trinitate* 8.1 (240). Kelly, *Early Christian Doctrines*, 273.

13. Pecknold, "How Augustine Used the Trinity," 134. See also Augustine, *De Trinitate* 6.9 (212n22).

14. See Gunton, *Promise of Trinitarian Theology*, 32–34. For a critical analysis of Gunton's position on Augustine, see Ormerod, "Augustine and the Trinity," 17–32.

An Indian Trinitarian Theology of *Missio Dei*

distinctions in Augustine's thought. One of those clear assertions comes from a mature period of Augustine's writings: "That the Father, Son, and Holy Spirit are a Trinity inseparable; One God, not three Gods. But yet so One God, as that the Son is not the Father, and the Father is not the Son, and the Holy Spirit is neither the Father nor the Son, but the Spirit of the Father and of the Son."[15] The other strongest example may be seen at the outset of the *De Trinitate*:

> [A]ccording to the scriptures Father and Son and Holy Spirit in the inseparable equality of one substance present a divine unity; and therefore there are not three gods, but one God: although indeed the Father has begotten the Son, and therefore he who is the Father is not the Son; and the Son is begotten by the Father, and therefore he who is the Son is not the Father; and the Holy Spirit is neither the Father nor the Son, but only the Spirit of the Father and of the Son, himself also coequal to the Father and the Son, and belonging to the threefold unity.[16]

Augustine traces distinctions within the Godhead in the mutual and eternal relationship as well as relations of origin of the trinitarian persons. The unity of the Trinity is affirmed in the one divine substance; yet each one is distinguished from the other in their being related to each other. The Father is differentiated from the Son as the begetter of the Son, the Son is distinct from the Father as begotten by the Father. The Holy Spirit is distinguished from the Father and the Son as their "inexpressible communion or fellowship" and as the Spirit of both of them.[17] While making distinction in the Trinity, Augustine is not quite comfortable with the use of "persons," designated as *hypostasis* in the Greek, perhaps because the term carries a sense of being individuals in the distinctions.[18] However, Augustine feels that "persons" along with "substance" can be used as terms of convenience in order to distinguish the trinitarian persons and to ward off the heresy of Sabellianism.[19]

---

15. Augustine, *Sermon* 2.2 (NPNF1/6:259). See Ayres, "Fundamental Grammar," 59–60; Augustine, *Letters 100–155*, 136, 138; *Sermon* 53.4 (NPNF1/6:428).

16. Augustine, *De Trinitate* 1.7 (70); 5.6 (192). See also Ormerod, *Trinity*, 35.

17. Augustine, *De Trinitate* 5.6 (192); 5.12 (199); Augustine, *Letters 156–210*, 114–17.

18. Kelly, *Early Christian Doctrines*, 274.

19. For detailed discussion of "persons" and "substance," see Augustine, *De Trinitate* 7.7–11 (227–34).

St. Augustine and Trinitarian Missio Dei Theology

One of the central concerns of Augustine, within the inseparability and the distinction of the trinitarian persons, is the place of the Holy Spirit in the Godhead. He calls the Holy Spirit the mutual love of the Father and the Son, a concept that he is not quite able to demonstrate from Scripture.[20] This idea emerges from his assertion that the Holy Spirit is of both the Father and the Son and it leads Augustine to regard the Holy Spirit as communion and fellowship between the Father and the Son.[21] In this relation of the Holy Spirit to the Father and the Son, Augustine traces the double procession of the Spirit. In the mutual relationship of the Father and the Son, the Father is the origin in reference to the Son, since the former has begotten the latter. Father is also the origin of the Holy Spirit because the Holy Spirit comes forth (proceeds) from the Father (John 15:26). The procession of the Spirit from the Father, says Augustine, does not imply begetting and hence the Spirit is *not* another son. The Spirit proceeds from the Father "as *being given*" and "*not as being born*" as the Son.[22] The Son was *begotten* timelessly by the Father. In begetting the Son, the Father gave him (Son) life which is coeternal with him (Father). Therefore, "just as the Father has it in himself that the Holy Spirit should proceed from him, so he gave to the Son that the Holy Spirit should proceed from him too, and in both cases timelessly."[23] Thus, in this double procession of the Spirit, the Father and the Son constitute one single origin (*principium*) of the Spirit.[24]

Augustine, while attempting to understand the Trinity, is conscious of the infiniteness of the mystery of the Trinity and the inadequacy of human finiteness in comprehending this ineffable being of God. However, he regarded the Trinity as a very central doctrine of Scripture, and believed that efforts must be made to deepen one's understanding about this vital teaching. Augustine made a significant contribution toward this dimension in a number of psychological analogies drawn from the interiority of the human person. A comprehensive analysis of this broad theme in Augustine's treatment of trinitarian analogy is beyond the scope of this chapter. Hence, this discussion will be confined to a brief overview of a few important analogies.

---

20. See Augustine, *Of Faith and the Creed* 9.19; *De Trinitate* 15.29 (421). See also Coffey, "Holy Spirit as the Mutual Love," 195–96.

21. Augustine, *De Trinitate* 5.12 (199); *Homilies on the Gospel of John* 19.6.

22. Augustine, *De Trinitate* 5.15 (201); *Letter* 170.4–5. Emphasis added.

23. Augustine, *De Trinitate* 15.47 (438); *Homilies on the Gospel of John* 99.9.

24. Augustine, *De Trinitate* 5.15 (201).

Augustine believes that there are vestiges of the Trinity in the created order where everything that exists derives its existence from the Triune God.[25] The human being, created in the image of the Triune God (Gen 1:26), according to Augustine, is by far the closest to the image of the Trinity, and thus bears resemblance to the triunity of God. Therefore, Augustine bases his analogies on this divine image in the human person.[26] He seeks the resemblance of the Trinity within the inner being, namely, in the human mind.

Possibly one of the most prominent trinitarian analogies is the one which Augustine develops from the Johannine text on love: *God is love* (1 John 4:8, 16). Prior to this, Augustine has already developed the idea that God is truth and good, and the highpoint of the articulation of these divine qualities is that God is love.[27] Love, for Augustine, is essentially triadic in nature and expression since it involves the one who *loves*, the one who is *loved*, and finally the *love* itself which unites the lover and the loved: "There you are with three, the lover, what is loved, and love. And what is love but a kind of life coupling or trying to couple together two things, namely lover and what is being loved?"[28] Augustine, in the ninth book, makes a transition and seeks to expand the image of love, making the human mind as the subject of love.

Three aspects of the human mind are traced out which, according to Augustine, show resemblance to the Trinity. In the being of the mind, there are the mind's knowledge (understanding) of itself and the mind's love for itself. There is the triad of the mind, its understanding, and its love corresponding to the Trinity. The mind's love of itself necessitates that the mind know its own self, the self-understanding. Thus, within the being of the mind, there is self-understanding and self-love constituting a Trinity of mind, understanding, and love.[29] For Augustine, this triadic nature of the mind serves as an image of the Triunity of God: "the Father as Being, the Son as Consciousness, and the Spirit as Love."[30] Augustine further de-

---

25. Augustine, *Of True Religion* 7.13 (232).

26. Augustine, *Sermon* 2.17–19 (NPNF1/6:263–64). See also *City of God* 11.26 (NPNF1/2:220).

27. See Drilling, "Psychological Analogy of the Trinity," 324; Augustine, *De Trinitate* 8.2–5 (242–46); 8.10–14 (253–57); 9.2 (272–73).

28. Augustine, *De Trinitate* 8.13 (257); 9.2 (272).

29. Augustine, *De Trinitate* 9.2–3 (272–73); Augustine, *Confessions* 13.12. See Rea, "Trinity," 409.

30. O'Collins, *Tripersonal God*, 136. See Augustine, *De Trinitate* 9.3–4.

St. Augustine and Trinitarian Missio Dei Theology

veloped this trinitarian model and suggested a more favored trinitarian analogy. He discovers within the human mind three things which, while being separate, are inseparable in operation: the memory of the mind which has the capacity of retention, the understanding which provides the ability to comprehend what is retained, and the will with which the mind attains understanding of itself from memory.[31] While being conscious of the inadequacy of these tentative expositions of the trinitarian imageries drawn from human interiority, for Augustine, they are founded on the human image and likeness as indicated earlier. They serve no more than as pointers to the divine mystery of the Trinity.

AUGUSTINE'S TRINITARIAN THEOLOGY AND *MISSIO DEI*

The *missio* (sending) of God as a theological category is a significant theme in Augustine's trinitarian doctrine. As a divine activity, *missio* is quite central to the revelation of the Triune God and God's redemptive work through which humanity is reconciled to God. This revelation and redemption are accomplished through the sending of the Son and the Holy Spirit in mission who reveal the inner life of the Triune God in the generation (*generatio*) of the Son and the procession also called spiration (*spiratio*) of the Spirit. Thus, mission in Augustine's trinitarian doctrine brings together, as it were, the inner trinitarian life of God and human reconciliation with God.[32]

The idea of the *missio Dei* traced out in Augustine has captured the attention of theologians and missiologists in recent times as indicated in the latter part of the first chapter. Augustine has helped us, albeit inadvertently, to situate mission in the trinitarian being of God. Mission receives its trinitarian structure from the *missio* of God who is not only the sender but also "the Content of the sending," the one being sent.[33] In Augustine's trinitarian thoughts, God sends himself in the Son and the Holy Spirit revealing himself to the world and redeeming the human race through the *missio* of God. The subsequent section of this chapter will seek to unearth this *missio* (sending) of God in relation to the triune being of God in Augustine's thought.

---

31. Augustine, *Sermon* 2.18–19; *De Trinitate* 10.13–19 (298–302). See Rea, "Trinity," 409.

32. Gioia, *Theological Epistemology*, 17; Ayres, *Augustine and the Trinity*, 181–85; Augustine, *De Trinitate* 2.7 (102); 4.29 (182).

33. Vicedom, *Mission of God*, 8. See Engelsviken, "Missio Dei," 483.

An Indian Trinitarian Theology of *Missio Dei*

THE TRINITY, *MISSIO DEI*, AND THEOPHANIES

The equality, consubstantiality, and inseparability of the Father, the Son, and the Holy Spirit are very central to Augustine's doctrine of the Trinity. The unity of the Godhead underlined by these three indispensable aspects of the Trinity, however, does not suggest the absence of distinctions in the Trinity. Augustine clearly distinguishes between the Father, the Son, and the Holy Spirit as distinct persons within the Godhead. The Son is distinct from the Father as the begotten of the Father, and therefore, he is not the Father; the Holy Spirit is distinguished from the Father and the Son, but is of both the Father and the Son, being coequal, coeternal, and consubstantial with the Father and the Son.[34]

An important context that raises questions about the equality of the Son with the Father was the alleged sending of the Son in the theophanies of the Hebrew Scriptures and the consequent contention by Augustine's opponents, those of Arian persuasion, about the Son's ontological subordination to the Father. The opponents denied the Son the immutability and invisibility ascribed to God in Scripture (Wis 7:27; 1 Tim 1:17; 6:15 –16). Accordingly, they attributed the divine manifestations in the Hebrew Scriptures to the Son of God, and thus sought to establish that the Son was made visible even prior to his incarnation. Hence, the Son is not regarded properly God as the Father is God, because unlike the Father, the Son is thought to be mutable and visible.[35] Augustine seeks to refute these arguments of the Arians through a thorough investigation of the theophanies, an exegetical exercise that occupies most of book 2 of the *De Trinitate*. Even prior to Augustine, theophanies occupied a significant space in the patristic Christological discourse. Before probing Augustine's thought on theophanies, it seems appropriate to examine the historical background of the theology of theophanies in early Christian thought.

Historical Background of the Theology of Theophanies in the Hebrew Scriptures

The attempts to relate theophanies to Christ may be traced back to polemical contexts of the pre-Augustinian patristic writings of both the Greek and Latin fathers. With the rise of heresies, such as Adoptionism, Arianism, Sabellianism, Marcionism, particularly on the Christological front, the

---

34. Augustine, *De Trinitate* 1.7 (70–71).
35. Augustine, *De Trinitate* 2.14–15 (110–11).

St. Augustine and Trinitarian Missio Dei Theology

fathers of the early church felt it incumbent upon them to defend the deity and the distinction of the personhood of Christ within the Godhead. To this end, the fathers employed polemical exegesis on theophanies in order to counter the heresies and to affirm the divinity of the Son as well as to distinguish him from the Father. Their writings evince the tendency to ascribe to Christ any manifestations, actions, and speeches of God or angels in anthropomorphic forms.[36]

The early Christian apologists, Justin Martyr and Theophilus of Antioch seemed to have believed what is called "Yahweh Christology," which attributes the manifestations of Yahweh to Christ. Justin identifies theophanies with the pre-incarnate Christ who is distinct from the Father, who according to Justin, is inaccessible as the one "who remains ever in the supercelestial places." He believed that the Son was sent as the judge over Sodom and Gomorrah as suggested by the following passage: "He who appeared to Abraham under the oak in Mamre is God [the Son], sent with the two angels in His company to judge Sodom by Another [Father] who remains ever in the supercelestial places."[37] According to Theophilus, it was the Word of the Father, the Son who assumed "the person of the Father and Lord of all, went to the garden in the person of God, and conversed with Adam."[38] Irenaeus, who possibly was a student of Justin and a devoted disciple of Polycarp, believed that the Son appeared in theophanies to the patriarchs. He makes two explicit references to Christ as having been revealed in the theophanies. He identifies the Son as speaking to both Abraham and Moses, and judging Sodom and Gomorrah for their wickedness.[39]

The third-century writers Tertullian and Novatian took the Christological approach to the theophanies of the Hebrew Scriptures in their defense against dualism and modalism. Tertullian, in distinguishing the Son from the Father, found it essential to affirm the visibility of the Son in the theophanies. The Father, for Tertullian, is invisible: "For God the Father none ever saw, and lived."[40] He goes as far as saying that Christ appeared

---

36. See Hanson, "Theophanies in the Old Testament," 67; Norwood, "Church Fathers," 17–33; Kloos, *Christ, Creation*, 14–15.

37. Justin, *Dialogue with Trypho* 56. See Trakatellis, *Pre-existence of Christ*; Kominiak, *Theophanies of the Old Testament*.

38. Theophilus of Antioch, *To Autolycus* (ANF2:2.22 [103]).

39. Irenaeus, *Against Heresies* (ANF1:3.6.1 [418–19]; 4.9.1 [472]).

40. Tertullian, *Answer to the Jews* (ANF3:9 [163]); *Against Praxeas* (ANF3:14 [609–10]).

An Indian Trinitarian Theology of *Missio Dei*

to Abraham "without being born, and yet in the flesh."[41] Distinguishing it from the incarnation, Tertullian believes that the appearance was in "truly *human* flesh, and yet *not born*."[42] In seeking to defend the divinity as well as the distinction of the Son from the Father against Sabellianism, Novatian turned to the theophanies. The Son, according to Novatian, while being God, is distinct from the Father and appeared as "the Announcer of the Father's mind" and thus made himself visible to the human race. He maintains the distinction as well as the visibility of the Son as in the divine appearance to Hagar in the wilderness and to Abraham at the oak of Mamre prior to the destruction of Sodom and Gomorrah.[43]

The fourth-century church father, Hilary of Poitiers, regarded theophanies as a progressive development of doctrine. Writing against the Arians, Hilary turns to theophanies to establish the plurality and distinctions within the Trinity. For instance, referring to the appearance of the angel of the Lord to Hagar, Hilary asserts that the functions of the angel confirm that the angel is the Son of God and he is distinct from God the Father.[44] The divine appearance to Abraham and Sarah, Hilary believes, prefigures the incarnation of the Son (Gen 18:1–15).[45] Augustine's spiritual mentor and one of the staunch defenders of Christian orthodoxy against Arianism, St. Ambrose identifies theophanies with the Son who, he believes, was seen and worshipped by the patriarchs, and who wrestled with Jacob.[46] Ambrose makes explicit references to pre-incarnate Christ as having appeared to Moses in the burning bush and appeared in the burning furnace with the three Hebrew young men.[47] It is important to note as we conclude this brief overview of theophanies in the patristic writings that all of these fathers who took a Christological approach to theophanies also often applied the appellation of angel to Christ, an idea seemed to have been taken from Isaiah 9:6.[48] Theophanies could be seen as a form of God's/the Son's mission into the world anticipating the New Testament Incarnation.

---

41. Tertullian, *On the Flesh of Christ* (ANF3:6 [527]).

42. Tertullian, *Against Marcion* (ANF3:3.9 [329]).

43. Novatian, *On the Trinity* (ANF5:18 [628]). See also Kari Kloos, *Christ, Creation*, 32–41.

44. Hilary of Poitiers, *On the Trinity*, 4.23; 5.11.

45. Hilary, *On the Trinity*, 4.27.

46. Ambrose, *On the Holy Spirit*, 1.4.55; *On the Duties of the Clergy*, 1.25.120.

47. Ambrose, *Exposition of the Christian Faith*, 1.13.80, 83.

48. Junker, "Christ as Angel," 221–50. See also Junker, "Christ as Angel," 225n13.

Augustine's Analysis of Theophanies

The pre-Augustinian theologians understood theophanies in terms of their Christological nature. Augustine, being grounded in his conviction of the inseparability and the invisibility of the Trinity, made a shift away from the theory of Christophanies advocated by his predecessors. For Augustine, viewing theophanies as Christophanies would be tantamount to giving up the inseparability of the Trinity as well as tending towards subordinationism.[49] Augustine's predecessors used theophanies to demonstrate to the heretics of their day, the preexistence of Christ, his deity as well as the distinctions within the Trinity. In this logos-centric hermeneutics of theophanies, the opponents of the Nicene doctrine readily found opportunity to establish their stance on the deity of the Son. For the Arians, who believed in the essential invisibility of God, the fathers's interpretation of the visibility of the Son in the theophanies effectively vindicated their position that the Son is not true God as the Father is God since he was manifested in the theophanies.[50]

Interestingly, Augustine consented to the essential invisibility of God as held by the Arians and rejected the Christological interpretation of his predecessors because of its subordinationist tendencies. Augustine found that his predecessors's logos-centric hermeneutics only reinforced the contention of the Arians that the visibility of the Son in the theophanies proves his subordination to the invisible Father, and hence the Son is of a different nature than the Father. Contesting the standpoints of the fathers as well as his Arian opponents on the theophanies in the Hebrew Scriptures, Augustine brought a new interpretation which marked a turning point in the Western Church's understanding of theophanies.[51]

Augustine believes from his careful analysis of theophanies that the Scripture does not warrant identifying theophanies with the sending of any of the persons of the Trinity. The theophanies should not, in his view, be regarded as physical manifestations of the Trinity. Therefore, for Augustine, the question of the identity of the subjects of theophanies cannot be answered with any certainty.[52] Following the New Testament revelation of the

---

49. Wassmer, "Trinitarian Theology of Augustine," 262. Augustine, *De Trinitate* 2.12–16 (109–12).

50. See Barnes, "Visible Christ and the Invisible Trinity," 330.

51. Bucur, "Exegesis of Biblical Theophanies," 104–5.

52. Augustine, *De Trinitate* 2.18–19 (113–15); 2.35 (126). See Manoussakis, "Theophany and Indication," 77–79.

An Indian Trinitarian Theology of *Missio Dei*

trinitarian persons, one might conjecture about the appearance of the Father, the Son, and the Holy Spirit in the theophanies. For instance, perhaps one could attribute the voice that spoke to Adam to the three divine persons retrospectively, following the divine voice in the New Testament in John 12:28.[53] Such presumptions might seem possible in the event of the divine encounters that Abraham experienced in his divine call (Gen 12:1), the divine visitation under the oak of Mambre (Gen 18), and subsequently the divine visit to Lot before the destruction of Sodom and Gomorrah.[54] Yet, in another instance of the giving of the Law on the mount of Sinai which is said to have been "written with the finger of God" (Exod 31:18), Augustine is wondering why should this divine act not be attributed to the Holy Spirit who is referred to as the "finger of God" in the gospels (Luke 11:20; cf. Matt 12:28). Extending this conjecture further, Augustine points to the correspondence between the fiftieth day from the Passover and slaying of the lamb to the events of Mount Sinai, and the descent of the Holy Spirit on the fiftieth day from the passion of Christ. Furthermore, the symbolism of fire in the events of Pentecost (Acts 2:1) and Sinai (Exod 19:18) seems to add more probability to the conjecture.[55]

In Augustine's judgment, the New Testament hints are inadequate to attribute theophanies of the Hebrew Scriptures either to any one particular person of the Godhead or to the Trinity as a whole.[56] However, Augustine contends that there is sufficient scriptural basis to believe that God is invisible in God's essential nature and essence. In explaining theophanies, at best, one could believe that the Triune God being the creator "could offer the senses of mortal men a token representation of himself in bodily guise or likeness."[57] These divine encounters, wonders Augustine, could also be from the angels sent to represent the Trinity in their manifestation who either appropriated the bodily guise of the creatures for that purpose or changed their own bodies into whatever shapes required by their divine commission.[58]

These conjectures apart, Augustine refuses to acknowledge theophanies as representing the sending of the second person of the Trinity as

---

53. Augustine, *De Trinitate* 2.18 (113–14); 2.35 (126). See Gioia, *Theological Epistemology*, 29.

54. Augustine, *De Trinitate* 2.19–22 (114–16).

55. Augustine, *De Trinitate* 2.26 (119).

56. Gioia, *Theological Epistemology*, 29.

57. Augustine, *De Trinitate* 2.35 (126).

58. Augustine, *De Trinitate* 3.3 (129).

St. Augustine and Trinitarian Missio Dei Theology

advocated by the Arians. For Augustine, "the divinity of the Son is made manifest only at the end-time and that there are, properly speaking, no theophanies of the Son (or of any other Person of the Trinity)."[59] Therefore, for Augustine, theophanies of the Hebrew Scriptures are not to be taken as the manifestations of the Son. He discounts the attempts to establish the Son as the visible member of the Trinity who appeared in theophanies. The proper manifestations of the Son as well as the Holy Spirit, according to Augustine, took place only in the incarnation and at Pentecost. Yet, these appearances to human bodily senses do not reveal the substance of the Son and the Spirit in which they are coequal and coeternal with the Father and with each other.[60]

However, on the other hand, Augustine brings out an important dimension of theophany to the mission of the Son in the New Testament. While theophanies themselves were not the manifestations of the Son, nevertheless he saw them as playing a critical role in the divine scheme of the unfolding of God's mission to the world in the incarnation. Reversing the tendency of the early Christian tradition to trace back Christ in the theophanies in order to demonstrate his divinity, Augustine sought to interpret theophanies as pointing forward to Christ.[61] Thus, he regards theophanies as likeness of the Son, which, like the rest of the creation, pointed forward to the mission of the coming Savior. "All the sacred and mysterious things that were shown to our fathers by angelic miracles, or that they themselves performed, *were likeness of him*, so that all creation might in some fashion utter the one who was to come and be the savior of all who needed to be restored from death."[62] The *missional objective* of theophanies may be found in its being a pointer to the senses of human beings of knowing God from whom they are separated. Therefore, Augustine sees theophanies as *sights* that God sent us "suited to our wandering state, to admonish us that what we seek is not here, and that we must turn back from the things around us to where our whole being springs from—if it did not, we would not even seek these things here."[63] Therefore, Augustine assigns a special space for theophanies in the divine scheme which were divinely ordained in order that they might point beyond themselves to God's future mission through Christ.

---

59. Barnes, "Visible Christ and the Invisible Trinity," 342.
60. Augustine, *De Trinitate* 3.27 (146).
61. Kloos, *Christ, Creation*, 151.
62. Augustine, *De Trinitate* 4.11 (164). Emphasis added.
63. Augustine, *De Trinitate* 4.2 (153). See also Kloos, *Christ, Creation*, 151.

An Indian Trinitarian Theology of *Missio Dei*

THE TRINITY AND DIVINE MISSIONS

Theologically, mission refers to the *economic* activity of the trinitarian sending in the New Testament where the Father sends the Son, and the Father and the Son together send the Holy Spirit.[64] This mission, for Augustine, is identified with the generation and the procession of the Son and the Holy Spirit, a thought we will discuss in this chapter. The sending of the Son and the Spirit in mission is located in their being (*filiation* and *spiration*) from the Father. Yet the Father is never said to have been sent because like the Son and the Holy Spirit, the Father "has not got anyone else to be from or proceed from."[65] Mission is the self-communication of the Father, his sending forth of the Son and the Holy Spirit in their visible manifestations in the world—the permanent visible manifestation of the Son and the transitory visible manifestation of the Holy Spirit.[66] More specifically, God's mission (*missio Dei*) takes place *only* in the incarnation of Christ and at Pentecost of the Holy Spirit. It is in the incarnation, the Son's divine nature is united with human nature, and the inner trinitarian identity of the Holy Spirit is revealed in the Spirit's procession from the Father. The mission of God that occurred in the incarnation and Pentecost is the central event in the economy of salvation because it reveals the inner trinitarian life and God's reconciliation of humanity to God.[67] Therefore, Augustine insists that God's mission is not to be sought in the theophanies of the Hebrew Scripture, but in the context of the incarnation and Pentecost.

Nevertheless, the visible divine appearances in the Hebrew Scriptures are important since they prefigured God's salvific plan through the death and resurrection of Christ.[68] Accordingly, the Word which was

---

64. Augustine, *De Trinitate* 4.29 (181–82).

65. Augustine, *De Trinitate* 4.28 (181). Darwish, "Concept of the Mediator," 71.

66. See Augustine, *De Trinitate* 2.7–9 (101–8); Clark, "*De Trinitate*," 93.

67. Gioia, *Theological Epistemology*, 34, 114–16; Augustine, *De Trinitate* 4. 28–29 (181–83). In a recent work on Trinitarian Missiology, Stephen Holmes does not see that for Augustine, the sending of the Son and the Holy Spirit is "illustrative or definitive of the inner-triune relations" (Holmes, "Trinitarian Missiology," 78). A careful reading of Augustine, as demonstrated in this chapter, will yield sufficient ground to believe that the divine economy of salvation through the mission of the Son and the Holy Spirit (in the incarnation and Pentecost) reveals the inner-trinitarian life. In his forceful work on "History and Faith in *De Trinitate*," Studer has convincingly demonstrated that "the temporal economy in fact manifests an eternal theology" (Studer, "History and Faith," 35, 38). See also Gioia, *Theological Epistemology*, 116.

68. Augustine, *De Trinitate* 2–3; see especially 3.26–27 (145–46).

then delivered through the angels in the Hebrew Scriptures (theophanies) is *now delivered through the Son* in the incarnation (Heb 2:1–3).[69] Thus, the mission (sending) of the Trinity takes place in the New Testament in the appearance of the Son and the Spirit. However, the sending of the Son and the Holy Spirit raises the issue of their equality with the Father which Augustine seeks to resolve.

The equality of the persons of the Godhead comes into sharp focus in Augustine's discussion of the divine missions, where he refutes the contention of his opponents that "the *one who sends* is greater than the *one sent*."[70] The consequence of such a claim, according to Augustine, is that because the Father sends the Son, the Father is greater than the Son; the Father and the Son are greater than the Holy Spirit as they together send the Holy Spirit. Refuting the proposition that sending implies inequality, Augustine seeks to demonstrate the inseparability and equality of the trinitarian persons. Inseparability entails that sending (*missio*) is the activity of all the three persons of the Godhead. The sending of the Son is the activity of both the Father and the Son: "But God's Word is his Son. So when the Father sent him by word, what happened was that he was sent by the Father and his Word. Hence, it is by the Father and the Son that the Son was sent, because the Son is the Father's Word."[71] The Word "without any beginning of time" was with God and was God (John 1:1).[72] The presence of the Father implies the presence of both the Son and the Holy Spirit. Augustine asks: "Is there anywhere he [Father] could be without his Word and his Wisdom, who *stretches mightily from end to end, and disposes all things properly* (Wis 8:1)? Nor for that matter could he be anywhere without his Spirit. . . . [Therefore] both Son and Holy Spirit are sent to where they already are."[73]

The trinitarian mission is historically demonstrated in the Father's sending of the Son in *the fullness of time, made of woman* (Gal 4:4). The Son was *sent from* the Father *into* the world as attested in the Gospel of John: *I came from the Father and have come into the world* (John 16:28). Accordingly, mission is the "going forth [of the Son] from the Father and

---

69. Augustine, *De Trinitate* 3.22 (142–43). See also Gioia, *Theological Epistemology*, 30.

70. Augustine, *De Trinitate* 2.7 (101). Emphasis added. See Clark, "*De Trinitate*," 93.

71. Augustine, *De Trinitate* 2.9 (103).

72. Augustine, *De Trinitate* 2.9 (103). The two other important passages that Augustine quotes to establish the equality of the Son with the Father are John 10:30 and Phil 2:6. See *De Trinitate* 2.3 (98).

73. Augustine, *De Trinitate* 2.7–8 (102). See Gioia, *Theological Epistemology*, 162.

An Indian Trinitarian Theology of *Missio Dei*

coming into this world."[74] For Augustine, this going forth of the Son needs to be seen in relation to the assertion that the Son "was in the world, and the world came into being through him. . . . He came to what was his own" (John 1:10–11). Accordingly, the Son was sent to the world where he already was. The same principle applies to the Holy Spirit: "If God is everywhere, his Spirit is everywhere too. So the Spirit also was sent to where he was already."[75]

The mission of the Son was not without the Holy Spirit, because the Son was born of the Holy Spirit (Matt 1:18). Thus, the incarnation and the virgin birth of Christ are the indivisible works of the Father, the Son, and the Holy Spirit.[76] Since the Father *who begot* and the Son *who was begotten* are one, the *one who sends* and the one *who is sent* are also one along with the Holy Spirit: "Just as the Father, then, begot and the Son was begotten, so the Father sent and the Son was sent. But just as the begetter and the begotten are one, so are the sender and the sent, because the Father and the Son are one; so too the Holy Spirit is one with them, because *these three are one* (1 John 5:7)."[77] This undifferentiated work of the Trinity in divine mission, for Augustine, presupposes the unity in substance of the Godhead and hence, the equality of the Father, the Son, and the Holy Spirit.

The equality of the Son and the Holy Spirit with the Father stems from their inseparability and unity within the Trinity which, as discussed earlier, only affirm the fact that the mission of the Son and the Holy Spirit is the work of all the persons of the Godhead. The fact of their being sent does not undermine the equality of the Son and the Holy Spirit, but in fact, it signifies the mission of the Trinity. More specifically, trinitarian mission constitutes the sending forth of the Son and the Holy Spirit by the Father. It is the manifestation in history of the second and the third persons of the Trinity. It was their going forth from the essential *hidden invisibility* of the Triune God to public gaze. The trinitarian mission testifies to the essential invisibility of God as well as God's historical manifestation in the Son and the Holy Spirit. Therefore, the Father remains invisible as the *sender*, who is never said to have been sent, and the Son and the Holy Spirit are manifest to the world in

---

74. Augustine, *De Trinitate* 2.7 (102). See also Ayres, *Augustine and the Trinity*, 181.

75. Augustine, *De Trinitate* 2.7 (102).

76. Augustine, *De Trinitate* 2.8–9 (102–3). Spicer, *Mystery of Unity*, 26.

77. Augustine, *De Trinitate* 4.29 (181–82). For Augustine, the oneness of God rests upon the inseparability, equality, and the consubstantiality of the Father, the Son, and the Holy Spirit. Yet, each person of the Trinity is differentiated from each other. See *De Trinitate* 1.7.

St. Augustine and Trinitarian Missio Dei Theology

their being sent forth by the Father.[78] The following two passages are central to this invisibility and the mission of the Trinity:

> The Son is not less than the Father simply because he was sent and the Father did the sending; and that the Holy Spirit is not less than either of them simply because he is declared in the gospel to have been sent by each . . . what constituted the sending of the Lord was his being born in the flesh, his issuing, so to speak, from the hidden invisibility of the Father's bosom and appearing to the eyes of men in the form of a servant; and likewise for the Holy Spirit his being seen as a dove in bodily guise and as fire in divided tongues. So what their being sent would mean is their *coming forth from the hidden world of the spiritual into the public gaze of mortal men in some bodily shape*; and as the Father never did this, he is only said to have sent, not also to have been sent.[79]

> The Son is not less than the Father just because he was sent by the Father, nor is the Holy Spirit less simply because the Father and the Son sent him. We should understand that these sendings are not mentioned in scripture because of any inequality or display or dissimilarity of substance between the divine persons, but because of the created *visible* manifestation *of the Son and the Holy Spirit*; or better still, in order to bring home to us that the Father is the source and origin of all deity.[80]

It is not unimportant that in these passages, while affirming the equality of the divine persons, Augustine accentuates the fact that the Father is the source of the Godhead. Ultimately, it is the Father who sends the Son and the Spirit, and it is from his hidden invisibility that they are sent forth. The Son and the Spirit, in their essential oneness with the Father, share in his invisibility and immutability.[81] The Son, who was jointly invisible with the Father, is made visible in mission in the incarnation. While the Son "appeared outwardly in created bodily form," (*in creatura corporali*) he always remains invisible "in uncreated spiritual form" (*intus in natura spirituali*).[82] The visibility of the Son in the incarnation was accompanied by the visibility of the Holy Spirit at Pentecost. The Holy Spirit appeared

---

78. See Augustine, *De Trinitate* 3.3 (128–29).

79. Augustine, *De Trinitate* 3.3 (128–29). Emphasis added.

80. Augustine, *De Trinitate* 4.32 (185). Emphasis added.

81. Gioia, *The Theological Epistemology*, 25. See Augustine, *De Trinitate* 1.11 (74); 2.9–10 (106–7); 2.14–16 (110–11).

82. Augustine, *De Trinitate* 2.9–10 (106–7).

in *created guise* like *the dove* (Matt 3:16) at the baptism of Jesus and again appeared as *tongues of fire* at Pentecost (Acts 2:3). Augustine calls these visible manifestations as the mission (sending) of the Holy Spirit. Yet, the substance of the Spirit as that of the Son is concealed which points to the essential invisibility and immutability of the Spirit like that of the Son and the Father.[83] However, there is a distinction, according to Augustine, between the manifestations of the Son and the Holy Spirit. The Holy Spirit did not manifest in a creaturely form, as did the Son who assumed human flesh and form in his manifestation. There was no hypostatic union as in the case of the Son where human nature was united with the divine in Christ. The Spirit did appear as *a dove, a violent wind, tongues of fire*, but the "Spirit did not make the dove blessed, or the violent gust, or the fire; he did not join them to himself and his person to be held in an everlasting union," as did the Son who is eternally God and human.[84] Thus, according to Augustine, while the visible manifestation of the Son is permanent, the manifestation of the Holy Spirit is transient. In the following section, we will expound the mission of the Trinity with special reference to the Son and the Holy Spirit in Augustine's trinitarian theology.

INCARNATION, PENTECOST, AND *MISSIO DEI*

Augustine's discussion on the divine sending (*missio*) and theophanies occupied most of the second and the third books of De Trinitate. He had already rejected the traditional Christological interpretation according to which the second person of the Trinity appeared in the theophanies. Nevertheless, he believed in the trinitarian character of the theophanies, and accordingly, he understood these visions as a symbolic representation of the Trinity. Augustine concludes that the theophanies "were produced through the changeable creation subject to the changeless God, and they did not manifest God as he is in himself, but in a symbolic manner as times and circumstances required."[85] "Whenever God was said to appear to our ancestors before our savior's incarnation, the voices heard and the physical manifestation seen were the work of angels."[86]

Having ruled out the appearance of the Trinity, particularly the mission of the Son and the Holy Spirit in the theophanies, Augustine returns to

---

83. Augustine, *De Trinitate* 2.10 (107).
84. Augustine, *De Trinitate* 2.11 (107).
85. Augustine, *De Trinitate* 2.32 (124). See also Kloos, *Christ, Creation*, 141–42.
86. Augustine, *De Trinitate* 3.27 (146).

the mission of the Trinity as evidenced in the incarnation and at Pentecost. Two themes are inseparably linked to each other in Augustine's discourse on the mission of the Son, namely, the trinitarian revelation and reconciliation (mediation). This suggests that for Augustine, mission is essentially revelatory and redemptive. No revelation is conceivable without the mediation of the Son, and no human reconciliation with God is possible without revelation. Hence, the mission of the Son is the mediation of revelation and reconciliation—revealing God to humanity and reconciling humanity to God.[87] God who reveals himself to us is also the one who reconciles us and thus enables us to know the self-revelation of God in Christ. In other words, God makes himself known to us (God's revelation) in the mission of the Son as well as heals our inability to perceive (i.e., God's reconciliation) God's self-manifestation.[88]

One might see the aspect of reconciliation by the Son as the most prominent theme which occupies most of the fourth book of the *De Trinitate*. However, there is a considerable discussion of the inner trinitarian revelation of the Godhead running through Augustine's discourse in relation to the mission (sending) of the Son. In the following sections, we will examine the inner trinitarian relations within the Godhead in the context of the mission of the Son as well as the mediation (reconciliation) by the Son.

Missio Dei *and Trinitarian Revelation*

The equality and the inseparability of the trinitarian persons form the important subject matter in the first three books of the *De Trinitate*. However, one has to wait until the fourth book for Augustine's more serious discussion into the mystery of the inner trinitarian relations. The two important aspects of this inner trinitarian mystery are the eternal generation of the Son and the procession of the Spirit, which demonstrate the trinitarian

---

87. See Augustine, *De Trinitate* 4.11–12 (164–66).

88. The themes of revelation and reconciliation form the important topics in the fourth book, which we will discuss in the following two sections. Humanity, according to Augustine, cannot perceive the self-revelation of God in the mission of the Son without the mediation (reconciliation) of the Son (4.2). The Son is said to be sent when he is known and perceived by a rational soul. But the fact remains that human wisdom being darkened was incapable of perceiving God's self-manifestation. Therefore, God chose to redeem humanity and thereby enabled them to know God's self-revelation in Christ (Gal 4:4; John 1:5, 14; 1 Cor 1:21). Thus, human inability to perceive God's revelation is overcome by God's reconciliation of the human race; hence, for Augustine, both these divine acts are inseparable. *De Trinitate* 4.24, 28 (175, 181). Gioia, *Theological Epistemology*, 32–34, 113.

An Indian Trinitarian Theology of *Missio Dei*

revelation (knowledge of God) in relation to the mission (sending) of the second and the third persons.[89]

The incarnation is the most pivotal event in the divine economy that reveals the mission of the Son. While Augustine does not rule out the trinitarian significance of the theophanies, the mission of God, according to him, begins only in God's self-revelation in the incarnation of the Son. This is the topic to which Augustine returns in the latter part of the fourth book after a thorough exposition on the question of divine mission in the theophanies. Having rebutted the claim of theophanies as the sending (mission) of the Son, Augustine seeks to establish that God's mission (*missio Dei*) begins only *in the fullness of the time when God had sent God's Son made of woman* (Gal 4:4).[90]

The mission of the Son in the incarnation has opened up the possibility of human redemption as well as human knowledge of the Triune God. The human need for redemption from sin and their need for knowing God are interlinked. Despite God's revelation in the mission of the Son, humanity is incapable of perceiving it. Human inability to know God stems from sin because, "we were incapable of grasping eternal things, and weighed down by the accumulated dirt of our sins, which we had collected by our love of *temporal* things, and which had become almost a natural growth on our mortal stock; so we needed *purifying*. But we could only be purified for adaptation to eternal things by temporal means."[91]

According to Augustine, it is *temporal* things that have deluded us, bound us in servile adaptation, and rendered us incapable of contemplating the eternal things (divine mysteries). Interestingly, God has chosen to redeem us through the *temporality* into which God has entered in the mission of the Son. This is an act of divine grace where God has appeared in the temporal world of human existence subjected to change and time. We respond to this divine initiative and accord faith in the work of Christ, who being the eternal Son of God, became the Son of man. Thus, our minds having been purified by faith in what Christ has done, we are enabled to

---

89. See Edmund Hill's introduction to Book 4 of the *De Trinitate*, 148. For non-Augustinian treatment of the mission of God as providing trinitarian revelation, see Cunningham, *These Three Are One*, 82–86.

90. Augustine, *De Trinitate* 4.26 (178–79); 2.8 (102–3). The transition to this significant theme of the Son's mission is marked by 4.25 (178) and it continues to the end of the fourth book.

91. Augustine, *De Trinitate* 4.24 (175). Emphasis added. See also Gioia, *Theological Epistemology*, 33.

St. Augustine and Trinitarian Missio Dei Theology

contemplate the eternal things.[92] The contemplation of God, according to Augustine, is the eternal reward of the new covenant.[93] Faith itself is related to the realm of *temporality* and is generated by grace. Our faith is then transformed into truth, "when we come to what we are promised as believers," the eternal life which is to know the Father (John 17:3).[94] Knowing the Father involves knowing both the Son and the Holy Spirit, knowing God as the Trinity because the trinitarian persons are inseparable.[95]

Revelation would be impossible unless the eternal God enters into our created world and unites himself to our mutable human condition. Therefore, in the mission of the Son, God has "provided us with a bridge to his eternity" in order that we may "pass from being among the things that originated to eternal things."[96] Christ's mission has given us the knowledge of God who has bridged "the abyss between his immutability and our mutability."[97] Thus, in the incarnation as well as at Pentecost, humanity is given a glimpse of the mystery of the Trinity of God. It is significant to note that this revelation (knowledge) of the Trinity has become possible in the missions of the Son and the Spirit.[98] As indicated earlier, mission is both revelatory and redemptive. The transition to this significant theme in *De Trinitate* is marked by the following remarkable passage towards the close of the fourth book:

> There you have what the Son of God has been sent for; indeed there you have what it is for the Son of God to have been sent. Everything that has taken place in time in 'originated' matters

92. Augustine, *De Trinitate* 4.24 (175). See Edmund Hill's note in Augustine, *De Trinitate*, 175–176n75. *De Trinitate*. Hill's observation is important to capture the full meaning of what Augustine is saying about the contemplation of the divine mysteries.

93. Augustine, "Spirit and the Letter," 223.

94. Augustine, *De Trinitate* 4.24 (176). Poitras, "St. Augustine and the *Missio Dei*," 36.

95. See Augustine, *De Trinitate* 1.17–19 (80–83).

96. Augustine, *De Trinitate* 4.24 (177).

97. Gioia, *Theological Epistemology*, 33.

98. The early church regarded the saving mission of the Son as the revelation of the triunity of the Godhead. According to the second-century theologian Irenaeus of Lyons, distinctions within the Trinity are only revealed in what later came to be called "economic Trinitarianism." According to Irenaeus, the second and the third persons revealed in the economy of salvation are distinct from the Father and yet they are one being with the Father. See Irenaeus, *Demonstration of the Apostolic Preaching* 7; Irenaeus, *Against Heresies* 5.12.2; Rusch, *Trinitarian Controversy*, 7; Studer, *Trinity and Incarnation*, xiii. Augustine seems to be in agreement with this position of the early church, and for him, trinitarian revelation becomes the focal point of the mission of the Son and the Spirit.

An Indian Trinitarian Theology of *Missio Dei*

which have been produced from the eternal and reduced back to the eternal, and has been designed to elicit the faith we must be purified by in order to contemplate the truth, has either been testimony to this mission or has been the actual mission of the Son of God (*testimonia missionis huius fuerunt aut ipsa missio filii dei*).[99]

The passage refers to the theophanies (testimony to mission) as well as the incarnation and Pentecost which is the proper (actual) mission in the New Testament. For Augustine, the theophanies are not themselves the mission of God; but as important divine interventions in human history in the affairs of fallen human race, they bear witness to the mission of God in Christ.[100] The visibility of the Son in the incarnation, which marks the actual mission of God, and his visible nature and actions are intended to generate faith that it "may be consummated in the contemplation of eternity when we truly see that which the visible Christ represents."[101] The Son represents the Triune God, and his sending demonstrates the equality, consubstantiality, and co-eternality of the trinitarian persons.[102]

As noted earlier, one of the most central concerns of Augustine in *De Trinitate* is to establish the unity and equality of the Father, the Son, and the Holy Spirit from the authority of the Scripture. Hence, Augustine views the mission of the Son within the overarching context of his conviction in the equality and the inseparability of the persons of the Godhead. Therefore, for Augustine, the sending of the Son is compatible with his generation from the Father, and thus it underlines the essential unity and equality of the Father and the Son. "On this foundation," writes Ayres, "Augustine articulates the principle that one of the central purposes of this sending is the revealing of the Son and Word as Son and Word, that is a revealing of the Word as *from* the Father and as the Word *with* Father and Spirit."[103] This passage from Ayres suggests something quite fundamental to Augustine's understanding of mission, namely, the generation of the Son and the procession of the Spirit, which we have already referred to in the beginning of this section.

---

99. Augustine, *De Trinitate* 4.25 (178). See also Ayres, *Augustine and the Trinity*, 184.

100. Gioia, *Theological Epistemology*, 79.

101. Ayres, *Augustine and the Trinity*, 184.

102. Augustine, *De Trinitate* 4.27–29 (178–82). See also Ayres, *Augustine and the Trinity*, 184–85.

103. Ayres, *Augustine and the Trinity*, 185. Emphasis added.

St. Augustine and Trinitarian Missio Dei Theology

Mission refers to more than unity, equality, and inseparability of the trinitarian persons. Mission is the going/sending forth of the Son and the Spirit from the Father into the world (their manifestation). It is the outward movement of the Son and the Spirit into the world in visible forms which results in the temporal mission of God. Augustine writes, "*I went forth from the Father*, he (Jesus) says, *and came into this world* (John 16:28). So that is what being sent [*mitti*] is, going forth from the Father and coming into this world."[104] However, one must note that the divine mission points to the dimension of both the visibility and invisibility of the Son. The Son who was *timelessly* begotten by the Father was sent (mission) in *time* in the world. His appearance in time in the corporeal world was in created bodily form (human flesh) and yet being timeless in his eternal and essential (spiritual) being, the Son was always "hidden from mortal eyes."[105]

Mission, for Augustine, is the economy of salvation that reveals the mystery of the inner trinitarian life, the eternal generation of the Son and the eternal procession of the Spirit. Yet, generation and procession themselves are not mission; mission, as noted earlier, is the coming forth of the Son and the Spirit from the Father and coming into the world.[106] This mission of God takes place in the incarnation of the Son and at Pentecost of the Holy Spirit where the Father sent them. Insofar as mission is the going/coming forth of the Son and the Spirit from the Father into the world, revealing the inner life of God in their being sent, mission signifies the economic dimension of the Trinity. Hill's observation is quite pertinent here: "The divine missions in fact constitute the very form of the economy of redemption. God is not constituted a triad by the economy. . . . [God] is revealed as a triad by the economy, because in fact the eternal divine triad unfolds the saving economy according to a triadic pattern. So the mystery of the Trinity is of the essence of our redemption."[107]

Mission, as the revelation of the inner Triune life of God represented in the incarnation and Pentecost, reveals that in their being sent, the Son and the Spirit are known to be from and proceed from the Father. "And just as being born means for the Son his being from the Father, so his being sent means his being known to be from him. And just as for the Holy Spirit his

---

104. Augustine, *De Trinitate* 2.7 (102). See Coffey, "Holy Spirit as the Mutual Love," 200.

105. Augustine, *De Trinitate* 2.10 (106–7); 15.47 (438).

106. Augustine, *De Trinitate* 2.7 (102).

107. Hill, "St. Augustine's De Trinitate," 285–86. See also Jowers, "Divine Unity," 74.

being the gift of God means his proceeding from the Father, so his being sent means his being known to proceed from him."[108] While distinguishing mission from the eternal generation and procession, Augustine identifies mission with not only being sent, but being known in the world.[109] The Son was sent "in virtue of the Son being from the Father."[110] One of the most important affirmations of Augustine in his discussion on trinitarian sending is that the Father is never sent. It is only the Son and Spirit who are sent, because they are from the Father: the Son is generated from the Father and the Spirit proceeds from the Father. Therefore, their mission begins in their being from the Father. The Father is not sent because "he has not got anyone else to be from or to proceed from."[111]

Mission of the Son unfolds the inner life of the Trinity and it emerges from the inseparable trinitarian relation, particularly, of the Father and the Son. Mission, the appearance of the Son in the flesh, is the work of the Father and the Son, where the Father *sends* and the Son is *sent*. Augustine captures the trinitarian interiority and inseparability as follows: "Since then it was a work of the Father and the Son that the Son should appear in the flesh, the one who so appeared in the flesh is appropriately said to have been sent, and the one who did not to have done the sending. Thus events which are put on outwardly in the sight of our bodily eyes are aptly called *missa* because they stem from the inner designs [*apparatus*] of our spiritual nature."[112]

The mission of the Son is grounded in his being from the Father and in his being known or perceived to be from the Father. Therefore,

> the Son of God is not said to be sent in the very fact that he is born of the Father, but either in the fact that the Word made flesh showed himself to this world; about this fact he says, *I went forth from the Father and came into this world* (John 16:28). Or else he is sent in the fact that he is perceived in time by someone's mind. . . .

---

108. Augustine, *De Trinitate* 4.29 (182). Hill observes that this sentence along with the succeeding sentence about the procession of the Spirit—"And just as for the Holy Spirit his being the gift of God means his proceeding from the Father, so his being sent means his being known to proceed from him"—is the culmination of Augustine's discussion on divine missions that he began in Book 2. "They state that it is the missions which reveal the inner core of the trinitarian mystery" (Hill, "St. Augustine's De Trinitate," 182n98). See also Ayres, *Augustine and the Trinity*, 185.

109. Hill, "St. Augustine's De Trinitate," 282.

110. Augustine, *De Trinitate* 4.27 (180).

111. Augustine, *De Trinitate* 4.28 (181).

112 Augustine, *De Trinitate* 2.9 (105–6).

St. Augustine and Trinitarian Missio Dei Theology

That he [Son] is born means that he is from eternity to eternity—he is *the brightness of eternal light* (Wis 7:26). But that he is sent means that he is known by somebody in time.[113]

In the divine mission (sending), the Son is made known to be from the Father (generation, filiation) as well as he is made known to the world as the sent one in the flesh. This mission of God takes place in our temporal world. This also demonstrates the fact that in God's grace, humanity is given the privilege of knowing God through temporal reality.[114] The invisible, immutable, and unknowable God is made known to us in grace through the temporal missions of the Son and the Holy Spirit. In his remarkable study on Augustine's *De Trinitate*, Luigi Gioia states,

> [k]nowledge of the Trinity means that God can only be known in a Trinitarian way. Knowledge of God the Trinity, means the knowledge *of* the Father *in* the Son *through* the Holy Spirit. In other words, it means that, united to the Son through love, we are introduced into the love and the knowledge of the Son in relation to the Father. We should never lose sight of this notion of the Trinitarian shape of our relation with God, even when it is not explicitly stated.[115]

The mission of God accomplished in the incarnation of Christ and his redemptive work are central to the revelation of the Triune God and of eternity. The God whom the Son reveals in his mission is the Triune God. Therefore, the revelation of God in the incarnation is fundamentally a trinitarian revelation.

---

113. Augustine, *De Trinitate* 4.28 (181). Augustine distinguishes between the eternal generation (begottenness) of the Son from the Father and "the human experience of the Son's being sent in the mission of redemption" as testified in the New Testament. See Dunham, *Trinity and Creation in Augustine*, 146.

114. Gioia, *Theological Epistemology*, 80. We have already noted that for Augustine, the Father is never sent. Mission originates from the generation (filiation) of the Son and the procession of the Holy Spirit from the Father, and in their (Son and Spirit) being known in the world. Augustine distinguishes the knowing of the Father from the knowing of the Son and the Holy Spirit. He writes, "But when the Father is known by someone in time he is not said to have been sent. For he has not got anyone else to be from or to proceed from. Wisdom says, *I went forth from the mouth of the Most High* (Sir 24:5), and of the Holy Spirit he says, *He proceeds from the Father* (Jn 15:26), but the Father is from no one" [*De Trinitate* 4. 28 (181)].

115. Gioia, *Theological Epistemology*, 107.

An Indian Trinitarian Theology of *Missio Dei*

Missio Dei *and Reconciliation*

In the preceding discussion, we have noticed that the revelation of God occurring in the mission of the Son is God's own work. Similarly, it is God who enables humanity to perceive that revelation. Therefore, for Augustine, God's revelation to humanity and human comprehension of that revelation are both the work of God. The human incapability to perceive God's revelation is healed in the mediatorial work of the Son. This mission of the Son is reconciliatory, bringing humanity in union with God. Augustine expounds this reconciliatory (mediatorial) mission of Christ against the background of Plotinian metaphysics of "the one and the many." Many scholars would see the influence of Plotinus's philosophy on Augustine's trinitarian doctrine, particularly in his doctrine of the unity of God.[116]

The problem of *the one* and *the many* emerged as a prominent philosophical challenge in the ancient world, and it continues to defy simple solutions. It emerges from the assumption of an underlying unity behind the universe and in the diversity and the multiplicity in the world.[117] There have been attempts to discover the origin of the *multiplicity* (many-ness) in the world from the *one* universal principle (often termed as "idea," "mind," or "God,") behind everything, and to reconcile the *many* with the *one* (principle or reality). Augustine discovers the origin of the *multiplicity* in the *one* God from whom are all things.[118] The issue of the reconciliation of the *one* and the *many*, for Augustine, is resolved in the incarnation of Christ who mediated on behalf of humanity and reconciled them to the *one* God.[119]

---

116. See Wassmer, "Trinitarian Theology," 261–68. According to Thomas Wassmer, Augustine derives the principle of God's unity from Plotinus; yet he stressed on the Trinity of God. Wassmer writes: "Still, in stressing the Unity he [Augustine] equally affirms the Being and the Trinity of God. In considering the Trinity-in-Unity he lays the emphasis on the Unity of the Godhead and not, as the Cappadocian Fathers and the later East, on the Three Divine Persons. Augustine starts from the one and simple divine nature which is the Trinity" (Wassmer, "Trinitarian Theology," 262).

117. See Matthews and Cohen, "One and the Many," 630–55; Bussanich, "Plotinus's Metaphysics," 38–65.

118. Augustine, *De Trinitate* 4.3 (154).

119. Augustine, *De Trinitate* 4.2–6 (153–59); 4.11 (164–65). See Edmund Hill's introduction to Book 4 of the *De Trinitate* (Augustine, *De Trinitate*, 149). Humanity, according to Augustine, through sin "flowed and faded away from the one supreme true God into the many, divided by the many, clinging to the many." Christ came as the representative of the *One* and as savior for the *many*, offering hope to the *many* to be purified from sin. In the *One* (Christ) "we have been purified by faith and will then be made completely whole by sight, and that thus fully reconciled to God by him the mediator, we may be

Humanity, through sin, has fallen into the many, into discord and division, and consequently moved away from the *One true God*. The ultimate salvation of the disintegrated humanity lies in their being restored to unity and to the One true God. This, Augustine believes, has been accomplished through the mediation of Christ.[120]

The incarnation of Christ has demonstrated the depravity of human sin. In other words, God's revelation in the mission of Christ is also a revelation of human sinfulness. God's self-manifestation both brings in the knowledge of the Triune God and demonstrates the human situation of sin. Therefore, God's mission in Christ takes place in the context of human sin and estrangement, and the human inability to know God. God's revelation came down to us in Christ's incarnation without which we would be unable to know God because of our sinful nature and alienation from God.[121] In this mission of the Son revealing to us the Triune God, we are given to understand our own sinful nature and the depth of God's love in order for us to be led into God's way of humility. Therefore, according to Augustine,

> First we had to be persuaded how much God loved us, in case out of sheer despair we lacked the courage to reach up to him. Also we had to be shown what sort of people we are that he loves, in case we should take pride in our own worth, and so bounce even further away from him and sink even more under our own strength. So he dealt with us in such a way that we could progress rather in his strength; he arranged it so that the power of charity would be brought to perfection in the weakness of humility.... So we needed to be persuaded how much God loves us, and what sort of people he loves; how much in case we despaired, what sort in case we grew proud.[122]

Calling attention to the Pauline passage from Romans 5:8, Augustine underscores the necessity of incarnation as the demonstration of God's love and grace towards humanity and finally God's redemption of humanity.[123] In the divine mission, incarnation was indispensable for the hypostatic union of the divine and the human in Christ in order that he reconcile

---

able to cling to the one, enjoy the one, and remain for ever one" (Augustine, *De Trinitate*, 165). See also Spicer, *Mystery of Unity*, 47.

120. Augustine, *De Trinitate* 4.11 (164–65). See also Bochet, "Hymn to the One," 42.

121. Augustine, *De Trinitate* 4.2 (153); Gioia, *Theological Epistemology*, 32–33. See also Wisse, *Trinitarian Theology Beyond Participation*, 136.

122. Augustine, *De Trinitate* 4.2 (153–54).

123. Augustine, *De Trinitate* 4.2 (154).

An Indian Trinitarian Theology of *Missio Dei*

humanity to God through his death. It is only in the incarnation of the Son that God's mission presents a suffering God who identifies himself with the suffering and hurting humanity. There is a clearer expression of this found in Augustine's exposition on Psalm 64:

> For He would not have been held except He were man, or have been seen except He were man, or have been smitten except He were man, or have been crucified or have died except He were man. There drew near a man therefore to all those sufferings, which in Him would have been of no avail except He were Man. But if He were not Man, there would not have been deliverance for man . . . presenting before human faces Man, keeping within God: concealing the *"form of God,"* wherein He is equal with the Father, and presenting the form of a servant, wherein He is less than the Father. For Himself has spoken of both: but one thing there is which He says in the form of God, another thing in the form of a servant. He has said in the form of God, *"I and the Father are one:"* He has said in the form of a servant, *"For the Father is greater than I."* Whence in the form of God says He, *"I and the Father are one"*?[124]

The mission of Christ's mediation is itself a trinitarian work—the inseparable work of the Father, the Son, and the Holy Spirit—and grounded in the Trinity. While Christ is the Son of man and the mediator between God and humanity, he is also the Son of God, equal to the Father and consubstantial with him. The object of the Son's mediation on behalf of all who believe in him, as reflected in his high priestly prayer, is their ultimate oneness and reconciliation with the Triune God. Therefore,

> they are cleansed by the mediator that they may be one in him, not only by virtue of the same nature . . . but even more by virtue of one and the same wholly harmonious will reaching out in concert to the same ultimate happiness, and fused somehow into one spirit in the furnace of charity. This is what he means when he says *That they may be one as we are one* (John 17:22)—that just as Father and Son are one not only by equality of substance but also by identity of will, so these men, for whom the Son is mediator with God, might be one not only by being of the same nature, but also by being bound in the fellowship of the same love. Finally, he shows that he is the mediator by whom we are reconciled to God, when

---

124. Augustine, *Exposition on Psalm* 64.11. Gioia, *Theological Epistemology*, 114.

St. Augustine and Trinitarian Missio Dei Theology

he says, *I in them and you in me, that they may be perfect into one* (John 17:23).[125]

The apparent lack of oneness of the disciples implied in the prayer is reflective of the divided humanity because of their "clashing wills and desires, and the uncleanness of their sins."[126] The mediation of Christ offers hope for humanity that had alienated from the one true God to be united with God in Christ in the Spirit of love. The ground of their oneness with God is the unity that eternally exists in the Trinity. Their oneness with each other is derived from their oneness with the Triune God through Christ, and the reconciliation with God accomplished through his mediation.[127] Augustine's discourse on the mediation of the Son and the restoration of the divided humanity to unity and the oneness of God underlines the fact that the economy of salvation is grounded in the trinitarian mystery of the Godhead. It is in the Son, the *only one mediator* that human multiplicity finds its unity, and the Son himself is united with the Father through his equality and consubstantiality with the Father. The unity of human multiplicity in Christ is made possible through the equality and oneness between the Father and the Son. Therefore, human salvation through the mission of the Son as the mediator cannot be thought of apart from the mystery of the Trinity.[128]

In Augustine's view, as evident in the above passage, there is a particularity seen in this human reconciliation and unity with the Triune God which points to the being of the Church in the Trinity. One could see a profound relation between Augustine's doctrine of the Trinity and his ecclesiology in the sense of both being intertwined.[129] The Son who unites the human nature to himself in his incarnation is also the one who through his own mediatory work unties the Church with the Triune God. This unity of the Church with the Trinity is derived from the church's union with

---

125. Augustine, *De Trinitate* 4.12 (165–66). See Gioia, *Theological Epistemology*, 89. Strangely enough, Augustine does not talk about the Trinity in the fourth book until towards the end where he takes up the missions of the Son and the Holy Spirit. See Bochet, "Hymn to the One," 41.

126. Augustine, *De Trinitate* 4.12 (165).

127. See Augustine, *De Trinitate* 4.12 (165–66).

128. Bochet, "Hymn to the One," 42. According to Hill, the Trinity as a mystery of the divine economy is fundamental to Augustine's trinitarian theology. See Hill, "St. Augustine's *De Trinitate*," 284–86.

129. See a very recent study on Augustine's trinitarian theology and ecclesiology, Ployd, *Augustine*.

An Indian Trinitarian Theology of *Missio Dei*

Christ: "'The Word which was made flesh, and dwelt in us.' To that flesh the Church is joined, and so there is made the whole Christ [*Christus totus*], Head and body."[130] In the unity of the Son with the Father and the unity of the Son with the Church, Christians are "fused somehow into one spirit in the furnace of charity . . . bound in the fellowship of the same love."[131] According to Augustine, "the church shares in the life of the Trinity through the Son's giving of the Spirit to his own body."[132] The oneness of the Trinity is extended to the Church in the sacrifice of the Son as made explicit in the following passage: "And this one true mediator, in reconciling us to God by his sacrifice of peace, would remain one with him to whom he offered it, and *make one in himself those for whom he offered it*, and be himself who offered it one and the same as what he offered."[133] Through the sacrifice of the Son, as a redeemed and reconciled community, the Church shares in the divine-humanity of the Son and through whom in the Triune God. There is "a new level of oneness in which the many come together in the person of Christ. . . . We are united to Christ and in Christ, united to God."[134] In "becoming a partaker of our mortality he [Christ] made us partakers of his divinity."[135] Thus, in Augustine's thought, one might say that the Church has its existence in the Trinity.[136]

Missio Dei *and Pentecost*

The Holy Spirit was sent and manifested in the world, in a way similar to the Son, yet in a different manner. The manifestation of the Spirit was the Spirit's coming forth from the hiddenness of God into visibility in the

---

130. Augustine, *Homily 1 on the First Epistle of John* 1.2. *Christus totus*, according to Augustine, suggests that the head (Christ) and the body (Church) constitute one Christ. However, this does not imply that Christ is not "complete without the body, but that he was prepared to be complete and entire together with us too, though even without us he is always complete and entire." Augustine, *Sermon* 341.11, *Sermons* (341–400), 26.

131. Augustine, *De Trinitate* 4.12 (166).

132. See Ployd, *Augustine*, 3.

133. Augustine, *De Trinitate* 4.19 (171). Emphasis added. See Darwish, "Concept of the Mediator," 82–85.

134. Darwish, "Concept of the Mediator," 81–82.

135. Augustine, *De Trinitate* 4.4 (155).

136. See Gioia, *Theological Epistemology*, 91. Colin Gunton, underlining the importance of developing the ontology of the Church, which is grounded in the Trinity of the Godhead, concludes that the personal communion within the Trinity is the ontological foundation of the Church. See Gunton, "Church on Earth," 48–53.

St. Augustine and Trinitarian Missio Dei Theology

world in some bodily form as in the incarnation of the Son. This sending (mission) of the Spirit occurred at Pentecost, "as a dove in bodily guise and as fire in divided tongues."[137] However, Augustine is careful to underline that as in the incarnation of the Son, the Holy Spirit in the essential spiritual being always remains invisible to mortal eyes. One must also note the main difference between the manifestation of the Spirit and the incarnation of the Son. The Son becoming flesh (human) and assuming human form has a dimension of perpetuity, and hence he is eternally God and human. Unlike the incarnation, the manifestation of the Holy Spirit in corporeal form was transitory and served merely as temporary significations adapted to our mortal senses of vision. The Spirit did not become "dove" or "fire" so as to be united to them in eternal union as humanity was united eternally with divinity in the Son.[138] According to Augustine, the created things in which the Holy Spirit appeared on the day of Pentecost are unlike those things which symbolize Christ, such as rock, man, lamb, etc. The occurrence of dove and fire was just "to signify something (of the Holy Spirit) and then to pass away."[139]

Why was the Spirit sent? The sending of the Holy Spirit at Pentecost, like the incarnation of the Son, reveals the mystery of the trinitarian life of God. The mission of the Holy Spirit is essentially the Spirit's being sent forth by the Father into the world, and it emerges from the Spirit's coming forth (spiration) from the Father and the Son. Augustine says, "And just as for the Holy Spirit his being the gift of God means his proceeding from the Father, so his being sent means his being known to proceed from him."[140] Although the procession of the Spirit itself is not the mission of the Spirit, it is nevertheless an important aspect in Augustine's understanding of the mission of the Holy Spirit.

Augustine's views on the Holy Spirit's procession must be viewed in the light of his emphasis on the unity of God which was very central for him as he was battling Arianism. Augustine's emphasis, as stated earlier, is on the inseparability, equality, and consubstantiality of the Trinity. Within the distinctions of the Trinity, the unity of the persons is of paramount importance to Augustine. He regards the place of the Holy Spirit within

---

137. Augustine, *De Trinitate* 3.3 (129); 2:10 (106–7).

138. See Augustine, *De Trinitate* 2.10–11 (107–8); Spicer, *Mystery of Unity*, 26.

139. Augustine, *De Trinitate* 2.11 (108).

140. Augustine, *De Trinitate* 4.29 (182). See also Ayres, *Augustine and the Trinity*, 185.

An Indian Trinitarian Theology of *Missio Dei*

the triunity of God as very crucial in affirming the unity of the Godhead. Augustine refers to the Holy Spirit as the Spirit of both the Father and the Son, the communion and love of the Father and the Son, and their unity. "The Holy Spirit is something common to Father and Son, whatever it is, or is their very commonness or communion, consubstantial and coeternal. Call this friendship, if it helps, but a better word for it is charity [love]."[141] Being the Spirit of the Father and the Son, and as their common gift, the Holy Spirit proceeds from the Father *principally* and also from the Son.[142] Augustine affirms this double procession of the Spirit more convincingly in the final book of the *De Trinitate*. He argues that the generation of the Son from the Father and his consubstantiality with the Father necessitates the procession of the Holy Spirit from the Son as well. In other words, the procession of the Spirit from the Son is something given to him by the Father in his co-eternality and consubstantiality with the Father:

> And anyone who can understand that when the Son said, *As the Father has life in himself, so he has given the Son to have life in himself* (Jn 5:26), he did not mean that the Father gave life to the Son already existing without life, but that he begot him timelessly in such a way that the life which the Father gave the Son by begetting him is co-eternal with the life of the Father who gave it, should also understand that just as the Father has it in himself that the Holy Spirit should proceed from him, so he gave to the Son that the Holy Spirit should proceed from him too, and in both cases timelessly; and thus that to say that the Holy Spirit proceeding from the Son is something which the Son has from the Father. If the Son has everything that he has from the Father, he clearly has from the Father that the Holy Spirit should proceed from him.[143]

Augustine seems to base his argument for the procession of the Holy Spirit from the Father and the Son on two key Johannine texts: *Whom (Holy Spirit) I will send you from the Father* (John 15:26); *whom the Father will send in my name* (John 14:26). These statements, for Augustine, are

---

141. See Augustine, *De Trinitate* 6:7 (210); 15:27 (421). Augustine's view of the Holy Spirit as love between the Father and the Son followed in the Western Church has elicited strong criticism from the East. The Eastern Church has felt that in identifying the Holy Spirit as the mutual love of the Father and the Son, the West is depersonalizing the Holy Spirit and upsetting the personal relationships within the Trinity. See Bray, "Double Procession," 422–23.

142. Augustine, *De Trinitate* 15:29 (422–23).

143. Augustine, *De Trinitate* 15.47 (438).

St. Augustine and Trinitarian Missio Dei Theology

indicative of the following: (1) the Spirit is of both the Father and the Son; and (2) the Father is the origin (*principium*) of the Godhead. Here one must not ignore Augustine's emphasis on the purpose of missions which is to reveal the Father as the source of all.[144] Yet we must also guard against the possibility of misconstruing Augustine as subordinating the Son and Holy Spirit to the Father. Augustine is fully convinced that the three persons of the Godhead are united in love where the Spirit is the consubstantial bond between the Father and the Son.[145]

Perhaps we need to delve a little deeper into Augustine's thoughts to gain a clear picture of double procession. The fact that the Spirit is of both the Father and the Son, for Augustine, seems to convey the idea of procession. Although the two Johannine texts (14:26; 15:26) do not explicitly speak of double procession, but evidently refer to the Spirit's procession from the Father. Augustine comes back to John 15:26 in the final book of the *De Trinitate*, and asks: "So if the Holy Spirit proceeds from both the Father and the Son, why did the Son say *he proceeds from the Father* (John 15:26)."[146] Augustine builds his case for double procession in a somewhat convoluted manner. He goes on to say that it was characteristic of Jesus to attribute to the Father all that belonged to himself. For instance, Jesus said, "My teaching is not mine but his who sent me" (John 7:16). Augustine views it an adequate ground to surmise that the Spirit proceeds from Jesus as well, who certainly did not say that the "[the Holy Spirit] does not proceed from me." Therefore, according to Augustine, the Father "from whom the Son has it that he is God—for he is God from God—is of course also the one from whom he has it that the Holy Spirit proceeds from him as well; and thus the Holy Spirit too has it from the Father that he should also proceed from the Son as he proceeds from the Father."[147] Further, Augustine seeks to infer double procession in a nuanced manner from another Johannine passage where Jesus says, "As the Father has life in himself, so he has given the Son to have life in himself" (John 5:26). This is, Augustine says, the Father's eternal begetting of the Son and by virtue of his eternal begetting, the Father "gave to the Son that the Holy

---

144. See Augustine, *De Trinitate* 4.29 (182); see also 15.27 (421).

145. Augustine, *De Trinitate* 15.37 (NPNF1/3:219). Ayres, "Augustine on the Triune Life of God," 76.

146. Augustine, *De Trinitate* 15.48 (439); 4.29 (182).

147. Augustine, *De Trinitate* 15.48 (439).

An Indian Trinitarian Theology of *Missio Dei*

Spirit should proceed from him" as the Spirit proceeds from the Father.[148] Therefore, the Father and the Son together are the one "origin of the Holy Spirit (*patrem et filium principium esse spiritus sancti*); not two origins [since the] Father and Son are one God."[149]

Augustine also draws support for the double procession of the Spirit from another rather obscure Johannine passage: . . . *he (Jesus) breathed on them and said to them, "Receive the Holy Spirit"* (20:22). He believes the material sign of Jesus breathing on the apostles as "a convenient symbolic demonstration that the Holy Spirit proceeds from the Son as well as from the Father."[150] This post-resurrection action, for Augustine, also demonstrates that the Holy Spirit is a virtue that went out from the Son.[151] He seeks to ground his claims for double procession in the Scripture. However, his attempts to extrapolate immanent Trinity from a corporeal sign, rather than drawing it from the whole biblical data, especially from the New Testament, have not fared well with modern biblical scholarship.[152]

The mission of the Spirit is assumed to be emerging from the Spirit's procession from the Father and the Son as in the case of the mission of the Son occurring in his generation (filiation) from the Father. The mission (sending) of the Holy Spirit, for Augustine, is closely connected to the mission of the Son. We have earlier referred to the Spirit's role in the incarnation of the Son. Augustine has affirmed the indispensable role of the Spirit in the birth of Jesus and thereby in the mission of the Son prior to Pentecost. In the fullness of the time when God sent the Son, God did not send him without the Holy Spirit. There was the very active part of the Spirit in the conception of the child that Mary *was found to be with the child of the Holy Spirit* (Matt 1:18). Even prior to this, says Augustine, there was

---

148. Augustine, *De Trinitate* 15.47 (438).

149. Augustine, *De Trinitate* 5.15 (201). See also 2.5 (100). McCarthy, "On the Procession of the Holy Spirit," 4. The issue of the double procession of the Spirit was important for Augustine, and he wished to give it further consideration as indicated in 2.5 (100). However, towards the end of the *De Trinitate*, he admits that perceiving the mystery of the double procession of the Holy Spirit is beyond any human reasoning. He reconciles himself to the hope that the mystery of the procession will ultimately be revealed only in eternity, 15.45 (435).

150. Augustine, *De Trinitate* 4.29 (182).

151. Augustine, *De Trinitate* 15.45 (436).

152. See Coffey, "Holy Spirit," 194–95.

the Isaianic prophecy where the Son is said to have been sent by the Spirit: *And now the Lord, and his Spirit, has sent me* (Isa 48:16).[153]

However, the mission of the Holy Spirit was going to take a unique character to it at Pentecost which, according to Augustine, actually signaled the beginning of the mission of the Spirit. The Pentecost mission of the Spirit was awaiting, as it were, the glorification of the Son. The following passage from Augustine seems quite pertinent here: "As for what the evangelist says, *The Spirit was not yet given because Jesus was not yet glorified* (John 7:39), how are we to understand it, except as saying that there was going to be a kind of giving or sending of the Holy Spirit after Christ's glorification such as there had never been before?"[154] Does glorification of Christ imply an end to the mission of the Son? Or, does the sending of the Spirit signal a new aspect of God's mission in the Spirit, perhaps as a continuation of the Son's mission? Augustine views the sending forth of the Spirit at Pentecost as a distinct and unique event in the economy of God. The manifestation of the Spirit occurred in perceptible signs and languages. It indicated that the redemption accomplished in the mission of the Son would be realized in the life of nations and peoples through the mission of the Spirit, when they "believe in Christ by the gift of the Holy Spirit."[155] The saving work accomplished through the Son is actualized in the life of believing humanity through the work of the Spirit. This happens by faith that works through love, both of which come through the ministration of the Holy Spirit—faith is generated in us by the Spirit and love is poured out in our hearts by the same Spirit: "In order that faith might work through love, *the charity [love] of God has been poured out into our hearts through the Holy Spirit which has been given to us* (Rom 5:5). And he was given to us when Jesus was glorified in his resurrection."[156]

Augustine's identification of the Holy Spirit as love between the Father and the Son (mutual love) is a distinct manner of conceiving the mystery of the Trinity. According to Augustine, the Holy Spirit as love is the consubstantial bond between the Father and the Son. His contention is that "if the love by which the Father loves the Son, and the Son loves the Father, ineffably demonstrates the communion of both, what is more suitable than that

---

153. Augustine, *De Trinitate* 2.9 (103).
154. Augustine, *De Trinitate* 4.29 (182–83).
155. Augustine, *De Trinitate* 4.29 (183).
156. Augustine, *De Trinitate* 13.14 (355).

An Indian Trinitarian Theology of *Missio Dei*

He should be specially called love, who is the Spirit common to both?"[157] It is through this love that the redeemed humanity is united to one another in Christ and through him to the Father. More explicitly stated, the unity within the Godhead, the unity of the Father and the Son is not only because of the equality of divine substance, but it also comes through their unity of will, the mutual love that exists between the Father and the Son, which is the Holy Spirit.[158] However, Augustine himself admits that the inference of the Holy Spirit being the mutual love between the Father and the Son is not found in Scripture. Yet, he seeks to adduce an array of scriptural passages (e.g., 1 John 4:13) in a rather nuanced manner to substantiate his contention of the Holy Spirit as the mutual love of the Father and the Son. The following passage is quite pertinent which seems more like a conclusion on the topic: "So the love which is from God and is God is distinctively the Holy Spirit; through him the charity of God is poured out in our hearts, and through it the whole triad dwells in us."[159]

While the Spirit is of the same equality of divine substance, the Spirit is also the one through whom the Father and the Son are united to each other and love each other. The Holy Spirit is the "supreme charity conjoining Father and Son to each other and subjoining us to them, and it would seem a suitable name since it is written *God is love* (1 John 4:8, 16)."[160] The Holy Spirit is common to both the Father and the Son, their "communion, consubstantial and coeternal," whom he specifically refers to as "love."[161] This unity of the Trinity that comes through "love in the Holy Spirit provides the *content* of the metaphysical notion of unity of essence or consubstantiality."[162] This love of the Holy Spirit through which the Father and the Son are eternally united is translated through the missions of the Son and the Spirit into the redeemed humanity so that they are not only united with the Father, but are also reconciled to each other.[163]

The Holy Spirit as love of the Father and the Son demonstrates inner trinitarian relations at the deepest level. God's eternal plan to bring humanity

---

157. Augustine, *De Trinitate* 15.37 (NPNF1/3:219).

158. Augustine, *De Trinitate* 4.12 (166).

159. Augustine, *De Trinitate* 15.32 (425); 15.27–31 (421–24). For more on Augustine's mutual-love theory, see Coffey, "Holy Spirit," 194–201.

160. Augustine, *De Trinitate* 7.6 (226).

161. Augustine, *De Trinitate* 6.7 (210). See Gioia, *Theological Epistemology*, 130.

162. Gioia, *Theological Epistemology*, 130.

163. Gioia, *Theological Epistemology*, 126.

into that communion is accomplished through God's mission. The trinitarian communion of the Father, the Son, and the Holy Spirit is replicated in the communion of God with us where the Triune God abides in us and we in the Trinity because we are given the Holy Spirit, the spirit of love and unity.[164] Two crucial things emerge from the preceding discussion: It is only in the mission of the Son and the Spirit that humanity could have a glimpse of the inner trinitarian life; human communion with the Triune God and with each other would never be realized without *missio Dei*.

CONCLUSION

Augustine is possibly the first theologian to situate mission within the trinitarian nature of God. In his delineation of the doctrine of the Trinity, the divine *missio* emerges as a significant theme in his defense of the equality and unity of the divine persons in the Godhead. As an important move towards this, after a thorough investigation, Augustine repudiated the possibility of mission of the trinitarian persons in the theophanies. The essential invisibility of God renders it impossible for any member of the Trinity to manifest physically in substance or essence. At best, he is prepared to concede that theophanies were mediated through creatures divinely controlled or through the medium of angels. However, the ultimate point that Augustine seeks to drive home to his Arian detractors is the equality and inseparability within the Godhead which necessitate that the Father, the Son, and the Holy Spirit are equally invisible. Since, divine invisibility evidently presupposes that God is unknowable, how does God reveal himself to the world? Augustine seeks the answer to this question in the divine missions, the incarnation of the Son and the manifestation of the Holy Spirit at Pentecost. Mission becomes the pivotal point of trinitarian revelation in the generation of the Son from the Father and in the procession of the Holy Spirit from the Son and the Father. Mission is actualized visibly in the sending of the Son and the Spirit in order that through this mission the human race would be reconciled to God through the mediation of the Son. Thus, God's visibility in the economy of salvation becomes revelatory and reconciliatory to the extent that humanity is privileged to know God and be saved.

There is another dimension of the answer to the question raised above on the divine invisibility and knowability. Although the mission of the Son and the Holy Spirit is God's revelation, yet God remains invisible and

---

164. See Augustine, *De Trinitate* 15.31 (424).

An Indian Trinitarian Theology of *Missio Dei*

unknowable in God's essential nature. The Son in the incarnation is visible as the object of our faith, yet he is invisible and unknowable in his divine nature as God. The essential divine invisibility and the unknowable nature apply to the Spirit as well. Thus, the sending of the Son and the Spirit by the Father does not constitute their ontological inferiority since they are inseparably united with the Father in equality and consubstantiality.

What is the missiological significance of Augustine's trinitarian theology? Augustine locates *missio* as an activity of the Triune God in the interior filiation and procession and in the sending of the Son and the Holy Spirit in the economy of salvation. The objective of this divine mission (sending), as noted above, is the revelation of the Triune God as well as the reconciliation of humanity to God. From Augustine's view, mission is understood as the inner-trinitarian work, the work of the Father, the Son, and the Holy Spirit in a much wider sense of God's overarching plan of human redemption. Hence, mission belongs to the Triune God who is both the initiator and author of mission and thus, mission may be said to be the work of God the Father, through the Son, in the Holy Spirit. Recognition of mission as *missio Dei*, as the work of the Triune God, questions the contemporary perception that often tends to take its departure of mission and theology from the experiences, contexts, and existential realities of the suffering, the marginalized, and the oppressed groups, rather than the Triune God who is the author of mission.[165] In the divine *missio* manifested in the incarnation of the Son, the Triune God comes down to a suffering and hurting world. As Augustine says, the Son became human to suffer, to be smitten, and finally to be crucified and die as human. *Missio Dei*, in Augustine's thought, takes place in response to human need, and their need for God's love and ultimate union with the Triune God. Therefore, the answer to the physical suffering of the oppressed and marginalized cannot be sought apart from the mission of the Triune God.

Augustine introduced the idea of *missio Dei* in a somewhat ancillary fashion in his trinitarian doctrine, and certainly not as a missiological category. On the other hand, in the non-Western framework found in Brahmabandhab Upadhyay, we have observed a pioneering interpretation of trinitarian theology in the context of Hindu-Christian dialogue with a strong missiological overtone. Despite the absence of *missio Dei* in Upadhyay's delineation of *saccidānanda* as Trinity, his interpretation demonstrates a deep commitment to a mission that is instrumental in

---

165. See Poitras, "St. Augustine and the *Missio Dei*," 42.

building Christianity that is distinctively Indian. The following chapter seeks to bring together the theological insights of Upadhyay and Augustine that could contribute to a trinitarian *missio Dei* theology relevant to the contemporary Indian context.

5

Towards an Indian Trinitarian Theology of *Missio Dei*

INTRODUCTION

IT MIGHT SEEM STARTLING to see Augustine and Brahmabandhab Upadhyay being brought together in a study as this, since there is little comparison that one can make between these two theologians. Augustine is a very dominant figure in Christian history and theology with enormous influence in both the spheres. Upadhyay, on the other hand, was an Indian theologian, a revolutionary, and a social reformer who had fallen into oblivion, whose work is now being rediscovered and recognized. What unites Augustine and Upadhyay in this study is the fact they identified the centrality of the doctrine of the Trinity for the life of the Church. Yet their trinitarian interpretation moves in different directions with their distinct goals. Perhaps one striking similarity is in their teaching of the Trinity in the analogy of *being, knowledge,* and *love* for Augustine, and *being, intelligence (knowledge),* and *bliss* for Upadhyay.

The trinitarian thoughts of St. Augustine and Upadhyay were formulated in quite different circumstances and for diverse reasons, and they were separated by long centuries and historical contexts. Augustine wrote his exposition of the Trinity in a Greek philosophical environment in order to challenge the heretical trinitarian formulations of Arianism. In a Hindu philosophical context, Upadhyay saw his trinitarian restatement as an important tool for indigenizing the Christian Gospel in India. While Upadhyay seeks a cultural and indigenous framework in a trinitarian context for building an

Towards an Indian Trinitarian Theology of Missio Dei

Indian Christianity, Augustine is expounding the doctrine of the Trinity and grounding it in the Scripture and in the Nicene and Athanasian creeds. An important distinction about Augustine and Upadhyay needs to be kept in mind while examining their views on the Trinity in relation to the *missio Dei*. The concept of *missio* as a theological category is a very important theme in Augustine's delineation of the doctrine of the Trinity. Augustine, in his treatment on the Trinity, seeks to portray *missio* (sending) as an important activity within the Triune God that establishes the unity, equality, and the inseparability of the Father, the Son, and the Holy Spirit. The generation of the Son from the Father and the procession of the Holy Spirit from both the Father and the Son precede the divine sending (*missio*). Mission is the sending/going forth and the outward movement of the Triune God into the world in visible form, where the Father sends the Son, and the Father and the Son send the Holy Spirit. This *missio* as an outward movement of the Son and the Holy Spirit from the Father takes place with the objective of revealing the Triune God and reconciling humanity to God. In this sense, Augustine may be said to have pioneered the concept of the *missio Dei* as the work of the Triune God in revealing himself to the world and redeeming the world through the mission of the Son in the Spirit.

The modern understanding of the *missio Dei* is rooted in this important trinitarian articulation of Augustine. Interestingly, on the other hand, in Upadhyay's rather philosophical trinitarian restatement, the *missio Dei* as a trinitarian mission concept does not appear. However, the fact remains that Upadhyay's delineation of the Trinity was undertaken within the larger *missio Dei* scheme of developing an indigenous theology with a clearly stated position of bringing the gospel to India in a meaningful way. For a cursory reader, Upadhyay's attempt to articulate Christian theology from the Hindu philosophy might appear to be predominantly metaphysical and abstract. However, Upadhyay undertook his Vedantic restatement of the Christian doctrine of the Trinity with a clear mission objective. He visualized a Christianity that is free from the Western "coating" and its "scholastic garb," and made intelligible to the Indian context. In his attempt to expound the Trinity from the framework of *saccidānanda*, Upadhyay attempts to build upon Christian orthodoxy, as he understood it. An attempt will be made in this chapter to analyze the trinitarian thoughts of Augustine and Upadhyay, and explore the conceptual resources and perspectives for a Christian theology of *missio Dei* informed by the doctrine of the Trinity for the Indian context.

An Indian Trinitarian Theology of *Missio Dei*

BRAHMABANDHAB UPADHYAY: *SACCIDĀNANDA* AND THE TRINITY

One of the significant contributions of Upadhyay is his attempt to expound the meaning of the positive Advaita assertion of Brahman as *saccidānanda*. He accorded the Advaita concept a personal dimension—which was unperceived and rather ambiguous in the Advaita tradition—very much in line with the appropriation of *logos* and *persona* in the early Christian tradition. Upadhyay, from his own understanding of the Christian Trinity and its restatement, attempted to unearth the personal dimension of the *saccidānanda*.[1] He saw how Shankara has argued for the two aspects of Brahman: the qualified Brahman with distinctions and characteristics represented by the *saguṇa* Brahman (*Īśvara*), and the other, the true aspect of Brahman, the Absolute who is without qualities and relations, represented by the *nirguṇa* Brahman. In relating Shankara's Brahman to the personal and relational nature of the Christian concept of God, Upadhyay found the *nirguṇa* aspect to be an ontological necessity, whereas the *saguṇa* aspect was contingent to the being of God. Accordingly, Upadhyay regards *saguṇa* as superimposition on *nirguṇa* and superabundance which are not essential to the being of Brahman, and they do not affect the fullness of Brahman in any way. The infinite Brahman is free to relate to the finite through the contingent superimposition of divine essence, and yet there is nothing in the divine nature that impels Brahman to be related to creation. Thus, Upadhyay seeks to bring out aspects of the personal and relational dimensions of Brahman while maintaining the aseity of Brahman.

Upadhyay found that the Upanishad category of *saccidānanda* offers a more persuasive and convincing way of reconciling the absolute Brahman of the Vedanta with the personal and relational God of the Christian faith. He discovers in *saccidānanda* that while Brahman is "unrelated without" in relation to the external creation, Brahman is "related within" in the essential divine being. He seeks to relate the internal relations within Brahman as *Sat*, *Cit*, and *Ānanda* to the relations of the Father, the Son, and the Holy Spirit in the Christian Trinity. This interpretation, without negating the unrelatedness of Brahman, is able to affirm the personal and relational nature of God. This is regarded as a unique contribution of Upadhyay and is the fundamental premise for his exposition of *saccidānanda* and the Trinity.[2]

---

1. Lobo, "Tripersonalising the Parabrahman," 171–72. See also Ratzinger, "Concerning the Notion of Person," 439–41.

2. See Tennent, "Listening to Voices Outside," 72.

Towards an Indian Trinitarian Theology of Missio Dei

The personal and relational dimension of Brahman that Upadhyay seeks to expound through *saccidānanda* is critical for his restatement of the doctrine of the Trinity and for his larger objective of making the Christian gospel meaningful to the Indian mind. *Saccidānanda*, for Upadhyay, demonstrates the personal/relational dimension as well as distinctions within the Godhead. Employing the Thomist framework of *"persona est subsistens distinctum in natura rationali"*[3] (person is a distinct subsistent in a rational nature), Upadhyay seeks to show that God (Brahman) as *saccidānanda* is personal with distinctions and relations in its inner being. Unlike the *nirguṇa* aspect of Brahman, the *saccidānanda* concept, with its distinctions of being, intelligence, and bliss, demonstrates God as a triune being who is related within himself.

The personal and relational dimensions that he seeks to derive from his exposition of *saccidānanda* are central to Upadhyay's larger objective. They are vital for understanding *missio Dei* as it has unfolded in the person of Christ because one cannot understand God's dealings with the world and humanity without the relational and personal dimensions within the Triune God. God's mission does not make sense without the sonship of Christ and hence, the personal and relational aspect within the Trinity is crucial for Upadhyay.[4] We might recall from Augustine how divine mission originates from the trinitarian relationship between the divine persons. Relations are intrinsic to the trinitarian being of God. For Augustine, the Father is called Father in relation to the Son, the Son is called Son in relation to the Father, and the Holy Spirit is communion and love of the Father and the Son.[5] Upadhyay is very much rooted in this orthodox position on the Trinity.

The personal and relational nature that he attempted to expound, Upadhyay believes, is a divine mystery. The absolute nature of God, according to him, will ever remain a mystery to humanity. Yet, there is something that impels human beings to know the inner life of God and to contemplate God as in himself. Upadhyay would concur with Augustine that this knowledge of the mystery of the inner life of the eternal being, rather "a foreglimpse [sic] . . . of the inner life of God," is made possible in the incarnation

---

3. O'Collins, *Tripersonal God*, 176. See Aquinas, *Power of God*, 251–52.

4. Upadhyay, *Writings*, 1:147–50.

5. Augustine, *De Trinitate* 6.7 (210); 5.12 (199). See Barron, "Augustine's Questions," 45–46; Kotsko, "Gift and *Communio*," 5–6.

An Indian Trinitarian Theology of *Missio Dei*

of Christ.[6] Humanity is able to understand this inner life of God not by reason but only through revelation. While reason enables one to know that "the self-existent Being is necessarily intelligent," reason cannot tell "what distinguishes the generating self from the eternally generated self."[7]

Upadhyay has demonstrated that God is a self-sufficient being who is eternally related within himself without being in need of relating to anything external. God is infinite knowledge and the object of God's knowledge is God's own self since infiniteness of God necessitates that the object of God's knowledge must necessarily be infinite. Thus, God is the subject as well as the object of knowledge. God is infinite love which is satisfied in God's own self without God being in need of anything external to satisfy God's love. Reason cannot distinguish between God's objective self from God's subjective self, and one must seek its answer in the divine revelation.[8] This inner trinitarian life and mystery, according to Upadhyay, make sense when it is approached from the perspective of *saccidānanda*. He believes the Vedanta idea of God as *Sat* (being) *Cit* (intelligence, consciousness) and *Ānanda* (bliss) and their relation to each other could shed light on the inner relation within the Trinity between the Father, the Son and the Holy Spirit. While Upadhyay is careful to uphold the orthodox doctrine of the Trinity, he underlines the instrumentality of Hindu philosophy in his wider objective of indigenization.

AUGUSTINE: THE TRINITY AND *MISSIO DEI*

The Latin "missio" (mission) was used exclusively for the sending (*missio*) activity of the Trinity until the Jesuits used it in the sixteenth century to signify the spread of the Christian faith.[9] Augustine's use of *missio Dei* in his doctrine of the Trinity must be viewed in this historical context.[10] The trinitarian *missio Dei* designates mission as being rooted in the Triune God, the Father, the Son, and the Holy Spirit. The Trinity as the most fundamental doctrine of the Christian faith becomes meaningful and significant in the human context only in the incarnation of Christ. It is in the life and work of Christ and the mission of God accomplished in his incarnation that humanity is given the privilege as well as the opportunity to contemplate the

6. Upadhyay, *Writings*, 1:110.
7. Upadhyay, *Writings*, 1:137, 189.
8. Upadhyay, *Writings*, 1:109–10.
9. O'Malley, "Mission and the Early Jesuits," 3.
10. For an explicit use of *missio dei*, see Augustine, *De Trinitate* 4.25 (178); 15.5 (397).

Towards an Indian Trinitarian Theology of Missio Dei

mystery of the Trinity. Alluding to Philipp Melanchthon, the first systematic theologian of the Protestant Reformation, Klaus Schulz writes, "the doctrine of the Trinity is meaningful only in terms of highlighting its salvific intentions in Christ."[11] The *missio Dei* as a theological and missiological category makes sense only in the outward operation of the Trinity demonstrated through the sending (*missio*) of the Son in the economy of salvation.[12] One cannot comprehend mission as the sending and the salvific activity of God apart from the economy of the Trinity. We have noted that for Augustine, mission that occurred in the incarnation of Christ and the manifestation of the Holy Spirit is the work of the Trinity. This temporal mission of the Son and the Spirit (economic Trinity) reveals, although temporally, the inner trinitarian relations (the ontological Trinity or the immanent Trinity) in the generation of the Son and the procession of the Spirit.

Augustine located the origin of divine missions in the eternal distinctions within the Godhead, in the filiation of the Son, the procession of the Holy Spirit, and their outward movement into the world in the incarnation and the Pentecost. The divine revelation to humanity and their reconciliation to God hinge upon this *missio* of God, the sending forth of the Son and the Holy Spirit in the divine economy of salvation. Contrary to the general perception that Augustine emphasized the immanent Trinity to the exclusion of the economic Trinity, his treatment of the divine missions demonstrates how God *in se* (immanent Trinity) is related to God *quoad nos* (economic Trinity). The preceding chapter on Augustine's *missio Dei* has demonstrated that God's mission takes place in the sphere of trinitarian economy, in the appearance of the Son and the Holy Spirit, revealing the mystery of the inner trinitarian life. Augustine has often been held responsible for sacrificing the economic Trinity and elevating the immanent Trinity. Critics have accused Augustine of having centered his trinitarian theology on the divine essence and the inseparability of the divine persons, leading to what they perceive to be the abandonment of the distinctions within the Trinity and the economic Trinity.[13] Contrary to this criticism, Augustine's treatment of the doctrine of the Trinity and the divine missions amply demonstrate the distinctions and economic Trinity.

---

11. Schulz, *Mission from the Cross*, 91.

12. See Schulz, *Mission from the Cross*, 92–93.

13. See Rahner, *Trinity*, 10–19; Gunton, *Promise of Trinitarian Theology*, 30–55; LaCugna, *God for Us*, 81–104.

An Indian Trinitarian Theology of *Missio Dei*

One of the most significant developments in the modern trinitarian renaissance has been the conversation it has effected between trinitarian theology and the Christian mission as delineated in the first chapter of this book. The relation between the doctrine of the Trinity and mission received a new impetus in the IMC conference in 1952 where mission was sought to be grounded in the Triune God. The idea of mission as being rooted in the nature of the Triune God which surfaced at Willingen was a very significant development. Mission is understood as *missio Dei*, the mission of the Trinity where the Church is seen as participating in the sending activity of the Triune God.

The attempts in this recent trinitarian renewal to locate the foundation and origin of mission go back to divine missions in Augustine. The fourth chapter of this book has shown that the temporal mission of the Son and the Spirit as a divine activity, for Augustine, makes sense only in the context of the trinitarian relation between the Father, the Son, and the Holy Spirit. While mission signifies the temporal visibility of the Godhead in the appearance of the Son and the Holy Spirit, it points back to the inner trinitarian relations, the generation of the Son and the procession of the Holy Spirit, where mission truly originates. In other words, the fact that the second and the third persons of the Trinity are sent in mission reveals that they are eternally (the Son is generated and the Spirit proceeds) from the Father. This inner trinitarian relation, represented in the generation of the Son and the procession of the Holy Spirit from the Father, becomes foundational for the mission (sending) of the Son and the Spirit.[14] Thus, mission, in Augustine's view, has its source in the being of the Triune God, in the sending forth of the Son and the Holy Spirit *by* the Father. The most fundamental position from where he begins his concept of the trinitarian *missio* (sending) is his conviction of the Father being the *principium* (origin) of the Godhead, and therefore the Father always remains the *unsent* one in the Trinity. The Father as the *principium* of the Trinity is the central doctrine affirmed by both the Greek and Latin fathers.[15] Hence, Augustine refers to mission as the going/sending forth of the Son and the Spirit from the Father into the world. Mission occurs in this outward movement of the Son and the Spirit from the hiddenness of God into visibility in the incarnation and at Pentecost.

---

14. For a history of filioque controversy, see Siecienski, *Filioque*.

15. See Barnes, "Latin Trinitarian Theology," 71; McGuckin, "Trinity in the Greek Fathers," 62; Clark, "De Trinitate," 94.

Towards an Indian Trinitarian Theology of Missio Dei

Inseparability, which forms one of the essential aspects of Augustine's trinitarian discourse, entails that the incarnation of Christ is the indivisible work of the Father, the Son, and the Holy Spirit. The mission of the Son is seen as originating in his being generated and sent from the Father, and it is inseparably related to the Holy Spirit. It is important to note that just as the Spirit was involved in the sending of the Son, the Spirit was also sent by the Son. The mission of the Spirit originates in the Spirit's procession from the Father and the Son, just as the Son's mission occurs in his generation from the Father. Augustine further accentuates the inseparable relation between the Triune persons by bringing in the idea of the Holy Spirit as the love between the Father and the Son. The love that unites the divine persons is transferred to human community through the divine missions bringing humanity into communion with the Triune God and with each other. Mission is integral to what God is in God's inner trinitarian life as Father, Son, and Holy Spirit who are not only consubstantial, equal, and inseparable, but united in the love of the Holy Spirit. This Trinity is a community, a loving communion of the Father, the Son and the Holy Spirit, according to Augustine, which unites (reconciles) humanity to that communion of God through the divine *missio*. Mission that originates in God is extended to humanity revealing himself to the world and uniting humanity to the trinitarian communion of God. Augustine's trinitarian theology of missions is a significant contribution which has implications for an Indian theology of mission rooted in the doctrine of the Trinity.

TRINITARIAN THEOLOGY AND INDIAN THEOLOGY OF *MISSIO DEI*

The reception of the *missio Dei* concept is regarded as a corrective to the traditional understanding of mission, particularly the triumphalist and paternalistic view of Western mission. The conceptualization of mission as belonging to God and grounded in the triune nature of God has defined mission as participation in what God is doing in the world and in human history. In Karl Hartenstein's words, "Mission is not just the conversion of the individual, nor just obedience to the word of the Lord, nor just the obligation to gather the church. It is the taking part in the sending of the Son, *missio Dei*, with the holistic aim of establishing Christ's rule over all redeemed creation."[16] The emphasis of *missio Dei* as the mission of the Tri-

---

16. Hartenstein quoted in Engelsviken, "*Missio Dei*," 482.

An Indian Trinitarian Theology of *Missio Dei*

une God reinforced the foundation of the Scripture and Christian tradition as the point of departure in theological and missiological formulation. On the other spectrum, particularly in the non-Western contexts, the emphasis is often laid on the anthropocentric view of mission where the approach is from the perspective of existential realities of human context.[17] These two polarizing trends, often referred to as "missiology from above" and "missiology from below," are very much present in the Indian theology of mission. While on the one side, there is an overemphasis on personal piety and evangelism without being sensitive enough to the social realities of human suffering and deprivation, on the other, there is an equal degree of emphasis on social concerns without reference to evangelism and piety.[18] The idea of trinitarian *missio Dei*, mission as participation in the sending activity of God, comes as a corrective to these divergent tendencies. Mission originates in God, in the Father's sending of the Son and the Spirit, continues in the participation of the Church in *missio Dei*, and moves towards the ultimate goal of God's kingdom. This trinitarian *missio Dei* provides an integrated approach to mission and encompasses all of human life, temporal as well as transcendental realities of life.[19] The following words of the Indian theologian and the metropolitan of the Orthodox Syrian Church, late Geevarghese Mar Osthathios is pertinent here:

> Holistic theology is trinitarian theology, and holistic mission is trinitarian mission comprising both personal ministry and social ministry, conversion and Christian nurture, the whole person and the whole world, meeting the material needs, physical requirements, cultural enlightenment, political liberation, historical and eschatological dimensions of life, secular and spiritual hunger, personal freedom and social justice, and the quest for equality, fraternity, and liberty.[20]

Indian Christian theology does not have a trinitarian shape that has traditionally characterized western theology. For instance, pneumatology has not emerged as a distinct field of study in Indian theology; it is very much part of Christological discussions. In fact, Indian doctrine of the Holy Spirit is fused somewhat with Christology which is close to the

---

17. Poitras, "St. Augustine and the *Missio Dei*," 41–42.
18. See Hrangkhuma, "Protestant Mission Trends in India," 51–53. See also Jongeneel and Engelen, "Contemporary Currents in Missiology," 447–57.
19. See Verkuyl, "Kingdom of God," 168–75.
20. Osthathios, "More Cross-currents in Mission," 176.

Towards an Indian Trinitarian Theology of Missio Dei

Spirit Christology of the ante-Nicene Christian doctrine in which the Holy Spirit is often equated with Christ.[21] Discourse on the person of Christ has been dominant in the Indian Christian theology as evidenced in such well-known works as *The Acknowledged Christ of the Indian Renaissance* by M. M. Thomas, *The Unknown Christ of Hinduism* by Raymond Panikkar, *The Hindu Response to the Unbound Christ* by Stanley Samartha, *The Undiscovered Christ* by Marcus Braybrooke, and others. The second chapter of this book has demonstrated how Christology has been dominant in Indian theology right through its development. Indian theology has generally been defective on its emphasis on the persons of the Father and the Holy Spirit. Excessive emphasis on any one person of the Trinity makes a truncated view of Christian doctrine of God which could prove detrimental to the life and witness of the Church. The tendency to isolate the work of the trinitarian persons seems to downplay the relational dimension of the Trinity. *Missio Dei* originates in the Triune God and it is carried out in the sending activity of the Father through the sending of the Son in the incarnation and of the Spirit at the Pentecost.[22] A robust trinitarian theology is the one that brings together the Church's faith in the rule of the Father, in the salvific work of the Son, and the empowering work of the Spirit. A theology of mission informed by trinitarian theology envisages the mission of God, which is grounded in the trinitarian being of God. The trinitarian *missio Dei* comes as a corrective to the "kind of thinking which founds the whole missionary task solely upon the doctrine of the person and work of Christ" or upon the power of the Holy Spirit.[23] The doctrine of Christ and the Holy Spirit, important as they are, need to be firmly anchored in the Father as the *principium*, to use the Augustinian term, from whom the Son and the Spirit are sent out in *missio Dei*. It is not the mission of the Son or the mission of the Spirit alone, but that of the Triune God. The Church is "invited to become, through the presence of the Holy Spirit, participants in the Son's loving obedience to the Father."[24]

The following sections will seek to show the significance of trinitarian *missio Dei* theology for the context of mission in India, with particular

---

21. See Appasamy, "Indwelling God," 24; Chenchiah, "Christianity and Hinduism," 217; Chakkarai, "Jesus the Avatār," 121. See also Joseph, *Indian Interpretation of the Holy Spirit*.

22. Gelder and Zscheile, *Missional Church in Perspective*, 108.

23. Newbigin, *Trinitarian Faith*, 77.

24. Newbigin, *Trinitarian Faith*, 78.

emphasis on three areas, which I regard as important: the trinitarian *missio Dei* in relation to the emerging indigenous church movements represented in the Pentecostal and charismatic churches, the trinitarian love and relationality with reference to the Indian subaltern communities, and the trinitarian *missio Dei* and dialogue. Furthermore, this will also reflect on the value of the Sanskrit tradition as a paradigm for doing theology and mission as represented in Upadhyay's work, and finally, the space of Indian theology in the landscape of global theology.

The Trinity, Ecclesiology, and Missio Dei

The rediscovery of the trinitarian foundation of the *missio Dei* marked a shift from an *ecclesiocentric* view of mission to a *trinitarian-centric* approach. This does not, however, undermine the place of the Church in the larger *missio Dei*, but rather reaffirms the Church as the *sent* community by the Triune God, which participates in the mission of God. If *missio Dei*, as expounded in this work, originates in the trinitarian being of God and in the Father's sending of the Son and the Holy Spirit in the incarnation and the Pentecost, it presupposes that it is the Triune God who has a mission, and not the Church. As Moltmann observes, "It is not the church that has a mission of salvation to fulfill to the world; it is the mission of the Son and the Spirit through the Father that includes the church, creating a church as it goes on its way."[25] Mission here is seen in terms of "a movement from God to the world, and the church is seen as an instrument for that mission."[26] The Church is more than an instrument of mission or a participant in *missio Dei*. One might say that the constitution of the Church itself is the result of the mission of God through which the church is brought into union with the Trinity. Church is a communion of people who are brought into the unity of the Triune God, the Father, the Son, and the Spirit. It is "a communion-in-mission" and its identity comes from the mission of God.[27] As observed by the Catholic Missiologist Stephen Bevans, "trinitarian understanding of mission turns ecclesiology on its head. It makes mission prior to and constitutive of the church."[28] Although a sense of ambiguity surrounds Augustine's view of the Church in relation to the Trinity, he does point to the Church as being rooted in the Trinity.

25. Moltmann, *Church in the Power of the Spirit*, 64.
26. Aagaard, "Trends in Missiological Thinking," 13.
27. Bevans and Schroeder, *Constants in Context*, 298.
28. Bevans, "Wisdom from the Margins," 28.

Augustine's ecclesiology, developed in response to the Donatist controversy, is rooted in his view of the Church as being temporal and heavenly, visible and invisible. The visible Church, according to him, is made up of carnal as well as spiritual people, sinners as well as saints (*corpus mixtum*) who will be separated at the Day of Judgment as in the parable of the net in Matthew 13:47–50. Augustine calls the visible Church the *Communio Sacramentorum* (*Societas Sacramentorum*) which is the sacramental institution understood in a social dimension.[29] But the sacramental participation in the visible Church does not make a person part of the invisible Church, the *Communio Sanctorum* (*Societas* or *Congregatio Sanctorum*), which constitutes the true (invisible) Church, unless s/he receives the word of Christ into the heart.[30] Church, in Augustine's view, is essentially a heavenly reality. It is the invisible true Church, the *Communio Sanctorum*, according to Augustine, which is united in the trinitarian communion in Christ, whose members are united by the Holy Spirit in love.[31]

As the Church's foundation is grounded in the communion of the Trinity, the Church may be said to be the image or icon of the Triune God in this world witnessing to "the mystery of the unity and diversity" in the Godhead.[32] Just as humanity is created in the image of the Triune God, the Church could also be understood as constituted in the image of the trinitarian God. This is generally explored in the three principal images of the Church in the New Testament that reflect the Trinity of God: *The people of God, the body of Christ, and the temple of the Holy Spirit*.[33] Theologically these ecclesial images "express the essence of the church and its true nature.... They reveal the real mystery of the church: the Holy Trinity."[34] The Church is a "theanthropic" and spiritual-temporal reality which is both divine and human at the same time. It is constituted of people who "have their identity and purpose defined and grounded by a real ontic bonding

---

29. See Augustine, *City of God* 18.49; *Sermon* 306 C; Lancel, *St. Augustine*, 284; Grabowski, *Church*, 499. See also Sparrow-Simpson, *St. Augustine*, 76.

30. Augustine, *Tractate* 50.2; *City of God* 1.35. See McCarthy, "Ecclesiology of Groaning," 28.

31. Faul, "Donatism," 863-4; Augustine, *De Trinitate* 4.12 (165–66); *Homily 1 on First John* 1.2; *Sermon* 341.11, *Sermon* 341.

32. Limouris, "Church as Mystery," 37.

33. See Küng, *Church*, 107–260. See also Chan, *Liturgical Theology*, 21–40; Davis, *Worship and the Reality*, 60–66.

34. Fuellenbach, *Church*, 64.

An Indian Trinitarian Theology of *Missio Dei*

with the triune God, mediated by Word, Spirit and sacrament."[35] Thus, the Church drawn from among men and women in a temporal realm becomes a trinitarian reality in its being made as the people of God, the body of Christ, and the temple of the Holy Spirit.[36]

The fact that the Church is the community that shares in the life and fellowship of the Trinity is quite fundamental for the Church's participation in *missio Dei*. The Church receives its mandate for mission from the trinitarian *missio* and its very being as the redeemed community of God is founded in mission of God. Mission, therefore, is the most indispensable task of the Church. The Luther theologian, Carl Braaten, has put it quite thoughtfully: "[Mission] is a matter of life and death; it goes to the heart of the question whether to be or not to be truly the church. To question the permanent validity of the church's call to mission is to tear it out of its proper trinitarian and christological framework."[37] The Church's task of continuing *missio Dei* flows from its triune origin and therefore, one "cannot separate the church's triune origins from our mission to the world."[38] The identity of the Church in the Triune God is quite central to understand God's mission and its praxis in the context of the global expansion of Christianity into the non-Western world.

This study of *missio Dei* theology and ecclesiology grounded in the doctrine of the Trinity holds special implication for the context of India. The twentieth century witnessed the emergence of vibrant indigenous independent church movements, which continue to be the fastest growing section of the Indian church today.[39] The indigenous church movements in India share pietistic theology, characteristics of Western evangelicalism, which emphasize individual conversion, inner spiritual experience, and commitment to mission often perceived as evangelism. This pietistic influence is perhaps true about much of the contemporary indigenous evangelical and Pentecostal Christianity across the world. Indigenous church movements are often criticized for their weak ecclesiology; the Church is perceived as having only an instrumental role in mission; the Church as

---

35. Davis, *Worship and the Reality*, 63–64.
36. Thompson, *Modern Trinitarian Perspectives*, 80.
37. Braaten, "Triune God," 426.
38. Lang'at, "Trinity and Missions," 170.
39. See Hedlund, *Christianity is Indian*; "Indian Instituted Churches," 33–37.

Towards an Indian Trinitarian Theology of Missio Dei

being part of the meta-story of God and as being the embodiment of the gospel is underplayed.[40]

One of the most significant indigenous church movements with a growing mission presence in the contemporary Indian scene is constituted of Pentecostal-Charismatic churches. Indian Pentecostalism, as in the case of global Pentecostalism, has not developed a robust ecclesiology. What the Pentecostal theologian Simon Chan has said about the global Pentecostal movement holds true for Indian Pentecostalism as well: "Pentecostals have been focusing on how to keep their communities vibrant through revival meetings, new techniques of church growth and new strategies. What they generally lack is a coherent theology of the Church which allows for the truths that they hold dear to be systematically extended from one generation to the next."[41] Indian Pentecostals have always distanced themselves from the larger Christian tradition which, in fact, would provide the framework for developing a Pentecostal theology, and in this context, a Pentecostal ecclesiology.[42] It is not within the purview of this chapter to initiate a discussion of Pentecostal ecclesiology. The concern here is to call attention to the necessity of a healthy ecclesiology informed by the doctrine of the Trinity.

In developing a healthy ecclesiology, it is important to trace the constitution of the Church as a spiritual reality to the *missio* (sending) of the Trinity. Pentecostal churches tend to overemphasize the work of the Holy Spirit, hence the emphasis on individual and private spiritual experience. The person of the Holy Spirit, as emphasized in the ecumenical councils such as Chalcedon, has not received adequate attention in Pentecostal

---

40. One of the criticisms leveled against pietistic theology has been the alleged sense of individualism and a weak ecclesiology. See Tennent, *Invitation to World Missions*, 62; Horton, "To Be or Not to Be." However, recent scholarships on Pietism have claimed that far from being an individual-centered spirituality, Pietism was a communitarian spiritual movement. See Olson, "Pietism," 3–16.

41. Chan, *Pentecostal Ecclesiology*, 7. See Hedlund, "Critique of Pentecostal Mission," 86–90.

42. Simon Chan, himself a Pentecostal theologian, says that Pentecostals have taken their cue from scholastic Protestantism and later evangelicalism which felt that "doctrine can be divorced from its ecclesiastical context." He believes that Pentecostals have much to learn from the Eastern Orthodox in recovering its ecclesiology. See Chan, *Pentecostal Ecclesiology*, 7–8. The lack of a robust ecclesiology often leads to mushrooming of independent churches by self-appointed leaders and custodians without any centralized leadership or administration. Such systems do not promote democratic principles in the organization and administration of Pentecostal churches. See Bergunder, *South Indian Pentecostal Movement*, 209–12.

An Indian Trinitarian Theology of *Missio Dei*

theology of the Spirit. Rediscovering the work of the Holy Spirit in the life and witness of the Church is regarded as a significant contribution of Pentecostalism to the global church. Yet, "the work of the Spirit in the church must ultimately reference the work of the Father and the Son since the church is the result of the Trinitarian economy and not exclusively the economy of the Spirit."[43] As Simon Chan further notes, the descent of the Spirit on Pentecost reveals "the full Trinitarian nature of God," as well as "a fuller understanding of the church."[44] The existence of the Church as the community of God's people is seen grounded in the mystery of the Triune God. "The loving initiative of the Father calls it [the Church] into being. Its form and meaning derive from living union with Christ, crucified and risen. Its structure is animated by the Holy Spirit, the principle of its life and growth."[45] The Church is the creation of the Triune God, the result of *missio Dei*, and is the community of people who are redeemed through the salvific work of Christ and sanctified by the Holy Spirit. Thus, the Church is made into a community of God's people, united to the Triune God and to one another. It is more than a fellowship of believers; it is community of people united within the communion of the Trinity (1 John 1:3). "It is the communion of the faithful united by the Holy Spirit, joined to Christ, and called . . . into the kingdom of God the Father."[46] Along with its pneumatological strength, recognizing this trinitarian foundation of the Church is quite vital for Indian Pentecostalism in its mission.

The Church in its reconciliation through the mediatory work of Christ is called into the trinitarian fellowship of the Father, the Son, and the Holy Spirit. It is an expression of God's deep love for humanity. God in himself is a loving communion to which God invites women and men out of love for them. The Church, which is called into the fellowship of the Triune God, is again sent out in God's mission to the world. While the Church by its nature and being is in the communion of the Trinity, it is simultaneously also in the world by its divine commission and sent into the world in *missio Dei*. The Church is gathered into the trinitarian communion in worship and in sacrament—in the celebration and remembrance of that event which brought the Church into the Triune fellowship in the breaking

---

43. Chan, *Pentecostal Ecclesiology*, 8.
44. Chan, *Pentecostal Ecclesiology*, 9.
45. Kelly, *Trinity of Love*, 3.
46. Fuellenbach, *Church*, 64.

Towards an Indian Trinitarian Theology of Missio Dei

of the bread and sharing of the cup—only to be sent again into the world.[47] The identity of the Church as the people of God, the body of Christ, and the temple of the Holy Spirit is shaped in the economy of the Trinity, and its mission flows in its being sent by the Triune God. This trinitarian dimension of the Church and its mission is not a prominent theme in the emerging indigenous church movements in India. The dearth of an adequate ecclesiological grounding has given way to a concept of mission that seems to be characterized by a sense of individualism, where the Church is not adequately emphasized as the *sent* community. The Church is seen no more than a fellowship and the Church as participant in God's mission is often underplayed. The emphasis is often given on individual's calling to mission rather than the calling of the Church into mission.[48] An ecclesiology informed by the trinitarian *missio Dei* conceives the Church as an image of the Triune God and "as a sent community that witnesses to God's reign in Christ through the power of the Spirit."[49] It is important that the Indian church in general and indigenous church movements in particular recapture this vision of the relation between the Trinity, the Church, and its mission as it seeks to witness in such a religiously, culturally, and socially plural society as India.

Trinitarian Life and Missio Dei

The preceding chapters on Upadhyay and Augustine have demonstrated the inner relationship within the Trinity that is fundamental to the life of the Godhead. Augustine traces the dimension of *missio* in the interior filiation and procession and in the sending of the Son and the Holy Spirit in the economy of salvation. Upadhyay attempted to expound the distinctions within the Vedanta description of God as *saccidānanda* which, according to him, demonstrates the inner relationship within the Triune God who is "happy in his self-colloquy."[50] Thus, contrary to a static ontological conception of God, both Augustine and Upadhyay show a more active, engaged relational model of the Trinity. This dimension of dynamic divine relationality is quite important for the understanding of mission as *missio Dei*. Just as God's mission within the Godhead is inconceivable without relationship, *missio Dei* in respect to humanity is unthinkable apart from it. "Mission is

47. Hoffmeyer, "Missional Trinity," 109–10.
48. See Bergunder, *South Indian Pentecostal Movement*, 191–208, 209–30.
49. Gelder and Zscheile, *Missional Church in Perspective*, 106.
50. Upadhyay, *Writings*, 1:130.

An Indian Trinitarian Theology of *Missio Dei*

... the entering into relational webs that transform us even as we engage in shaping others. The agency involved is God's, ours, and our neighbor's."[51] There is a trinitarian imagination undergirding mission in the recent renewal of trinitarian doctrine which, in my view, has not been adequately appropriated in Indian theology of mission. Capturing the trinitarian vision is of great consequence for the Church's mission in the most diverse and divisive context of India, particularly for the Church's mission to the poor and the marginalized. In the following section, I will examine the trinitarian aspects of love, relationality, and communion, and will attempt to draw its implications for a trinitarian *missio Dei* theology with special reference to the subalterns in India.

TRINITARIAN LOVE AND *MISSIO DEI*

The trinitarian relationship is communion of love between the Father, the Son, and the Holy Spirit. Hence, in Augustine's conception, one cannot think of the Trinity apart from love. Augustine calls for translating this trinitarian love into neighborly love and into human relationship. Drawing on John's first epistle, Augustine links in an inseparable fashion one's love for God and neighbor:

> This passage [1 John 4:7] shows clearly and sufficiently how this brotherly love ... is proclaimed on the highest authority not only to be from God but also simply to be God. When therefore we love our brother out of love, we love our brother out of God; and it is impossible that we should not love especially the love that we love our brother with. Thus we infer that those two commandments cannot exist without each other: because God is love the man who loves love certainly loves God; and the man who loves his brother must love love.... So with one and the same charity we love God and neighbor; but God on God's account, ourselves and neighbor also God's account.[52]

Love represented by the Holy Spirit as the mutual love of the Father and the Son, for Augustine, plays a foundational role in the trinitarian communion as demonstrated in the fourth chapter of this book. One must see the above passage in relation to Augustine's exposition on Jesus' commandment on love (John 13:34–35) which he extends and relates with the Great Commandment to love God and to love one's neighbor (Matt 22:37–40).

---

51. Gelder and Zscheile, *Missional Church in Perspective*, 121-22.
52. Augustine, *De Trinitate* 8.12 (256).

Towards an Indian Trinitarian Theology of Missio Dei

One also needs to bear in mind that the origin of this love, recalling the trinitarian love, is in God and was made manifest only in *missio Dei*. The standard of love underlined in the commandment of love is to "love as I have [God has] loved," and "love your neighbor as yourself." The standard in both acts of human love is God's love: "on the one hand, he that loves God cannot despise His commandment to love his neighbor; and on the other, he who in a holy and spiritual way loves his neighbor, what does he love in him but God? That is the love, distinguished from all mundane love, which the Lord specially characterized, when He added, 'as I have loved you.'"[53] The emphasis on "as God" in relation to God's love makes true sense only in the death of Christ, the ultimate expression of God's love as indicated by Jesus in John 15:12-13. In a trinitarian sense, it is the giving of the Triune God's own self, in which the Father gives away the Son to die and the Son gives himself up to death. It is the self-giving of God to the world, and the sharing of God's best for humanity. A very pertinent thought in this context comes from Mar Osthatios, who speaks of the eternal sharing of God. He says, "God is sharing this very nature of love in eternity in God's infinite self and into time and history through creation and the salvific action of the Son and the Holy Spirit."[54] The "as of God" that Jesus has emphasized points to the ultimate expression of God's sharing of himself, a model the Church is called to emulate, to "love as I have loved."

The command to love "as God" has loved is a profound teaching because it deprives the disciples of any choice as to whom they love. "Since man is not God and never attains equality with God, the 'as God' deprives him of any chance to choose his neighbor."[55] It is because God has already showed us that we cannot "take pride in our own worth" as the recipients of God's love, and therefore we must love others regardless of their merit.[56] For Augustine, this implies that everyone is a neighbor and therefore everyone is an object of neighborly love: "You should consider every person your neighbor, even before he is a Christian. For you do not know how he stands with God."[57] Augustine recognizes that because love originates and flows from God, one cannot love the neighbor unless s/he receives divine enablement to love. "Who can love his neighbour—that is, everyone—as himself, if he

---

53. Augustine, *Tractates on John's Gospel* 65.2.
54. Osthathios, "Divine Sharing," 19.
55. Arendt, *Love and Saint Augustine*, 94.
56. Augustine, *De Trinitate* 4.2 (153–54). Gioia, *Theological Epistemology*, 87–88.
57. Augustine, *Commentaries on the Psalms* 25, ii, 2.

does not love God, by whose command and gift he is able to fulfil the love of neighbour?"[58] This neighborly love, in Augustine's view, is closely related to one's love towards God and it has a trinitarian dimension. He calls it "true love" which originates from God, exemplified through Christ's death, and poured out in our hearts through the Holy Spirit.[59] This trinitarian love is important as it embraces all of humanity without any distinctions whatsoever. This important aspect of trinitarian love has implications for the Church's mission and even more so for the Indian church's mission in a socially disintegrated and caste-ridden society which has perpetuated inequality and injustice for millions of subalterns, the Dalits and Tribals.[60]

Regrettably, love as the essential hallmark of Christian discipleship (cf. John 13:35) does not find expression in the community of believers when inequality of Dalits and Tribals prevails within the church. The trinitarian mystery teaches that a divine relationality is built on mutual love between the divine persons. This holds true in human relationship as well and more so within the body of the Church where, to use Augustine's often quoted Romans passage, *the love of God has been poured out into our hearts through the Holy Spirit* (Rom 5:5). God's *missio* itself, in Augustine's view, was an expression of God's love as demonstrated in the mission of the Son.[61] The divine love expressed in *missio Dei* is the self-giving of the Triune God in the Son of God and his identifying with the poor and the marginalized. This is the vision of love that must characterize the mission of the Church, expressed in concrete and credible actions for the sake of those who have been victims of structural oppression both within and outside the church. Speaking on the deplorable state of the subaltern communities within the Indian church as well as outside, the Catholic Bishop's Conference of India (CBCI) has called upon the Indian church to make "personal and

---

58. Augustine, *Commentary on Paul's Epistle to the Galatians*, 45.

59. Augustine, *De Trinitate* 8.10 (253–54).

60. The word "subaltern" is generally used as a self-designation for "Dalits," formerly called "untouchables," and "Tribals" (Adivasi) who are considered the aboriginals of India. According to the latest census data, Dalits and Tribals together constitute 24.2 percent of the Indian population. See Office of the Registrar, "Census of India 2011." The Indian church is comprised predominantly of the Dalit and Tribal communities. In Indian Christian theological discourse, which has traditionally been dominated by the elitist Brahminical tradition, the subaltern communities and their concerns have rarely been the subject matters of Christian theology in India until recently. The marginalization, deprivation, and inequality of the subaltern communities in the social, economic, and political spheres of India continue in a subtle manner.

61. See Augustine, *De Trinitate* 4.2 (153–54).

Towards an Indian Trinitarian Theology of Missio Dei

institutional sacrifices ... for the poor, the Dalits and the Tribals."[62] In the words of an Indian Catholic missiologist, "when the manifestation of God's love is experienced by dalits [sic], we can say that the church is alive and the people can have hope for the reign of God."[63] Speaking on the context of the struggles of Dalits and Tribals in India, yet another Indian Catholic missiologist observes that we suffer "not so much from a lack of the sense of the divine but a lack of the sense of the neighbour, fellow human beings."[64] Human sense of the divine finds its true expression in human relationship only when it is characterized by divine love.

Christianity was perceived to be a more egalitarian religion which offered the possibility of liberation to subaltern communities in India. The main context of the subaltern's conversion to Christianity was their experience of long-standing inequality and injustice at the hands of the prevailing caste Hindu social order, and the hope and promise of an egalitarian way of life they saw in Christianity. In reality, the Indian church is not certainly an egalitarian society where the caste system as a social and cultural structure does exist.[65] One may not deny the fact that conversion to Christianity did contribute to a measure of emancipation to some among the subaltern groups in terms of education and economic well-being, and the consequent elevation of their social status. Nevertheless, a true sense of equality and justice has always evaded the Dalits and the Tribals. The fact remains that the Indian church in its hierarchy and leadership has failed to reflect the true meaning of Christian love in creating an ecclesial environment for the liberation of the subaltern communities.

Trinitarian Relationality and *Missio Dei*

In the modern renewal of trinitarian theology, divine relationality has replaced the traditional ontology of divine substance as the most important approach to the mystery of the Trinity and its implications for Christian life and mission. This significant development marked a shift from the metaphysical and intellectual understanding of faith in the Trinity to an attempt that seeks to discover the meaning and the practical relevance of the doctrine of the Trinity to the wider spheres of human life and society.[66] The

---

62. Gorantla and Thumma, "Dalit Christians in the Third Millennium," 152.
63. Stanislaus, "Dalits and the Mission of the Church," 189.
64. Kavunkal, "Indian Perspectives in Mission and Missiology," 155.
65. Amaladoss, *Life in Freedom*, 25. See Christopher, "Between Two Worlds," 10.
66. See Franke, "God is Love," 105; Boff, *Trinity and Society*, 100–110.

An Indian Trinitarian Theology of *Missio Dei*

belief in God as a relational being in God's trinitarian nature who reaches out to humanity in relationship is a hallmark of the Christian faith. The modern renewal of trinitarian theology has helped change misperceptions of God as an isolated monad to that of a God who is internally related within and who invites people into the sweet communion and loving relationship of the Trinity through God's mission to the world.

God is a community bound in eternal relations between the Father, the Son, and the Holy Spirit who give themselves to and dwell in each other. The oneness and plurality of God are interwoven, as it were, in God's eternal being without erasing either the oneness or the plurality. The relationship of the divine persons is so dynamic and deeply intimate that they coinhere and mutually dwell in each other. This deeper sense of inner divine relatedness of the Trinity is explained by the term "perichoresis," used first by Gregory of Nazianzus and later popularized by the Greek theologian, John Damascene. Perichoresis is the mutual interdependence, interpenetration, and reciprocal indwelling of the persons in the Trinity. It is the "being-in-one-another" of the divine persons, their permeation into one another, and yet being distinct from each other.[67] It expresses the trinitarian unity of the Godhead in its deepest sense. Leonardo Boff explains it succinctly: "[Perichoresis] means that the Father is ever in the Son, communicating life and love to him. The Son is ever in the Father knowing him and lovingly acknowledging him as Father. Father and Son are in the Holy Spirit as mutual expression of life and love. The Holy Spirit is in the Son and the Father as source and manifestation of life and love of this boundless source. All are in all."[68]

---

67. Boff, *Trinity and Society*, 135–36. See LaCugna, *God for Us*, 270–72.

68. Boff, *Holy Trinity*, 15. The meaning of perichoresis is traced back to the New Testament, to the statements of Jesus on his relation with God the Father. The following NT passages are important in this regard: "The Father and I are one" (John 10:30); "the Father is in me and I am in the Father" (John 10:38; 4:11); "I ask . . . that they may all be one. As you, Father, are in me and I am in you, may they also be in us" (John 17:20–21). A careful analysis of the term *perichoresis* is important in discovering its meaning fully and its use within the trinitarian thought. Leonardo Boff has given a quite helpful explanation of *perichoresis*. Since it has two meanings, it is translated into two Latin words, *circuminsessio* and *circumincessio*. From these two Latin words are coined the two English words, "circuminsession" and "circumincession." The meaning of *circuminsessio* is "one thing being contained in another, dwelling in being in another—a situation of fact, a static state." *Circuminsessio* comes from two words, *sedere* and *sessio* which mean, "being seated, having its seat in, seat." When applied to Trinity, this would signify "one Person is in the others, surrounds the others on all sides (*circum-*), occupies the same space as the others, fills them with its presence." The second Latin word, *circumincessio* comes from

Towards an Indian Trinitarian Theology of Missio Dei

One may see the appropriation of perichoresis of the Eastern theologians reflected in Augustine's use of the inseparability and consubstantiality of the trinitarian persons where he understands the Holy Spirit as the mutual love of the Father and the Son. Although Augustine does not use the term "perichoresis" as such, his teaching on trinitarian inseparability points to the direction of perichoresis. In the inseparability of the Father, the Son, and the Holy Spirit, no person is alone, but each person is always in each other in a perichoretic unity. Pecknold notes, "Augustine modified Greek (Cappadocian) terms inappropriate to a Latin audience, but preserved their basic insights and continued . . . their relational principles grounded in the notion of *perichoresis*."[69] The Triune God, for Augustine, "is a co-inherent *communio* of three persons, each one constituted by its relation to the other two."[70] In his use of perichoretic inseparability, if one may use such a phrase, Augustine asserts the intrinsic communion of the Trinity as well as the distinction of the persons. In one of his writings in the mature period of his life, Augustine says, "That the Father, Son, and Holy Spirit are a Trinity inseparable; One God, not three Gods. But yet so One God, as that the Son is not the Father, and the Father is not the Son, and the Holy Spirit is neither the Father nor the Son, but the Spirit of the Father and of the Son."[71]

The idea of perichoresis is not quite absent from Upadhyay's treatment of the Trinity. The words that come closer to perichoresis in Upadhyay's exposition of the Trinity are "colloquy" ("conversation" or "dialogue") and "conjoin" which signify eternal and intimate relation within the Trinity. Upadhyay describes the trinitarian relation as "the mystery of the timeless Word-colloquy which sweetens the divine bosom and fills it with joy ineffable."[72] The Father and the Son are bound in the "Spirit of Love. Revelation has given us a fore-glimpse [sic] of the inner life of God and has declared how his knowledge and love are fully satisfied by the colloquy of God with God in Spirit."[73] In both Augustine and Upadhyay, love becomes

---

incedere, which means "to permeate, com-penetrate and interpenetrate." This meaning is active and suggests "the interpenetration or interweaving of one Person with the others and in the others" (Boff, *Trinity and Society*, 136).

69. Pecknold, "How Augustine Used the Trinity," 134. See Lytle, "Perichoretically Embodied Ethics," 93–105.

70. Barron, "Augustine's Questions," 45.

71. Augustine, *Sermon* 2.2 (NPNF1/6:259). See also Augustine, *Letters 100–155*, 136, 138; *Sermon* 53.4.

72. Upadhyay, *Writings*, 1:189.

73. Upadhyay, *Writings*, 1:189.

An Indian Trinitarian Theology of *Missio Dei*

the central theme in the eternal relation of the Triune God. The trinitarian persons are intimately and mysteriously bound to each other in the "spirit of Love which sweetens the divine Bosom with boundless delight,"[74] and in the "supreme charity conjoining Father and Son to each other."[75]

The trinitarian relationality and the idea of perichoresis have come to be regarded as a paradigm for relations that must characterize human society in the economic, sociopolitical, and ecclesial spheres of life. Advocates of this approach believe that trinitarian relation and communion have liberating impulses which have great significance for the life of subaltern communities.[76] "Relational trinitarian theology gives us a vision of God as a dynamic community of mutuality, openness, difference, and love that makes space for others to participate."[77] This "space" is one of invitation which is made possible through the Church, the body of Christ, which mystically participates in the very life of God because the Church is *in* Christ.

Trinitarian relationality comes as a critique of ideologies that promote hegemony and concentration of power by an elite minority, and disregard for diversity and plurality in society. This creates structures that are domineering, oppressive, and intolerant to the poor and the marginalized.[78] The Father, the Son, and the Holy Spirit are distinct persons within the Trinity, yet there is communion and unity which respect differences and otherness. This ought to reflect in human relationship and community where there are distinctions and otherness that must be honored. Trinitarian relationality and communion imply affirmation of diversity, convergence of differences, mutual acceptance, sense of community, and equality. It is "a society of sisters and brothers whose social fabric is woven out of participation and communion of all in everything [which] can justifiably claim to be an image and likeness (albeit pale) of the Trinity."[79]

A theology of mission informed by trinitarian relationality has significant implications for the Indian church's mission to the subaltern communities. The *missio*, as Augustine has demonstrated, flows from the inner trinitarian relations, from the generation of the Son and the

---

74. Upadhyay, *Writings*, 1:193.

75. Augustine, *De Trinitate* 7.6 (226).

76. Boff, *Trinity and Society*; Boff, *Holy Trinity, Perfect Community*; Moltmann, *Trinity and the Kingdom*.

77. Gelder and Zscheile, *Missional Church in Perspective*, 108.

78. Boff, *Trinity and Society*, 149–50.

79. Boff, *Trinity and Society*, 151.

Towards an Indian Trinitarian Theology of Missio Dei

procession of the Holy Spirit from the Father. Therefore, Christian mission cannot be conceived apart from relationality and love within the trinitarian persons. A divergent position of divine relationality may be seen in the Hindu system of thought which Upadhyay sought to expound through his restatement of the Trinity. Relationality, personhood, and qualities such as love are incompatible with the highest concept of the ultimate reality (Brahman) according to Advaita Vedanta of Shankara. Brahman is devoid of any qualities and is an unrelated being, hence cannot have relationship to the world. Employing the Vedanta category of *saccidānanda*, Upadhyay seeks to resolve the problem of the *unrelatedness* of Brahman by appealing to "the nature of *Brahman* as *Cit*, Thought, and in the fact that though God is 'unrelated without' he may yet be 'related within.'"[80] Yet one must understand that Hinduism and its social order, unlike Christian trinitarianism, operate in a worldview influenced by the concept of an unrelated and impersonal Brahman.

The most fundamental framework of the Hindu social order (caste system) in relation to the subaltern communities is structured on inequality. In this social order of caste structure, "people are placed in graded inequality which expresses itself in the social, political, economic, religious, and cultural dimensions."[81] All forms of injustices perpetrated on subaltern communities, such as subjugation, marginalization, exploitation, and discrimination spring from this structural inequality. The trinitarian *missio Dei* envisions an alternative structure grounded on trinitarian relationality and communion which makes sense to the subaltern communities because they have a strong sense of "relationships and interdependence in the community."[82] The trinitarian relationality and communion which form the bedrock of Christian *koinonia* are to become the substratum of an Indian trinitarian *missio Dei*. Trinitarian relationality which affirms the equality of all created in *imago Dei* provides the Church a paradigm of sharing with and embracing the subalterns. The Church as a reflection of the trinitarian relationality and communion is sent into the world in continuation of the trinitarian *missio Dei* to the vulnerable and the marginalized represented in the sufferings of the subaltern communities who are objects of God's priority. Trinitarian *missio* is God's self-giving in the suffering and the death of Christ, and the ultimate act of divinity identifying with human

---

80. Boyd, *Introduction to Indian Christian Theology*, 73.
81. Rosario, "Mission from the Perspective of Dalits," 282.
82. Gonsalves, *God of Our Soil*, 164.

An Indian Trinitarian Theology of *Missio Dei*

vulnerability and suffering, which the global church, the Indian church in particular, is called to emulate. The Church is to embody the new creation even in the present. Therefore, the final unity of the Trinity (that God might be all in all) is mirrored in our work as agents of reconciliation.

The Trinity, Dialogue, and Missio Dei

The question of religious pluralism and the Christian attitude and relation to non-Christian faiths has always been part of the self-identity of the Christian Church and its mission. This perhaps has become more pronounced in the contemporary globalized world, which has brought religious traditions to the church's doorways. One of the important developments in the modern trinitarian renewal has been the attempt to search for the relevance of the doctrine of the Trinity in the context of religious pluralism of the day. Raymond Panikkar is regarded as the first Christian theologian to have attempted to relate the Christian doctrine of the Trinity to other religions. Panikkar seems convinced of the universal dimension of the Trinity that he believes it embraces religious traditions beyond Christianity. Therefore, in his view the "Trinity . . . may be considered as a junction where the authentic spiritual dimensions of all religions meet."[83]

While the attempt to relate the Trinity to non-Christian religious traditions and pluralist context of today is a consequent development of the trinitarian renaissance, one could perhaps trace its premise to Augustine and Upadhyay. Augustine did not attempt to relate the Trinity to non-Christian traditions, but drew attention to the trinitarian vestiges that he found in the human mind. Accordingly, for Augustine, "man was not made to the image of God as regards the shape of his body, but as regards his rational mind."[84] The German Protestant theologian, Michael von Brück, finds a resonance between Augustine's trinitarian theology, his emphasis on divine unity in particular, and the Advaita Vedanta concept of *saccidānanda*.

In Advaita Vedanta, Brahman is "the one-without-a-second (*advitiya*), true being (*sat*), pure spirit (*cit*), and final bliss (*ananda*)."[85] "*Sat-cit-ananda* is neither a part nor a property of *brahman* [sic]. The three united are,

---

83. Panikkar, *Trinity and World Religions*, 42. Panikkar's work on Trinity and religious plurality was followed by others significant works as D'Costa, *Meeting of Religions and the Trinity*; Heim, *Depth of the Riches*; Vanhoozer, *Trinity in a Pluralistic Age*.

84. Augustine, *De Trinitate* 12.12 (331). See also Peters, *God as Trinity*, 73.

85. Brück, *Unity of Reality*, 17.

Towards an Indian Trinitarian Theology of Missio Dei

rather, the essential nature of *brahman*. *Saccidananda* is *brahman* itself."[86] Augustine's description of the inseparable unity of the Godhead by way of anthropological-psychological analogies, according to Brück, seems to correspond to this indivisible nature of Brahman, *saccidānanda*. Augustine affirms divine unity in terms of one being, one will, and inseparable operation where God is the subject as well as the object. This trinitarian life is beyond human reason and therefore Augustine's analogies, according to Brück, fail to explain satisfactorily the Godhead.[87] In Brück's opinion, moving beyond rational knowledge to contemplation of trinitarian unity "under three aspects, which are not properties but relational moments by which the whole becomes present in each of the particular notions," one could see "parallels in *saccidānanda* as the expression of the essence of the Absolute."[88] He believes *saccidānanda* as "being," "consciousness," and "bliss" is closer to Augustine's analogy of "Being," "Knowledge," and "Love" (Will). "The *cit* aspect of *brahman* reveals the same thing as Augustine's attempt at trinitarian analogies in consciousness. Consciousness is one and identical with itself insofar as it comprehends a multitude of contents."[89]

However, one cannot stretch Augustine's *vestigia trinitatis* so as to support an Augustinian theology of religions. Unlike the paradigms of trinitarian theology of religions represented by Panikkar and Brück, which move beyond the Christian dogmatic formulations, Augustine confined the trinitarian revelation to the incarnation and the Pentecost. For Augustine, the foundation of God's *missio* (sending) is in the trinitarian relation of the Godhead. This mission became a reality in God's revelation in the human and historical context in a dialogical form exemplified in the incarnation of Jesus, in his life, and ministry. As Pope Paul VI notes in his encyclical, *Ecclesiam Suam*, "the noble origin of this dialogue [is] in the mind of God Himself. . . . Indeed, the whole history of man's salvation is one long, varied dialogue, which marvelously begins with God and which He prolongs with men in so many different ways."[90] *Missio Dei* that began in the Triune God and unfolded in the incarnation of Christ reflects God's continuing dialogue

---

86. Brück, *Unity of Reality*, 26.

87. Brück, *Unity of Reality*, 90–91.

88. Brück, *Unity of Reality*, 91. For a detailed discussion on the dialogue between the trinitarian understanding of God and the Advaita Vedanta, see Brück, *Unity of Reality*, 143–277.

89. Brück, *Unity of Reality*, 91.

90. Paul VI, "*Ecclesiam Suam*." See also Bevans and Schroeder, *Prophetic Dialogue*, 25.

An Indian Trinitarian Theology of *Missio Dei*

with the hurting and suffering world of humanity. It also envisages human reconciliation to God and to one another and a human society founded on the principles of communion and relationality. In a world of suffering caused by poverty, marginalization of the poor and the vulnerable, religious intolerance, and communal divide, a dialogue rooted in the trinitarian *missio Dei* has great significance. This is a call the Church as participant in God's mission cannot ignore especially in a context like India, which is a classic example of diversity in religion, ethnicity, and culture.

Turning to Upadhyay, one might say he pioneered a Hindu-Christian dialogue and was the first Indian Christian theologian to bring the doctrine of the Trinity in a dialogical mode, relating it to the Advaita Vedanta concept of *saccidānanda*. As Wayne Teasdale notes, Upadhyay "greatly advanced dialogue in a substantive way and positioned Christianity to develop an Indian Christian theology consonant with the genius of the Hindu tradition."[91] As already observed in the second and the third chapters of this book, the thoughts of Upadhyay's predecessors, Raja Ram Mohan Roy and Keshub Chunder Sen, on Christian faith became instrumental in bringing the Christian faith in dialogue with Hinduism. Upadhyay got the whole idea for his life project from the *Brahmo Samaj* of Roy and Sen and his trinitarian thought, in particular, from Sen. However, the difference with Upadhyay was his encounter with Roman Catholicism that made him more orthodox. He was the first Indian Christian theologian to have employed the Advaita Vedanta framework of *saccidānanda* to restate the doctrine of the Trinity for the Indian context. This provides an important instance of employing the Hindu philosophical categories and language in order to expound the Christian gospel in the Indian context, thus bringing Christian Trinity in dialogue with Hindu thought. Upadhyay found a model to follow in Thomas Aquinas who used the system of Aristotelian philosophy for constructing Christian theology, and sought to replace Aquinas's use of Aristotelian philosophy with Shankara's Advaita Vedanta in an attempt to indigenize the Christian faith in India. The trinitarian restatement from the perspective of the Vedanta category of *saccidānanda* is regarded as an important step in this direction. Upadhyay's Sanskrit hymn on the Trinity is deemed as an important early attempt to dialogue with Hindu thoughts. Without reformulating or reconstructing the orthodox understanding of the trinitarian doctrine, Upadhyay sought to recast the trinitarian doctrine in Hindu categories and cultural forms.

91. Teasdale, *Catholicism in Dialogue*, 11, 127.

Towards an Indian Trinitarian Theology of Missio Dei

While integrating the Christian and Hindu imageries, he let the "Hindu resonance abound" and "steeped the hymn's vocabulary . . . in the language of the classical Upanishads and the *Gita*."[92] In bringing the Trinity in dialogue with Advaita Vedanta, Upadhyay was careful to relate it with the *nirguṇa* Brahman, the highest Hindu conception of God, rather than *saguṇa* Brahman. The true meaning of God as *saccidānanda*, according to Upadhyay, is known through the trinitarian revelation.[93]

What is the implication of the trinitarian dialogue for the *missio Dei* theology in the Indian context? The doctrine of the Trinity provides a classic example of languages and categories drawn from Greek philosophy in expounding the key doctrinal statements of the Christian faith. The Greek philosophical languages and terms such as *ousia, hypostasis, substantia, persona*, and *homoousion* found their way into the early church's formulation of classical trinitarianism. Upadhyay would regard these Greek categories and concepts as alien to religious and cultural contexts like India which is untouched by Greek philosophy. They appear to be what Sadhu Sunder Singh called the "foreign cup" containing the gospel which the Hindu rejects. They are more likely to obscure the true meaning of the gospel and thus present a distorted view of the Christian faith in India. In the case of the doctrine of the Trinity, terms such as "person," "substance," "begotten," and "procession" cannot be adequately translated into Indian languages so as to convey their precise meaning which they hold in Western formulation of the Trinity. In the Indian situation, there is an inherent danger of identifying "person" with individual, "begotten" with human procreation, and "substance" with material objects.[94] Similarly, the "procession" of the Holy Spirit, the philosophical concept situated in the theological confrontation of the Eastern and the Western Christian traditions, makes no sense to the Indian mind. Upadhyay, both as a Christian and an Indian, recognized the need for "capturing the essence of the [Christian doctrinal] formulation, but using the language and thought forms more familiar to Indians."[95]

The importance of Upadhyay's use of the Indian categories and thought-forms to restate the Christian faith must be seen in his attempts to

---

92. Lipner, *Brahmabandhab Upadhyay*, 203. Ipgrave, *Trinity and Inter Faith Dialogue*, 355.

93. Boyd, *Introduction to Indian Christian Theology*, 72–73. Ipgrave, *Trinity and Inter Faith Dialogue*, 356.

94. Tennent, "Listening to Voices Outside," 70–71.

95. Tennent, "Listening to Voices Outside," 71.

translate the Christian doctrine and its historic formulation in a way that makes sense to the Indian mind. It must be said to the credit of Upadhyay that much before the need for cultural and theological translatability of the gospel was ever recognized in view of the contemporary global expansion of Christianity, he was attempting what may be called theological contextualization or theological translatability—Upadhyay was certainly a pioneer in theological translatability. The challenge he took upon himself was the task of bringing Indian philosophy to the service of indigenizing the Christian faith in India without undermining the fundamentals of the Christian doctrines. Upadhyay would not "compromise in matters of dogmatic faith," which he believed is "the bulwark of truth."[96] Yet, his views were not only unrecognized in his lifetime and but were rejected by the church of the day. As the Franciscan historian, Achilles Meersman, has quite aptly put it, Upadhyay was "too much ahead of his times," and a genius "born before his time."[97]

SANSKRIT TRADITION AND CHRISTIAN THEOLOGY

One of the most important aspects of this study pertains to the use of Advaita Vedanta as an instrument of theological contextualization and its significance for mission in India. This section will highlight the continuing significance of the Sanskrit paradigm for Indian theological formulations in the face of attempts to challenge its utility as a paradigm for theological articulation. It is important to distinguish the constructive and affirmative aspects from the repressive and domineering strands within the larger matrix of the Sanskrit paradigm.

The criticism often directed against the pioneering efforts in Indian theology, including that of Brahmabandhab Upadhyay, has been the dominance of Sanskrit paradigm on theological formulation in India. Upadhyay has been particularly subjected to criticism for employing Advaita Vedanta in restating the Christian faith which is today seen as extraneous to the non-Sanskrit and counter-Sanskrit paradigms of other Hindu castes, Dalits, and Tribals who are outside the elite Hindu caste groups.[98] In view of the long association of the Sanskrit language and tradition with Brahminical ethnic particularity, Indian theological

---

96. Upadhyay, *Writings* 2:223.

97. Meersman, "Can We Speak of Indigenization," 82.

98. See Lipner, *Brahmabandhab Upadhyay*, 204; Lipner, "Brahmabandhab Upadhyay," 181–82.

Towards an Indian Trinitarian Theology of Missio Dei

reflections from the framework of the Sanskrit tradition came to be regarded as theology from the upper side as opposed to subaltern theologies from the underside. The pioneers of Indian Christian theology discovered in the Sanskrit tradition the possibility of employing a native and cultural framework to formulate an indigenous theology, and thus to break the dominance of Western theology over the Indian church. Brahmabandhab Upadhyay's use of Shankara's Advaita Vedanta and A. J. Appasamy's use of Rāmānuja's Vishishtadvaita Vedanta (qualified monism or qualified non-dualism) are the two earliest examples of Sanskritization of Christian theology in India.[99] These two representative attempts reflect a reaction against the dominance of Western theology as well as a growing consciousness about the need for articulating Christian faith employing cultural and religious traditions of India. The successors of these pioneering theologians followed their paths and Christian theological reflections in India continued to be informed by the Sanskrit paradigm.

The Sanskrit tradition being the dominant religious paradigm in India, it was quite natural that the early theologians were drawn to it and they found it valuable in interpreting the Christian faith in India. Importantly, this also marked a significant shift in the negative Christian perception about the Indian religious traditions on the one hand, and on the other, a critical approach towards transporting Western formulations of theology to India. There was a growing consciousness about the need for seeking a dynamic relationship between the Christian faith and the Indian culture in intelligibly communicating the message of the gospel in India.[100] Therefore, despite their divergent theological positions, Christian theologians of all confessions became convinced of the usefulness of the Sanskrit tradition in charting a way forward for the gospel into the Hindu world. They were optimistic about the usefulness of the Sanskrit language and employed it, "destigmatizing it as a vehicle of Brahminical ethnic domination and transformed it into a vehicle for Christian proclamation."[101]

However, the Sanskrit paradigm as an instrument of Christian theological articulation was challenged by the emergence of Indian liberation (subaltern) theologies. Theological formulations from the Sanskrit strand of thought largely founded on the experience of elite caste Hindu groups came to be seen as oppressive to the Dalit and Tribal communities. According to

---

99. See Tennent, "Contextualizing the Sanskritic Tradition," 344–45.

100. See Kuruvila, *Word Became Flesh*, 201.

101. Tennent, "Contextualizing the Sanskritic Tradition," 345.

An Indian Trinitarian Theology of *Missio Dei*

the subaltern theologians, theological constructs rooted in the experience of the upper caste elites of the Hindu society fail to reflect the subaltern communities's experience of age-long suffering and oppression caused by those forces that ironically the Sanskrit paradigm represents. The Sanskrit tradition has been instrumental at the hands of the Hindu elites in disenfranchising the subaltern communities. Therefore, Indian liberation theologies such as Dalit and Tribal theologies distanced themselves from the Sanskrit theological tradition.[102]

Despite the fact that the Sanskrit tradition was made to play a hegemonic and oppressive role, one cannot dismiss altogether a tradition that has over the centuries shaped the religious beliefs and culture as well as the worldview of the people of India including the subaltern communities, and exerted a pan-Indian intellectual and spiritual influence. Interestingly, the word "Dalit" itself is derived from the Sanskrit root, "dal" which means "split," "break," "crack," "crushed," "broken," and so on.[103] It is an indisputable fact that the Sanskrit paradigm has contributed immensely towards an indigenized theological expression of the Christian faith in India. This does not imply discounting the questions raised by counter theologies against the expediency of the Sanskrit strand in the contemporary theological and mission discourse in view of its association with Brahminism.

While one might concede the justification behind the subaltern theologies's rejection of Brahminical religion as oppressive, it is rather unrealistic to seek a wholesale rejection of the Sanskrit tradition as vitiated. It is quite important to note that the Dalits and other subaltern communities might find support from the anti-Brahminical strands within the Sanskrit tradition itself. There have been instances from within the Hindu scriptures that refute the supremacy and privileges of Brahmins. *Vajrasucika* Upanishad, for instance, denies that one becomes Brahmin by birth, or because of one's knowledge or duties. Privilege of greatness and wisdom, according to the Upanishad, are open to all regardless of their caste or birth.[104] Similarly, according to Shankara, right knowledge of the self is beyond any distinctions of caste.[105] One might notice subversive elements within Buddhism and Jainism which question the authority of the Vedas and reject the

---

102. See Tennent, "Contextualizing the Sanskritic Tradition," 345–46; Prabhakar, *Towards a Dalit Theology*; Nirmal and Devasahayam, *Reader in Dalit Theology*.

103. Sadangi, *Emancipation of Dalits*, 130.

104. *Vajrasucika Upanishad* 5–9 (Radhakrishnan, *Principal Upanishads*, 936–38).

105. Deutsch and Buitenen, *Source Book of Advaita Vedanta*, 153.

Towards an Indian Trinitarian Theology of Missio Dei

religious supremacy of the Brahmins.[106] Similarly, there have been groups within Hinduism while accepting the Vedas protested against the established Hindu doctrines and practices such as the caste system. Vishnavism and Tantrism, particularly, the Left-Handed Tantrism are the other two important dissenting movements within Hinduism that challenged Brahminical supremacy.[107] The Bhakti movement of the 12th and subsequent centuries represents a revolt against Brahmins's hegemony over spirituality often under Brahmin patronage. It was Brahmin *Acharyas* (teachers or scholars) like Rāmānuja, Mādhava, Rāmānanda, Vallabha, and Chaitanya who championed Bhakti movement which attracted Dalit spiritual leaders like Ravidass, Chokhamela, Namdev, and others.[108] Rāmānuja is said to have been sympathetically disposed towards the lowly and the poor. This is often illustrated by a story according to which Rāmānuja disclosed the meaning of the *Astakshari Mantra* to all people without discrimination based on caste or creed, much to the displeasure of his revered Master Tirukottiyar Nambi who revealed to him the *Mantra*. The sacred *Mantra* is believed to have the potential of liberating everyone who repeats it under proper guidance, and Rāmānuja did not want to exclude anyone from this spiritual benefit including the outcastes.[109] This sympathetic disposition as well as the instances of dissenting voices and protest movements must be seen as providing a historical continuity between subaltern theologies and Sanskrit tradition. One could see in the protest movements and subversive elements within the Sanskrit strands the aspirations of Dalits and Tribals for equality and freedom and their fight against the unjust social structures of contemporary times. Dalit and Tribal theologies would only stand to gain by searching for resources of knowledge and recapturing the insights available in the dissenting movements of the Sanskrit tradition and appropriating them. Perhaps these dissenting strands should form subject matter for contemporary Indian theological discourses and their usefulness or otherwise for the mission of the church be appraised.

The pioneers of Indian Christian theology recognized the importance of the Sanskrit tradition to serve the cause of Christian faith in India. Upadhyay was one of those earliest Christians to have explored the potential of

---

106. Kinsley, *Cultural Perspective Hinduism*, 56.

107. Kinsley, *Cultural Perspective Hinduism*, 59–63. Tantrism is a movement within Hinduism combining magical and mystical elements and with sacred writings of its own.

108. Paswan and Jaideva, *Encyclopaedia of Dalits*, 29–30.

109. Narasimhacharya, *Sri Ramanuja*, 30–31.

An Indian Trinitarian Theology of *Missio Dei*

the Sanskrit paradigm for the interpretation of the gospel and the building of an Indian Christianity. This provided him with a framework for restating the Christian faith in more intelligible ways and bringing Christian faith in dialogue with Vedanta philosophy. In this regard, Lipner observes that "the Hindu phenomenon is so malleable both as to *theoria* and *praxis* that it continues to provide endless opportunities for dialogue and indigenization through its Sanskritic forms."[110] Sanskrit tradition, which is largely representative of Hinduism, has a great sway over the culture of India. Upadhyay found the Sanskrit tradition was best suited to his objective of indigenizing the Christian faith in India. He recognized that religion is always closely related to the cultural environment where it finds itself and it is true for Christianity as well. Therefore, in Upadhyay's view, the Christian faith in India will not take root and grow unless it is grounded in the Indian culture which is significantly influenced by Sanskrit tradition. Indian culture is Hinduism, not as a religion, but as cultural and social reality.[111] In that sense, Upadhyay regarded Advaita Vedanta as instrumental in articulating the Christian faith in the Indian cultural frame for the mission of the Indian church, and for constructing Christianity on Indian foundations.

INDIAN TRINITARIAN THEOLOGY IN GLOBAL CONVERSATION

The shift of Christianity's center from the West to the global South is regarded as a very remarkable development in the modern history of the Church. With the unprecedented growth of the church in Asia, Africa, and Latin America, Christianity has now become predominantly a non-Western religion, truly a global religion. This demographic move of Christianity comes with significant implications for how the biblical faith and doctrines are interpreted and understood in a global context of varied cultural and religious traditions.[112] The Christian West has always remained the center of theological discourse, and the Western theological formulations have long been regarded as benchmark for the rest of the churches globally. The cross-cultural expansion of Christianity raises questions about this normativity of Western theology in the context of the

---

110. Lipner, "Brahmabandhab Upadhyay," 183.

111. See Tennent, *Building Christianity*, 300–354.

112. See Netland, "Introduction," 14–34. See also Tennent, *Theology*, 8–14; Jenkins, *New Face of Christianity*.

church's explosive growth in the global South.[113] These new situations underscore the necessity of formulating theologies that will be sensitive and pertinent to those particular contexts and cultures as well as address questions and challenges they pose. This would imply that the Christian theological discourse in the majority world would be informed by dialogue with the living traditions, culture, and social environments that condition the life of people who embrace the Christian faith.[114] It is important to note that today indigenous theologies emerge from mission engagements with non-Christian cultures which was characteristic of the early church's missionary encounter in the Graeco-Roman world.

In the early church's mission movements, the Christian faith was brought into conversation with other cultures in order that the message of the gospel would be made relevant and meaningful to those contexts. Precedents to this Christian dialogue with the Hellenistic culture are found in the New Testament itself. Christian theology in the New Testament began taking shape in mission engagements with the Hellenistic religious, cultural, and social milieus of the time. Thus, "in the New Testament theological concerns are grounded in the *missio Dei*."[115] As David Bosch observes, the early church, "because of its missionary encounter with the world, was forced to theologize."[116] Therefore, the "beginnings of a missionary theology" also became the "beginnings of Christian theology."[117]

As Andrew Walls observes, Christian concepts originated in the Jewish context had to be translated into the culture and language of the Greek world as Christianity began to expand beyond the confines of Palestine. In bringing the message of the gospel to the Greek world, "a new conceptual vocabulary had to be constructed. Elements of vocabulary already existing in that world had to be commandeered and turned towards Christ."[118] The new categories and languages, for instance, the idea of *logos*, began to shape the Christian doctrines in the changed environment and they received new meanings. This reception of new meaning and formation of theology's identity as a process in mission encounters with cultures and languages have continued even to our times. In Andrew Walls's words, "Christianity

---

113. Tennent, *Theology*, 11.
114. See Walls, *Missionary Movement*, 7.
115. Shenk, "Recasting Theology of Mission," 98.
116. Bosch, *Transforming Mission*, 16.
117. Kasting, *Die Anfänge der urchristlichen Mission*, 127.
118. Walls, *Missionary Movement*, xvii.

An Indian Trinitarian Theology of *Missio Dei*

is a generational process, an ongoing dialogue with culture," which continues to shape Christian theology across cultures in its contemporary global transmission.[119] Today, it is through such cultural conversation and the "theological translatability" that the message of the gospel is made meaningful and relevant to myriads of cultures, languages, and religious traditions and indigenous theologies are articulated.[120]

The beginning of Christian theological reflections in India offers a classic example of how theology emerges in mission encounter with religious and cultural settings. The second chapter of this book has revealed how Christian theological discourse was initiated not by Christians, but by English educated Hindu reformers in missionary situations of dialogue between Hinduism and Christianity. Interestingly, the Christian doctrine of the Trinity was an important part of that Hindu-Christian dialogue as may be seen in the different responses of Roy and Sen. Perhaps the Trinity could be termed as the starting point of Hindu-Christian dialogue and catalyst for the emergence of Christian theology in India. This dialogue, from the Christian side, was led not by native Indians, but by a Western missionary, Joshua Marshman. Christian theological reflection in a non-Western context, initiated by a Hindu, responded to by a Western missionary, and carried out further by Hindu converts to Christian faith is perhaps a unique development in modern Christian history. The pioneers of Indian Christian theology, such as K. M. Banerjea, Brahmabandhab Upadhyay, A. J. Appasamy, and many others further pursued this Hindu-Christian dialogue in their attempts to develop an indigenous theology.

However, despite the significant advances Indian Christian theology has made over a century, theological and missiological reflections in India have not been adequately recognized and brought on the global landscape of theological discourse. Indian Christian theology, like other non-Western world theologies, remains on the periphery of the global theological table. Western theology and Christian history continue to be regarded as points of departure to which non-Western theological contributions are considered ancillary at best. The continuing expansion and vibrancy of Christianity in the South and the emerging indigenous theological expressions from the experience and life situations of the majority world call for more recognition and respectable

---

119. Walls, *Missionary Movement*, xvii.

120. Tennent, *Theology*, 2. Tennent calls the process of "the shift in theological discourse, whereby the universal truths of the gospel are being revisited and retold in new, global contexts," "*theological translatability*."

Towards an Indian Trinitarian Theology of Missio Dei

space within the global theological enterprise. The study on Augustine and Brahmabandhab Upadhyay undertaken in this book demonstrates that such an attempt is both possible and necessary.

Upadhyay was a pioneer who dared to break new grounds for Christian theology and mission in India, which was pursued by the succeeding generation of Indian theologians. Despite the fact that a Protestant priest led Upadhyay to Christian faith, he was drawn to the Roman Catholic Church for its grander and more global vision. He felt that Protestantism was beholden to the British colonialist presence. On the other hand, he found trinitarianism in Catholicism as he discovered the *missio Dei* world of the Roman Catholic Church. He came under the profound influence of Thomas Aquinas, who became the source for much of Upadhyay's theology.[121] The reason he found Aquinas so compelling was that the latter's entire project was based on his reconciliation of Christian theology with Aristotelian philosophy. Since Upadhyay's project was to make Indian Christianity use the thoughts forms of Advaitism, he was drawn to Aquinas.

The theological formulation seen in the work of Upadhyay and the successive Indian theologians has a missiological mooring to it. The activity of theologizing has been undertaken with a view to the relevance of the gospel and its acceptability in the religious and cultural matrix of India. As observed in the third chapter of this book, Upadhyay's particular concern was to build an indigenous Christianity on Indian foundations. This, for him, was the Hindu philosophy as represented in the Advaita Vedanta of Shankara. Towards this objective, Upadhyay has made a significant contribution to the larger theological discourse by bringing the Christian faith in dialogue with the Advaita Vedanta. In particular, his restatement of the Christian doctrine of the Trinity in terms of *saccidānanda*, and his attempt to expound the trinitarian mystery in the Vedanta language without moving away from the Scripture and the ecumenical creeds of the Church constitute a remarkable achievement. Upadhyay's Vedantic interpretation of the Trinity was undertaken as part of his larger mission objective. To such an extent, his *saccidānanda* restatement prefigured the concept of the *missio Dei*. Trinitarian exposition of *saccidānanda* is a remarkable example of contextualizing Christian theology in the majority world, and it points to the need for indigenous expression of the Christian faith in the continuing expansion of Christianity.

---

121. Tennent, *Building Christianity*, 152.

An Indian Trinitarian Theology of *Missio Dei*

CONCLUSION

The trinitarian theologies of St. Augustine and Brahmabandhab Upadhyay offer thoughtful insights in formulating an Indian trinitarian *missio Dei* theology. The concept of the *missio Dei* drawn from the trinitarian theology of Augustine with its teaching on God's mission as originating in the trinitarian nature of God, the Father, the Son and the Holy Spirit, and their inner trinitarian relationality and communion is an important resource for formulating an Indian theology of mission informed by the doctrine of the Trinity. As discussed earlier, trinitarian theology is yet to gain a central place in Indian theological discourse which has often been Christology-centered. Similarly, the doctrine of the Holy Spirit has not been sufficiently brought to bear upon Indian theological reflection. A trinitarian undergirding of theological and missiological discourse is important as discussed in this chapter and it has great implications for the Indian church's contexts of mission. There are certain key identifiable areas in the life of the Indian church and its witness that would require trinitarian underpinning. This necessity is particularly visible in the Indian indigenous church movements represented in the remarkable growth of Pentecostal/charismatic churches. A robust ecclesiology and a conception of mission informed by the doctrine of the Trinity is quite central for the indigenous church movements in capturing the vision of the Church as founded on the trinitarian communion of God and its mission flowing from that trinitarian foundation of the Church. A trinitarian imagination is also important for the Indian church's mission in the context of struggle for freedom, equality, and justice represented in the suffering of the Dalit and Tribal communities. The dimension of relationality founded in the loving communion and self-giving of the Triune persons of the Godhead must form an important component of an Indian trinitarian *missio Dei*.

The study of *saccidānanda* in relation to the Trinity that Upadhyay has undertaken in missional context points to the need of contextualizing Christian theology in terms of Indian tradition and culture for the larger purpose of mission. Hence, Upadhyay's appropriation of the Advaita Vedanta offers the possibility of contextualizing the Christian faith in an effort to build Christianity on Indian foundations. His restatement of *saccidānanda* is regarded as an example of how the appropriation of categories from the Sanskrit tradition can contribute to the indigenization of Christianity and thus serve the mission of the church in India. This Sanskrit paradigm as an instrument in restating Christian theology in India continues to be relevant even in the face of the emerging liberation/subaltern theologies which are often dismissive of the Sanskrit paradigm and seek to distance from it. The Sanskrit tradition appropriated by Upadhyay demonstrates the richness of the religious and cultural categories that can be appropriated for developing indigenous theological expression in the context of the global expansion of Christianity. However, these indigenous theological formulations are yet to be granted a hearing in the global scene and brought into conversation with mainstream theological discourse.

Conclusion

THIS MONOGRAPH, UNDERTAKEN IN the larger context of modern trinitarian renaissance and Indian Christian theology, has sought to demonstrate that the trinitarian theologies of St. Augustine and the Indian theologian, Brahmabandhab Upadhyay, could provide conceptual resources for the construction of a Christian theology of mission relevant for the Indian context. The trinitarian theology of Augustine lays the foundation for a Christian theology of mission understood as *missio Dei*. The appropriation of the Advaita Vedanta concept of *saccidānanda* in the trinitarian theology of Upadhyay offers terminology and concepts for contextualizing a Christian understanding of God for an Indian setting. In this process, this study has illustrated the importance of the universal dimension of the Christian faith and its contextual articulation by attempting to study Augustine's trinitarian theology in relation to its indigenous representation explored by Upadhyay for an Indian context. While Augustine can be regarded as representing a classical Western expression of the Christian doctrine, Upadhyay calls for its indigenous expression and cultural relevance. As part of this exercise, this book has sought to explore how trinitarian theologies of these two Christian thinkers can provide perspectives that can inform a trinitarian theology of *missio Dei* for the Indian context.

Although the modern concept of the *missio Dei* is relatively a recent theological and missiological development, this book has attempted to show that its root could be traced back to Augustine's trinitarian doctrine. In Augustine's trinitarian thought, God's mission takes place in the outward movement of the Triune God, in the Father's sending (*missio*) of the Son and the Holy Spirit into the world which occurs in the manifestation of the Son in the incarnation and the Spirit at Pentecost. This *missio* of God is a central event in the economy of salvation which is revelatory wherein mission itself is a revelation of the Triune God, as well as reconciliatory, as humanity is reconciled to God through the redemptive work of the Son. In Augustine's construal of the Trinity, mission is located in the relational and communal life of the Triune God. This study has argued that the doctrine of the Trinity, particularly its relational and communitarian dimensions, should be seen as essential to an Indian theology of mission.

This work has underscored the importance of a trinitarian imagination in the expression of Christian faith and practice of Christian mission. This trinitarian vision has implications for how mission should be perceived in an Indian context and beyond. Mission theology informed by the doctrine of the Trinity helps create a holistic view of Christian mission integrating the vertical and horizontal dimensions of life, the cultural and evangelistic mandate, where the gospel is proclaimed both in word and deed. God's mission, as Augustine has shown, flows out of the trinitarian self-relatedness and love of the Triune God and is manifested in the incarnation of the Son. Mission is the display of God's openness to the world in salvation history and the plenitude of the trinitarian love in which the Father goes out to redeem the world in the sending (*missio*) of the Son and the Spirit. God's mission focuses on the restoration of creation and humanity to the communion of the Trinity and to the worship and glory of the one and only God. This is the overarching vision to which the Scripture points and to which mission bears witness.

Therefore, mission must be seen beyond salvation and humanization of evangelical and ecumenical polarities. God's mission transcends individual salvation of Christian piety and the social gospel of theological liberalism. The ultimate goal of mission is to gather everything in Christ, into the eternal relationship and communion of the Triune God (Eph 1:10; John 17:21–26). The restored creation and the redeemed humanity are taken on in the mystery of the trinitarian communion, within the perichoretic life of God. This trinitarian vision must be seen as a corrective to the contemporary obsession with the reductionism and radicalization (secularization and horizontalization) of mission. Since mission originates in the nature of the Triune God and in his sovereign intentionality, it ought to transcend the temporal reality of the here and now and must encompass a grand narrative of an eternal reality of the Triune God. As Newbigin points out, "All things have been created that they may be summed up in Christ the Son. All history is directed towards that end. All creation has this as its goal. The Spirit of God, who is also the Spirit of the Son, is given as the foretaste of that consummation, as the witness to it, and as the guide of the Church on the road towards it."[1] In the meantime, the Church is gathered into the trinitarian communion in worship and in sacrament in the here and now—in the celebration and remembrance of that event which brought the Church into the triune fellowship in the breaking of the bread and sharing of the cup—only to be sent again into the world to bear witness to God's mission until the final gathering in the *eschaton*.[2]

Augustine's insistence on the inseparability of the Father, the Son, and the Holy Spirit in their being and operations could well be taken as a corrective to the deficiency of an adequate patrology and pneumatology, and to a virtual and exclusive focus of Christology in mission theology. As noted by the renowned Russian Orthodox theologian, Sergius Bulgakov, "*In concreto*, trinitarian theology is patrology, Christology, and pneumatology, all three."[3] Then, if mission is the *missio Dei*, it must be seen as patrological, Christological, and pneumatological—of the Father, of the Son, and of the Holy Spirit. As noted by Lesslie Newbigin, a true doctrine of mission is not Christological only, but it must also make large space for the Father and the Holy Spirit.[4] This triadic pattern underlies the New Testament witness to mission. God the Father is the initiator and source of the *missio Dei*; God the Son is the embodiment of the *missio Dei*; God the Holy Spirit is the empowering presence of the *missio Dei*.[5] This primacy of all three divine persons in mission is beautifully encapsulated by the Catholic theologian, Kilian McDonnell thus: "The Father sends the Son in the Spirit to touch and transform the world and church, leading them in the Spirit, through the Son / Christ to the Father."[6] It is only a trinitarian theology that can safeguard the centrality of the place of the three persons of the Godhead in mission.

While in Augustine we find a theological framework for a trinitarian *missio Dei* theology, Upadhyay's restatement of the Christian concept of

1. Newbigin, *Trinitarian Faith and Today's Mission*, 78.
2. Hoffmeyer, "Missional Trinity," 109–10.
3. Bulgakov, *Comforter*, 7.
4. Newbigin, *Trinitarian Faith and Today's Mission*, 31.
5. For a detailed exposition of this, see Tennent, *Invitation to World Missions*, 75–101.
6. McDonnell, *Other Hand of God*, 91.

Conclusion

Trinity using the Upanishadic and philosophic category of *saccidānanda* may be seen as accentuating the necessity of a contextual theology that takes into consideration the Indian philosophical and cultural categories for the expression of Christian faith in India. This trinitarian exposition in the Indian thought forms and cultural categories was a pioneering experiment aimed at indigenizing the Christian gospel with a much larger missional objective. In dialogue with Advaita Vedanta, Upadhyay has enriched Indian Christian theology with languages and expressions from the Sanskrit tradition in translating the Christian doctrine for the Indian context. This attempt is regarded as an important step forward in demonstrating the usefulness of the Indian philosophical and cultural thought-forms and languages in indigenizing Christian theology in India.

However, indigenized expression of theology, for Upadhyay, did not mean the dilution of the central message of the Christian faith or its universal validity. Rather, he was attempting at what is today called cultural and theological translatability, restating the universal truths of the gospel which is culturally sensitive and contextually relevant.[7] His restatement of the Trinity through the use of Advaita Vedanta may be regarded as a classic example of cultural and theological translatability. This may be seen as a balancing act. Balancing of the universal truth of the Christian faith and the particular demands of the local contexts is very important in the context of global Christianity as well as in view of the native and contextual theologies that emerge from different locations. It is a necessary and important part of Christian mission that the gospel address the local concerns of particular contexts. Applying the biblical truth to local issues or situations shows the ongoing and universal relevance of the gospel.

However, the appropriation of the Sanskrit paradigm as a tool for indigenization has often been challenged for its long association with Brahminical ethnic particularity. This book has attempted to argue that, while recognizing the association of the Sanskrit tradition with Brahminical ethnicity, one cannot overlook voices of dissent within the Sanskrit tradition against Brahminism, which in itself could be regarded as a liberating resource for the subaltern movements, providing them with historical continuity with past anti-Brahminical movements.

Upadhyay's theological articulation for an Indian context is part of a larger Indian theological project, spanning over a century. During this period, India has produced remarkable indigenous theological reflections which

---

7. See Tennent, *Theology*, 2.

An Indian Trinitarian Theology of *Missio Dei*

are slowly finding their rightful place in global theological discourse. The development of indigenous theologies signifies the necessity for contextual theologies and it is all the more important in view of the momentous movement of Christianity from the global north to the global south.

The two theological figures examined in this study—Augustine and Upadhyay—while differing in their historical contexts and particular concerns, shared a common conviction regarding the centrality of the doctrine of the Trinity for Christian faith. Augustine employed a trinitarian *missio Dei* concept within his larger purpose of defending the Nicene doctrine of the Trinity against Arianism. On the other hand, Upadhyay used the trinitarian discourse within his larger mission objective as a tool to show the way forward for the mission of the church in India. Despite these different historical contexts, mission and Trinity became quite central in their respective theological projects. I have argued that their trinitarian insights can be brought together as independent voices in providing conceptual resources for a Christian theology of mission in India that can help to remedy perceived defects of existing mission theology and practice in the Indian churches. The lines of arguments presented in this book invite further development and research. As such, this book is understood as a prolegomena to and preparation for a future development of an Indian *missio Dei* theology such as the one introduced here.

Sanskrit Glossary

Advaita Vedanta: A school of Hindu philosophy often called a monistic or non-dualistic system, according to which Brahman is the only one reality, the impersonal Absolute about which one cannot posit any qualities. The chief exponent of Advaita Vedanta was Shankara (Adi Shankara or Shankaracharya).

Aham Brahmāsmi: A great saying in the Upanishad which means "I am Brahman (the Absolute)." It is used to describe the unity of the Atman (individual self or soul) with Brahman (the Absolute).

Antaryāmin: The inner spirit, the inner principle, the inner guide, the indweller who/which dwells within. It is the form in which the ultimate reality exists in a very subtle manner in the hearts of all living beings.

Asanga: Used to express the unrelated-ness or nonattachment of Brahman to anything outside of itself. Brahman cannot be defined by relationship because Brahman is *asanga*.

Atman: The innermost essence of individual self which is identical with the universal self, the eternal principle. Brahman as the universal principle and Atman as the human essence are regarded as ultimately the same.

Avatār: Descent, a term used to describe the manifestation of God in physical form for the restoration of righteousness (dharma) in the world.

Sanskrit Glossary

Bhakti: Loving devotion, faith, and surrender to a personal god in Hinduism. *Bhakti* was also a movement in Hinduism which was marked by mutual intense emotional attachment and love between a devotee and a personal god.

Brahman: The Supreme, the Absolute, and the all-pervading reality in Hinduism, apart from whom, there is no reality, and as described in the Upanishads, the one which is the source of all things. (See Advaita Vedanta). Brahman is devoid of all qualities and distinctions within or outside Brahman.

Brahman, *Nirguṇa*: This refers to Brahman conceived as being impersonal without any attributes and external relations.

Brahman, *Saguṇa*: This is Brahman conceived as having qualities referring to the ultimate reality in personal terms.

Brahmo Samaj (Society of Brahma): A theistic reform movement within Hinduism, founded by Raja Ram Mohan Roy in the early part of the nineteenth century. Roy was influenced by the teachings of Christ as well as Islam and sought to incorporate them into his newly formed *Samaj*. *Brahmo Samaj* denounced polytheism, idol worship, and caste system practiced in Hinduism, and sought to reform Hinduism from within.

***Maya*:** Fundamental concept in Hinduism, especially in Shankara's Advaita Vedanta philosophy, which refers to misperception of the phenomenal world as being real whereas it is not.

Parabrahman: It refers to Brahman as the supreme, the highest, and totally transcendent reality. For Shankara, the Brahman is Parabrahman, the "higher Brahman" who is distinguished from the "lower Brahman," *aparabrahman* (*Īśvara*). This distinction between a higher and lower Brahman is one of the hallmarks of Shankara's advaita.

***Paramārthika*:** Absolutely real, the highest level of reality in Advaita Vedanta.

Prajāpati (Lord of creatures): A name often appears in the early Vedic texts referring several gods; but in the later texts, *Prajapati* is referred to as a single deity, a supreme god, creator of heaven and earth, and the lord of creatures, who is frequently identified with Brahman.

Sanskrit Glossary

Rāmānuja: Hindu philosopher (ca. 1017–1137 AD), who is regarded as the chief proponent of the *Vishishtadvaita* (modified non-dualism or qualified monism) branch of Vedanta and widely regarded as one of the most influential Indian thinkers.

Saccidānanda: A compound form of three Sanskrit words, *Sat* (being) *Cit* (intelligence or consciousness), and *Ānanda* (bliss) which refers to the ultimate reality. This is regarded as a complete description of Brahman in the Hindu scriptures.

Sāyujya: The final stage of spiritual progress where the devotee feels him/herself as being identical with God.

Shankara (Shankaracharya): Eighth-century Hindu thinker who is regarded as the most renowned Indian philosopher and theologian and the chief exponent of the Advaita Vedanta School of philosophy. Shankara consolidated the doctrine of Advaita Vedanta and is believed to have laid the foundations of modern Hindu philosophical thought.

Tantrism: System of ritual exercise followed in certain sects in Hinduism and Buddhism. It is believed that this spiritual practice leads the practitioner to liberating knowledge.

Tat tvam asi: One of the great sayings (*mahavakyas*) in the Chandogya Upanishads of the *Sāma Veda*, translated as "that thou art" or "you are that," which is used to reinforce the identity of the individual self (atman) with the absolute self (Brahman), the all-pervading reality of the universe.

Upanishads: The final part of the Vedic corpus. The term literally means "to sit near devotedly." Upanishads are also called Vedanta because they are the concluding part of the Vedas.

Vishishtadvaita (modified non-dualism or qualified monism): One of the major schools of Vedanta, an orthodox school of Indian philosophy. The most prominent exponent of *Vishishtadvaita* was Rāmānuja.

Vyavahārika: Relative reality or dependent or contingent reality in Advaita Vedanta.

Bibliography

Aagaard, Johannes. "Trends in Missiological Thinking During the Sixties." *International Review of Mission* 62.245 (1973) 8–25.
Ables, Travis E. "The Decline and Fall of the West? Debates about the Trinity in Contemporary Christian Theology." *Religion Compass* 6.3 (2012) 163–73.
Aleaz, K. P. *Christian Thought Through Advaita Vedanta*. Delhi: ISPCK, 1996.
———. "The Theological Writings of Brahmabandhav Upadhyaya Re-Examined." *Indian Journal of Theology* 28.2 (1979) 55–77.
———. "Trinity as Sat-Chit-Ananda in the Thought of the Indian Theologian Brahmabandhav Upadhyaya." *Asia Journal of Theology* 23.1 (2009) 82–91.
Amaladoss, Michael. *Life in Freedom: Liberation Theologies in Asia*. Maryknoll, NY: Orbis, 1997.
Andersen, Wilhelm. *Towards a Theology of Mission: A Study of the Encounter Between the Missionary Enterprise and the Church and its Theology*. London: SCM, 1955.
Animananda, B. *The Blade: Life and Work of Brahmabandhab Upadhyay*. Calcutta: Roy & Sons, n.d.
Ann McDougall, Joy. "The Return of Trinitarian Praxis? Moltmann on the Trinity and the Christian Life." *The Journal of Religion* 83. 2 (2003) 177–203.
Appasamy, A. J. *Christianity as Bhakti Marga: A Study of the Johannine Doctrine of Love*. 3rd ed. Madras: Christian Literature Service, 1991.
———. *The Gospel and India's Heritage*. London: SPCK, 1942.
———. "The Indwelling God." In *The Christian Bhakti of A. J. Appasamy*, edited by T. Dayanandan Francis, 22–32. Madras: Christian Literature Society, 1992.
———. *Sadhu Sunder Singh*. 1958. Reprint, Cambridge: Lutterworth, 2002.
Aquinas, Thomas. *The Power of God*. Translated by Richard J. Regan. New York: Oxford University Press, 2012.
———. *The Trinity* (1a. 27–32). *Summa Theologiae*. Vol. 6. Edited by Ceslaus Velecky. London: Blackfriars, Eyre & Spottiswoode, 1965.
Arendt, Hannah. *Love and Saint Augustine*. Edited and with an Interpretative Essay by Joanna Vecchiarelli Scott and Judith Chelius Stark. Chicago: University of Chicago Press, 1995.

Bibliography

Athanasius. *Letters Concerning the Holy Spirit.* Translated by C.R B. Shapland. London: The Epworth Press, 1951.

Augustine. *Commentary on Paul's Epistle to the Galatians*, 45. Translated by Eric Antone Plumer. Oxford: Oxford University Press, 2003.

———. *Letters 100–155.* New York: New City, 2003.

———. *Letters 156–210.* New York: New City, 2004.

———. "Of True Religion." In *Earlier Writings*, edited by John H. S. Burleigh, 218–83. Library of Christian Classics. London: SCM, 1953. Reprint, Louisville: 2006.

———. *Sermons (341–400) on Various Subjects.* Translated by Edmund Hill. Edited by John E. Rotelle. New York: New City, 1995.

———. "The Spirit and the Letter." In *Augustine: Later Works.* Vol. 8. Library of Christian Classics. Philadelphia: Westminster, 1955.

———. *Trinity (De Trinitate).* Translated by Edmund Hill. 1991. Reprint, New York: New City, 2012.

Ayres, Lewis. *Augustine and the Trinity.* 2010. Reprint, Cambridge: Cambridge University Press, 2012.

———. "Augustine on the Trinity." In *Oxford Handbook of the Trinity*, edited by Giles Emery and Matthew Levering, 123–37. Oxford: Oxford University Press, 2011.

———. "Augustine on the Triune Life of God." In *The Cambridge Companion to Augustine*, edited by David V. Meconi and Eleonore Stump, 60–77. 2nd ed. Cambridge: Cambridge University Press, 2014.

———. "The Fundamental Grammar of Augustine's Trinitarian Theology." In *Augustine and His Critics: Essays in Honour of Gerald Bonner*, edited by Robert Dodaro and George Lawless, 51–76. London: Routledge, 2000.

———. "'Remember that You are Catholic' (serm. 2.2): Augustine on the Unity of the Triune God." *Journal of Early Christian Studies* 8.1 (2000) 39–82.

Baago, Kaj. "Indian Indigenous Theology." *International Review of Mission* 55.218 (1966) 221–25.

———. *Pioneers of Indigenous Christianity.* Bangalore: Christian Institute for the Study of Religion and Society; Madras: CLS, 1969.

Baillie, D. M. *God was in Christ: An Essay on Incarnation and Atonement.* New York: Scribner's Sons, 1948.

Balmes, James. *Fundamental Philosophy.* Vol. 2. Translated by Henry F. Brownson. New York: D. & J. Sadlier, 1856.

Banerjea, K. M. *Two Essays as Supplements to the Arian Witness.* Calcutta: Thacker, Spink & Co., 1880.

Barnes, Michel René. "Augustine in Contemporary Trinitarian Theology." *Theological Studies* 56 (1995) 237–50.

———. "Exegesis and Polemic in Augustine's *De Trinitate* I." *Augustinian Studies* 30 (1999) 43–60.

———. "Latin Trinitarian Theology." In *The Cambridge Companion to the Trinity*, edited by Peter Phan, 70–84. Cambridge: Cambridge University Press, 2011.

———. "The Visible Christ and the Invisible Trinity: Mt 5:8 in Augustine's Trinitarian Theology of 400." *Modern Theology* 19 (2003) 329–55.

Barron, Robert. "Augustine's Questions: Why the Augustinian Theology of God Matters Today." *Logos: A Journal of Catholic Thought and Culture* 10. 4 (2007) 35–54.

Barth, Karl. *Church Dogmatics.* Vol. 1.1. Translated by G. W. Bromley. 2nd ed. Edinburgh: T & T Clark, 1975.

Bibliography

———. *Church Dogmatics*. Vol. 1.2. Translated by G. T. Thomson and Harold Knight. Edinburgh: T & T Clark, 1956.
———. *Church Dogmatics*. Vol. 3.4. Translated by A. T. Mackay, et al. Edinburgh: T & T Clark, 1961.
———. *Church Dogmatics*. Vol. 4.3. Translated by G. W. Bromiley. Edinburgh: T & T Clark, 1962.
———. "Die Theologie und die Mission in der Gegenwart." *Zwischen den Zeiten* 10. 3 (1932) 189–215.
Barua, Ankur. "God's Body at Work: Rāmānuja and Panentheism." *International Journal of Hindu Studies* 14.1 (2010) 1–30.
Bauckham, Richard. "'Only the Suffering God can Help': Divine Passibility in Modern Theology." *Themelios* 9 (1984) 6–8.
Bassham, Rodger C. "Development and Tensions in Mission Theology: 1948–1975." PhD diss., Southern Methodist University, 1978.
Beckwith, Carl L. *Hilary of Poitiers on the Trinity: From De Fide to De Trinitate*. Oxford: Oxford University Press, 2008.
Bergunder, Michael. *The South Indian Pentecostal Movement in the Twentieth Century*. Grand Rapids: Eerdmans, 2008.
Berkhof, Hendrikus. *The Christian Faith: An Introduction to the Study of Faith*. Translated by Sierd Woudstra. Grand Rapids: Eerdmans, 1979.
Bevans, Stephen. "Wisdom from the Margins: Systematic Theology and the Missiological Imagination." *CTSA Proceedings* 56 (2001) 21–42.
Bevans, Stephen, and Roger P. Schroeder. *Constants in Context: A Theology of Mission for Today*. Maryknoll, NY: Orbis, 2004.
———. *Prophetic Dialogue: Reflections on Christian Mission Today*. Maryknoll, NY: Orbis, 2011.
Beyerhaus, Peter. "Mission and Humanization." *International Review of Mission* 60.237 (1971) 11–24.
Birkeli, F. "Svenska Prästforbundet." *Meddelande* 1 (1968) 28. Quoted in Aagaard, Johannes. "Trends in Missiological Thinking During the Sixties." *International Review of Mission* 62.245 (1973) 8–25.
Bochet, Isabelle. "The Hymn to the One in Augustine's *De Trinitate* IV." *Augustinian Studies* 38.1 (2007) 41–60.
Boff, Leonardo. *Holy Trinity: Perfect Community*. Translated by Philip Berryman. Maryknoll, NY: Orbis, 2000.
———. "Trinitarian Community and Social Liberation." *Cross Currents* 38.3 (1988) 289–308.
———. *Trinity and Society*. Translated by Paul Burns. Maryknoll, NY: Orbis, 1988.
Bonaventure. *The Works of Bonaventure*. Vols. 1 & 2. Translated by José de Vinck. New Jersey: St. Anthony's Guild, 1960–63.
Bosch, David J. *The Transforming Mission: Paradigm Shifts in Theology of Mission*. 1991. Reprint, Maryknoll, NY: Orbis, 2002.
Boyd, Robin. *India and the Latin Captivity of the Church: The Cultural Context of the Gospel*. Cambridge: Cambridge University Press, 1974.
———. *An Introduction to Indian Christian Theology*. Rev. ed. 1979. Reprint, Delhi: ISPCK/ITL, 1991.
Braaten, Carl E. "The Triune God: The Source and Model of Christian Unity and Mission." *Missiology: An International Review* 18.4 (1990) 415–27.

Bibliography

Brahma-Sūtra-Bhāṣya of Sri Śaṅkarācārya. Translated by Swami Gambhirananda. Calcutta: Advaita Ashram, 1965.

Bray, Gerald. "The Double Procession of the Holy Spirit in Evangelical Theology Today: Do We Still Need It?" *Journal of Evangelical Theological Society* 41.3 (1998) 415–26.

Bromiley, Geoffrey W. *Introduction to the Theology of Karl Barth*. Grand Rapids: Eerdmans, 1979.

Brück, Michael von. *The Unity of Reality: God, God-Experience, and Mediation in the Hindu-Christian Dialogue*. Translated by James V. Zeitz. New York: Paulist, 1986.

Bucur, Bogdan G. "Exegesis of Biblical Theophanies in Byzantine Hymnography: Rewritten Bible?" *Theological Studies* 68 (2007) 92–112.

———. "Theophanies and Vision of God in Augustine's *De Trinitate*: An Eastern Orthodox Perspective." *St Vladimir's Theological Quarterly* 52.1 (2008) 67–93.

Bulgakov, Sergius. *The Comforter*. Translated by Boris Jakim. Grand Rapids: Eerdmans, 2004.

Bürkle, Horst, and Wolfgang M. W. Roth. *Indian Voices in Today's Theological Debate*. Lucknow, India: Lucknow Publishing House, 1966.

Bussanich, John. "Plotinus's Metaphysics of the One." In *The Cambridge Companion to Plotinus*, edited by L. P. Gerson, 38–65. 1996. Reprint, New York: Cambridge University Press, 1999.

Calvin, John. *Institutes of the Christian Religion*. Translated by Henry Beveridge. 2008. Reprint, Peabody, MA: Hendrickson, 2009.

Cary, Philip. "On Behalf of Classical Trinitarianism: A Critique of Rahner on the Trinity." *Thomist* 56 (1992) 365–405.

Chakkarai, Vengal. "The Cross and Indian Thought." In *Vengal Chakkarai*, edited by P. T. Thomas, 199–383. Vol. 1. Bangalore: United Theological College, 1981.

———. "Jesus the Avatar." In *Vengal Chakkarai*, edited by P. T. Thomas, 42–198. Vol. 1. Bangalore: United Theological College, 1981.

Chan, Simon. *Liturgical Theology: The Church as Worshiping Community*. Downers Grove, IL: InterVarsity, 2006.

———. *Pentecostal Ecclesiology: An Essay on the Development of Doctrine*. Dorest, UK: Deo, 2011.

The Chandogya Upanishad and Sri Sankara's Commentary. Vol. 4. Translated by Ganganatha Jha. Madras: V. C. Seshacharri, 1923.

Channing, William E. "Unitarian Christianity." In *The Works of William E. Channing*. 367–84. Boston: American Unitarian Association, 1900.

Chatterjee, Sunil Kumar. "Our Theological Task VI: Review and Re-statement." *The Guardian* 25.6 (1947) 67–68.

———. "The Vedanta Philosophy and the Message of Christ." *India Journal of Theology* 4.2 (1955) 18–23.

———. *William Carey and Serampore*. Calcutta: Ghosh Publishing Concern, 1984.

Chenchiah, Pandipeddi. "Christian Message in a Non-Christian World." Appendix. In *Rethinking Christianity in India*, edited by D. M. Devasahayam and A. N. Sudarisanam, 1–54. Madras: Hogarth, 1938.

———. "Christianity and Hinduism." In *The Theology of Chenchiah: With Selections from His Writings*, edited by D. A. Thangasamy. Bangalore: CISRS and YMCA, 1966.

———. "Church and the Indian Christian." In *Rethinking Christianity in India*, edited by D. M. Devasahayam and A. N. Sudarisanam. Madras: Hogarth, 1938.

———. "Indian Christian Spiritual Discipline." In *The Theology of Chenchiah: With Selections from His Writings*, edited by D. A. Thangasamy. Bangalore: CISRS and YMCA, 1966.

———. "Jesus and Non-Christian Faiths." In *Rethinking Christianity in India*, edited by D. M. Devasahayam and A. N. Sudarisanam. Madras: Hogarth, 1938.

———. "Protest Against Barthianism." In *The Theology of Chenchiah: With Selections from His Writings*, edited by D. A. Thangasamy. Bangalore: CISRS and YMCA, 1966.

Chenchiah, Pandipeddi, et al. *Asramas: Past and Present*. Madras: Indian Christian Book Club, 1941.

Chia, Roland. "Trinity and Ontology: Colin Gunton's Ecclesiology." *International Journal of Systematic Theology* 9.4 (2007) 452–68.

Christopher, K. W. "Between Two Worlds: The Predicament of Dalit Christians in Bama's Works." *The Journal of Commonwealth Literature* 47.7 (2012) 7–25.

Clark, Mary T. "De Trinitate." In *The Cambridge Companion to Augustine*, edited by Eleonore Stump and Norman Kretzmann, 91–102. Cambridge: Cambridge University Press, 2001.

Clarke, Sathianathan. "Hindutva, Religious and Ethnocultural Minorities, and Indian-Christian Theology." *Harvard Theological Review* 95.2 (2002) 197–226.

———. "The Jesus of Nineteenth Century Indian Christian Theology: An Indian Inculturation with Continuing Problems and Prospects." *Studies in World Christianity* 5.1 (1999) 32–46.

Coffey, David. "The Holy Spirit as the Mutual Love of the Father and the Son." *Theological Studies* 51 (1990) 193–229.

Comer, Kim, et al., eds. *Wisdom of the Sadhu: Teachings of Sundar Singh*. Farmington, PA: Plough, 2007.

Cox, Harvey. *The Secular City: Secularization and Urbanization in Theological Perspective*. New York: Macmillan, 1965.

Cunningham, David S. *These Three Are One: The Practice of Trinitarian Theology*. 1998. Reprint, Oxford: Blackwell, 1999.

D'Costa, Gavin. *The Meeting of Religions and the Trinity*. Maryknoll, NY: Orbis, 2000.

Danam, B. "Indian Church: Its Response to Dalit Movement." *National Council of Churches Review* 120.3 (2000) 257–77.

Daniel, J. T. K. "Ecumenical Pragmatism of the Serampore Mission." In *Mission Paradigm in the New Millennium*, edited by W. S. Milton Jaganathan, 106–7. Delhi: ISPCK, 2000.

Darwish, Linda. "The Concept of the Mediator in Augustine's Understanding of the Trinity." *Didaskalia* 13.1 (2001) 61–86.

Davis, John Jefferson. *Worship and the Reality of God's Presence: An Evangelical Theology of Real Presence*. Downers Grove, IL: InterVarsity, 2010.

Detlev Schulz, Klaus. *Mission from the Cross: The Lutheran Theology of Mission*. St. Louis: Concordia, 2009.

Deutsch, Eliot, and J. A. B. van Buitenen. *A Source Book of Advaita Vedanta*. Honolulu: University Press of Hawaii, 1971.

Devanandan, P. D. *Christian Concern in Hinduism*. Bangalore: CISRS, 1961.

———. *I Will Lift up Mine Eyes unto the Hills: Sermons and Bibles Studies*. Edited by S. J. Samartha and Nalini Devanandan. Bangalore: CISRS, 1963.

Bibliography

———. *Preparation for Dialogue: A Collection of Essays on Hinduism and Christianity in New India*. Edited by Nalini Devanandan and M. M. Thomas. Bangalore: CISRS, 1964.
Devasahayam, D. M., and A. N. Sudarisanam, eds. *Rethinking Christianity in India*. Madras: Hogarth, 1938.
Devasahayam, V. "Doing Dalit Theology: Basic Assumptions." In *Frontiers of Dalit Theology*, edited by V. Devasahayam, 270–82. Madras: ISPCK/GURUKUL, 1996.
Dhavamony, Mariasusai. *Hindu-Christian-Dialogue: Theological Soundings and Perspectives*. Amsterdam/New York: Rodopi, 2002.
Drilling, Peter. "The Psychological Analogy of the Trinity: Augustine, Aquinas, and Lonergan." *Irish Theological Quarterly* 71 (2006) 320–37.
Dunham, Scott A. *The Trinity and Creation in Augustine: An Ecological Analysis*. Albany, NY: State University of New York Press, 2008.
Elders, Leo J. *The Philosophical Theology of St. Thomas Aquinas*. Leiden: Brill, 1990.
Engelsviken, Tormod. "*Missio Dei*: The Understanding and Misunderstanding of a Theological Concept of European Churches and Missiology." *International Review of Mission* 92.367 (2003) 481–97.
Faul, D. "Donatism." In *New Catholic Encyclopedia*, edited by Berard L. Marthaler, et al., 861–64. Vol. 4. Washington, DC: Catholic University of America Press and Gale, 2003.
Fallon, Pierre. "Christianity in Bengal." In *Studies in the Bengal Renaissance*, edited by Jagannath Chakavorty, 448–59. Rev. ed. Calcutta: National Council of Education, Bengal, 1977.
Feuerstein, Georg. *Tantra: The Path of Ecstasy*. Boston, MA: Shambhala, 1998.
Fiorenza, Francis Schüssler. "Schleiermacher's Understanding of God as Triune." In *Cambridge Companion to Friedrich Schleiermacher*, edited by Jacqueline Mariña, 171–88. Cambridge: Cambridge University Press, 2005.
Firth, Cyril Bruce. *An Introduction to Indian Church History*. Rev. ed. Madras: Senate of Serampore of College and CLS, 1989.
Flett, John G. *The Witness of God: The Trinity, Missio Dei, Karl Bath, and the Nature of Christian Community*. Grand Rapids: Eerdmans, 2012.
Flood, Gavin D. *An Introduction to Hinduism*. Cambridge: Cambridge University Press, 1996.
Fonseca, C. "A Prophet Disowned: Swami Upadhyaya Brahmabandhav." *Vidyajyoti Journal of Theological Reflection* 44 (1980) 177–94.
Fortman, Edmund J. *The Triune God: A Historical Study of the Doctrine of the Trinity*. Philadelphia, PA: Westminster, 1972.
Franke, John R. "God is Love: The Social Trinity and the Mission of God." In *Trinitarian Theology for the Church: Scripture, Community, Worship*, edited by Daniel J. Treier and David Lauber, 105–19. Downers Grove, IL: InterVarsity, 2009.
Freytag, Walter. "Changes in the Patterns of Western Missions." In *The Ghana Assembly of the International Missionary Council, 28th December, 1957 to 8th January, 1958: Selected Papers, with an Essay on the Role of the IMC*, edited by Ronald K. Orchard, 138–47. London: Edinburgh House, 1958.
———. *Reden und Aufsätze: Herausgegeben von Jan Hermelink und Hans Jochen Margull, Teil 2*. München: Kaiser Verlag, 1961. Quoted in Gensichen, Hans-Werner. "Walter Freytag 1899-1959: The Miracle of the Church Among the Nations." In *Mission*

Bibliography

Legacies: Biographical Studies of Leaders of the Modern Missionary Movement, edited by Gerald H. Anderson, et al. Maryknoll, NY: Orbis, 1994.
Frykenberg, Robert Eric. *Christianity in India: From Beginnings to the Present*. Oxford: Oxford University Press, 2008.
Fuellenbach, John. *Church: Community for the Kingdom*. Maryknoll, NY: Orbis, 2002.
Garbe, Richard. "St. Thomas in India." *The Monist* 25.1 (1915) 1–27.
Garg, Ganga Ram, ed. *Encyclopaedia of the Hindu World*. Vol. 2. New Delhi: Concept, 1992.
Gelder, Craig Van, and Dwight J. Zscheile. *The Missional Church in Perspective: Mapping Trends and Shaping the Conversation*. Grand Rapids: Baker Academic, 2011.
Giles, Kevin. *The Trinity & Subordinationism: The Doctrine of God and Contemporary Gender Debate*. Downers Grove, IL: InterVarsity, 2002.
Gioia, Luigi. *The Theological Epistemology of Augustine's De Trinitate*. 2008. Reprint, New York: Oxford University Press, 2009.
Gispert-Sauch, George. "The Sanskrit Hymns of Brahmabandhav Upadhyay." *Religion and Society* 19.4 (1972) 60–79.
Gladstone, J. W. "Mission and Evangelization in India: A Historical Perspective." In *Mission Paradigm in the New Millennium*, edited by W. S. Milton Jaganathan, 74–75. Delhi: ISPCK, 2000.
Gonsalves, Francis. *God of Our Soil: Towards Subaltern Trinitarian Theology*. Delhi: ISPCK/VIEWS, 2010.
Goodall, Norman, ed. *Missions under the Cross: Addresses Delivered at the Enlarged Meeting of the Committee of the International Missionary Council at Willingen, in Germany, 1952; with Statements issued by the Meeting*. Edinburgh House: London, 1953.
Gorantla, Johannes, and Anthoniraj Thumma. "Dalit Christians in the Third Millennium." In *The Church in India in the Emerging Third Millennium*, edited by Thomas D'Sa, 142–62. Bangalore: NBCLC, 2005.
Goreh, Nehemiah. *Letter to the Brahmos from a Converted Brahman of Benares*. Allahabad, India: Allahabad Mission, 1868.
———. *Objections to Catholic Doctrine*. Calcutta: Bishop's College, 1868.
———. *Proofs of the Divinity of Our Lord Stated in a Letter to a Friend*. n.p., 1887.
———. *A Rational Refutation of the Hindu Philosophical System*. Calcutta: Calcutta Christian Tract & Book Society, 1862.
Grabowski, Stanislaus J. *The Church: An Introduction to the Theology of St. Augustine*. St Louis, MO: B. Herder, 1957.
Grenz, Stanley J. *Rediscovering the Triune God: The Trinity in Contemporary Theology*. Minneapolis: Fortress, 2005.
Grimes, John A. *A Concise Dictionary of Indian Philosophy: Sanskrit Terms Defined in English*. New and rev. ed. Albany: State University of New York Press, 1996.
Guder, Darell L. "From Mission and Theology to Missional Theology." *Princeton Seminary Bulletin* 24.1 (2003) 36–54.
Günther, Wolfgang. "The History and Significance of World Mission Conferences in the Twentieth Century." *International Review of Mission* 92.367 (2003) 521–37.
Gunton, Colin E. "The Church on Earth: The Roots of Community." In *On Being the Church: Essays on the Christian Community*, edited by Colin E. Gunton and Daniel W. Hardy, 48–109. Edinburgh: T&T Clark, 1989.
———. *The Promise of Trinitarian Theology*. 3rd ed. Edinburgh: T & T Clark, 2003.

Bibliography

Gutiérrez, Gustavo. *A Theology of Liberation: History, Politics, and Salvation.* Translated and edited by Sister Caridad Inda and John Eagleson. Maryknoll, NY: Orbis, 1973.

Hanson, Anthony. "Theophanies in the Old Testament and the Second Person of the Trinity. A Piece of Early Christian Speculation." *Hermathena* 65 (1945) 67–73.

Hartenstein, Karl. "The *Augsburg Confession* and its Missiological Significance." Translated by Klaus D. Schulz. *Concordia Theological Quarterly* 65.1 (2001) 31–46.

———. "Theologische Besinnungen." In *Mission Zwischen Gestern und Morgen. Von Gestaltwandel der Weltmission der Christenheit im Licht der Konferenz des Internationalen Missionrates in Willingen*, edited by Walter Freytag, 54. Stuttgart: Evangelischer Missiosverlag, 1952. Quoted in Aagaard, Johannes. "Trends in Missiological Thinking During the Sixties." *International Review of Mission* 62.245 (1973) 8–25.

———. "Wozu nötigt die Finanzlage der Mission." *Evangelisches Missions-Magazin* 79 (1934) 217–29.

Hedlund, Roger E., ed. *Christianity is Indian: The Emergence of an Indigenous Community.* Delhi: ISPCK, 2000.

———. "Critique of Pentecostal Mission by a Friendly Evangelical." *Asian Journal of Pentecostal Studies* 8.1 (2005) 67–94.

———. "Glimpses of India Today: A Mission Approach for One Billion People." In *Mission at the Dawn of the Twenty-first Century: A Vision for the Church*, edited by Paul Varo Martinson, 122–33. Minneapolis, MN: Kirk House, 1999.

———. "Indian Instituted Churches: Indigenous Christianity Indian Style." *Mission Studies: Journal of the International Association for Mission Studies* 16.1 (1999) 26–42.

Hegel, G. W. F. *Lectures on the Philosophy of Religion.* Vol. 1. Translated by R. F. Brown, et al. Edited by Peter C. Hodgson. Berkeley: University of California Press, 1984.

———. *Lectures on the Philosophy of World History: Introduction.* Translated by H. B. Nisbet. 1975. Reprint, Cambridge: Cambridge University Press, 1984.

Heim, Mark. *The Depth of the Riches: A Trinitarian Theology of Religious Ends.* Grand Rapids: Eerdmans, 2000.

Hermann, Samuel Reimarus. *Fragments.* Translated by Ralph S. Fraser. Edited by Charles H. Talbert. 1970. Reprint, Chico, CA: Scholars, 1985.

Heron, A. C. "Who Proceedeth from the Father and the Son: The Problem of the Filioque." *Scottish Journal of Theology* 24.2 (1971) 49–167.

Hill, Edmund. "St. Augustine's De Trinitate: The Doctrinal Significance of its Structure." *Revue des Etudes Augustiniennes* 19 (1973) 277–86.

Hiriyanna, M. *The Essentials of Indian Philosophy.* London: George & Allen, 1960.

Hodgson, Leonard. *The Doctrine of the Trinity: Croall Lectures 1942-1943.* 1943. Reprint, London: Nisbet, 1951.

Hoedemaker, Bert. "The Legacy of J. C. Hoekendijk." *International Bulletin of Missionary Research* 19.4 (1995) 166–70.

Hoekendijk, J. C. "The Church in Missionary Thinking." *International Review of Mission* 41.3 (1952) 324–36.

———. *The Church Inside Out.* Translated by Isaac C. Rottenberg. Philadelphia: Westminster, 1966.

Hoffmeyer, John F. "The Missional Trinity." *Dialog: A Journal of Theology* 40.2 (2001) 108–111.

Holmes, Stephen R. "Trinitarian Missiology: Towards a Theology of God as Missionary." *International Journal of Systematic Theology* 8.1 (2006) 72–90.

Holzer, Vincent. "Karl Rahner, Hans Urs von Balthasar, and Twentieth-Century Catholic Currents on the Trinity." In *The Oxford Handbook of the Trinity*, edited by Gilles Emery and Matthew Levering, 314–27. Oxford: Oxford University Press, 2011.

Horton, Michael. "To Be or Not to Be: The Uneasy Relationship between Reformed Christianity and American Evangelicalism." *Modern Reformation* 17.6 (2008). http://www.modernreformation.org/default.php?page=articledisplay&var2=980.

Hrangkhuma, F. "Protestant Mission Trends in India." In *Mission Trends Today: Historical and Theological Perspective*, edited by Mattam, Joseph and Sebastian Kim, 37–54. Mumbai: St. Paul's, 1997.

Hudson, D. Dennis. *Protestant Origins in India: Tamil Evangelical Christian, 1706–1835*. Grand Rapids: Eerdmans, 2000.

Ipgrave, Michael. *Trinity and Inter Faith Dialogue: Plenitude and Plurality*. Bern: Peter Lang, 2003.

Jacobs, Stephen. *Hinduism Today*. New York: Continuum International, 2010.

Jaganathan, W. S. Milton, ed. *Mission Paradigm in the New Millennium*. Delhi: ISPCK, 2000.

Jathanna, O. V. "Indian Christian Theology: Methodological Reflections." *Bangalore Theological Forum* 18.2–3 (1986) 59–74.

Jenkins, Philip. *The New Face of Christianity: Believing the Bible in the Global South*. New York: Oxford University Press, 2006.

Jenson, Robert W. *Systematic Theology: The Triune God*. Vol. 1. New York: Oxford University Press, 1997.

———. *The Triune Identity: God According to the Gospel*. Philadelphia: Fortress, 1982.

Jeyaraj, Daniel. *Genealogy of the South Indian Deities: An English Translation of Bartholomäus Ziegenbalg's Original German Manuscript with a Textual Analysis and Glossary*. Oxford: RoutledgeCurzon, 2005.

Johanns, Pierre. *To Christ Through the Vedanta*. Vol. 1. Edited by Theo De Greeff and Joseph Patmury. Bangalore: United Theological College, 1996.

Johnson, Todd M. "Contextualization: A New-Old Idea Illustrations from the Life of an Italian Jesuit in Seventeenth-Century India." *International Journal of Frontier Missions* 4 (1987) 9–20.

Jongeneel, J. A. B., and J. M. van Engelen. "Contemporary Currents in Missiology." In *Missiology: An Ecumenical Introduction: Texts and Contexts of Global Christianity*, edited by A. Camps, et al., 438–57. Grand Rapids: Eerdmans, 1995.

Joseph, P. V. *Indian Interpretation of the Holy Spirit: An Appraisal of the Pneumatology of Appasamy, Chenchiah, and Chakkarai*. Delhi: NTC-ISPCK, 2007.

———. "Resurgence of Trinitarian Theology and Shaping of *Missio Dei* Theology." *Dharma Deepika: A South Asian Journal of Missiological Research* 20.2 (2016) 6–19.

Jowers, Dennis W. "Divine Unity and the Economy of Salvation in the *De Trinitate* of Augustine." *The Reformed Theological Review* 60.2 (2001) 68–84.

———. "An Exposition and Critique of Karl Rahner's Axiom: 'The Economic Trinity is the Immanent Trinity and Vice Versa.'" *Mid-America Journal of Theology* 15 (2004) 165–200.

Jüngel, Eberhard. *God as the Mystery of the World: On the Foundations of the Theology of the Crucified One in the Dispute Between Theism and Atheism*. Grand Rapids: Eerdmans, 1983.

———. *God's Being is in Becoming: The Trinitarian Being of God in the Theology of Karl Barth*. Edinburgh: T & T Clark, 2001.

Bibliography

Junker, Gunther. "Christ as Angel: The Reclamation of a Primitive Title." *Trinity Journal* 15.2 (1994) 221–50.
Kant, Immanuel. *Religion and Rational Theology*. Translated and edited by Allen W. Wood and George Di Giovanni. Cambridge: Cambridge University Press, 1996.
Kappen, Sebastian. *Jesus and Culture*. Vol. 1 of *Selected Writings of Sebastian Kappen*. Delhi: ISPCK, 2002.
———. *Jesus and Society*. Vol. 2 of *Selected Writings of Sebastian Kappen*. Delhi: ISPCK, 2002.
———. *Towards a Holistic Cultural Paradigm*. Tiruvalla, India: CSS, 2003.
Kasting, Heinrcih. *Die Anfänge der urchristlichen Mission*. Munich: Kaiser Verlag, 1969. Quoted in Bosch, David J. *The Transforming Mission: Paradigm Shifts in Theology of Mission*. 1991. Reprint, Maryknoll, New York: Orbis, 2002.
Kavunkal, Jacob. "Developing an Indian Missiology." *Vidyajyoti Journal of Theological Reflection* 63 (1999) 178–83.
———. "Indian Perspectives in Mission and Missiology." In *Emerging Indian Missiology: Context and Concepts*, edited by Joseph Mattaom and Joseph Valiamangalam, 155. Delhi: FOIM & ISPCK, 2006.
Kelly, Anthony. *The Trinity of Love: A Theology of the Christian God*. Wilmington, DE: Michael Glazier, 1989.
Kelly, J. N. D. *Early Christian Doctrines*. Rev. ed. New York: Harper & Row, 1978.
Kinsley, David R. *A Cultural Perspective Hinduism*. 2nd ed. Englewood Cliffs, NJ: Prentice-Hall, 1993.
Kirk, J. Andrew. *What is Mission? Theological Explorations*. Minneapolis: Fortress, 2000.
Klijn, Albertus Frederik Johannes. *The Acts of Thomas: Introduction, Text, Commentary*. Leiden: Brill, 1962.
Kline, Peter. "Participation in God and the Nature of Christian Community: Robert Jenson and Eberhard Jüngel." *International Journal of Systematic Theology* 13.1 (2011) 38–61.
Kloos, Kari. *Christ, Creation, and the Vision of God: Augustine's Transformation of Early Christian Theophany Interpretation*. Leiden: Brill, 2011.
Kolencherry, Antony. *Universality of Modern Hinduism: A Study of Brahma Samaj and its Contribution to Indian Christian Theology*. Bangalore: Asian Trading, 1984.
Kominiak, Benedict. *The Theophanies of the Old Testament in the Writing of St. Justin*. Washington: Catholic University of America Press, 1948.
Kopf, David. *British Orientalism and the Bengal Renaissance: The Dynamics of Indian Modernization 1773–1835*. Berkeley: University of California Press, 1969.
Kotsko, Adam. "Gift and *Communio*: The Holy Spirit in Augustine's *De Trinitate*." *Scottish Journal of Theology* 64.1 (2011) 1–12.
Krishnamacharya, V., and M. B. Narasimha Ayyangar, eds. *Vedāntasāra of Bhagavad Rāmānuja*. Translated by V. Krishnamacharya and M. B. Narasimha Ayyangar. Madras: Adyar Library, 1953.
Küng, Hans. *The Church*. Translated by Ray and Rosaleen Ockenden. New York: Sheed and Ward, 1967.
Kuruvila, K. P. *The Word Became Flesh: A Christological Paradigm for Doing Theology in India*. Delhi: ISPCK, 2002.
LaCugna, Catherine Mowry. *God for Us: The Trinity and Christian Life*. San Francisco: HarperSanFrancisco, 1991.

Bibliography

———. "Introduction." In Karl Rahner. *The Trinity*. Translated by Joseph Donceel, vii-xxi. New York: Crossroad, 2003.

———. "The Practical Trinity." *The Christian Century* 109.22 (1992) 678–82.

Lacy, Creighton. "The Legacy of Paul David Devanandan." *International Bulletin of Missionary Research* 5.1 (1981) 18–21.

Lancel, Serge. *St. Augustine*. Translated by Antonia Nevill. London: SCM, 2002.

Lang'at, Robert K. "Trinity and Missions: Theological Priority in Missionary Nomenclature." In *Trinitarian Theology for the Church: Scripture, Community, Worship*, edited by Daniel J. Treier and David Lauber, 161–81. Downers Grove, IL: InterVarsity, 2009.

Lehmann, Paul L., ed. "The Missionary Obligation of the Church." *Theology Today* 9.1 (1952) 20–38.

Limouris, Gennadios. "The Church as Mystery and Sign in Relation to the Holy Trinity in Ecclesiastical Perspectives." In *Church Kingdom World: The Church as Mystery and Prophetic Sign*, edited by Gennadios Limouris, 18–49. Geneva: WCC, 1986.

Lincicum, David. "Economy and Immanence: Karl Rahner's Doctrine of the Trinity." *European Journal of Theology* 14.2 (2005) 111–18.

Lipner, Julius J. "Brahmabandhab Upadhyay (1861–1907) and His Significance for Our Times." *Vidyajyoti Journal of Theological Reflection* 71.3 (2007) 165–84.

———. *Brahmabandhab Upadhyay: The Life and Thought of a Revolutionary*. Delhi: Oxford University Press, 1999.

———. Introduction to *The Writings of Brahmabandhab Upadhyay*, by Brahmabandhab Upadhyay. 2 vols. Edited and annotated by Julius J. Lipner and George Gispert-Sauch. Bangalore: United Theological College, 1991–2002.

Lobo, Bryan. "Tripersonalising the Parabrahman." In *A Hindu-Catholic: Brahmabandhab Upadhyay's Significance for Indian Christian Theology*, edited by Sebastian Painadath and Jacob Parappally, 154–85. Bangalore: Asian Trading, 2008.

Longchar, A. Wati. "The Need for Doing Tribal Theology." *Tribal Theology: A Reader*, edited by Shimreingam Shimray, 1–16. Jorhat, India: Eastern Theological College, 2003.

Lossky, Vladimir. *The Mystical Theology of the Eastern Church*. London: James Clarke, 1957.

———. *Orthodox Theology: An Introduction*. Translated by Ian and Ihita Kesarcodi-Watson. Crestwood, NY: St. Vladimir's Seminary, 1978.

Louth, Andrew. *St John Damascene: Tradition and Originality in Byzantine Theology*. New York: Oxford University Press, 2002.

Lytle, R. Matthew. "Perichoretically Embodied Ethics: A Biblical-Theological and Historical-Theological Analysis of the Importance of Perichoretic Relationship for Christian Ethics." PhD diss., Southern Baptist Theological Seminary, 2008.

Majumdar, A. K. "The Doctrine of Evolution in the Sankhya Philosophy." *The Philosophical Review* 34.1 (1925) 51–69.

Malkovsky, Bradley. "The Personhood of Śaṁkara's 'Para Brahman.'" *The Journal of Religion* 77.4 (1997) 541–62.

Manoussakis, John Panteleimon. "Theophany and Indication: Reconciling Augustinian and Palamite Aesthetics." *Modern Theology* 26.1 (2010) 77–89.

Marmion, Declan, and Rik Van Nieuwenhove. *An Introduction to the Trinity*. Cambridge: Cambridge University Press, 2011.

Bibliography

Mattaom, Joseph, and Joseph Valiamangalam, eds. *Emerging Indian Missiology: Context and Concepts*. Delhi: FOIM & ISPCK, 2006.

Matthews, Gareth B., and S. Marc Cohen. "The One and the Many." *The Review of Metaphysics* 21.4 (1968) 630–55.

Matthey, Jacques. "Missiology in the World Council of Churches: Update: Presentation, History, Theological Background and Emphases of the Most Recent Mission Statement of the World Council of Churches (WCC)." *International Review of Mission* 90.359 (2001) 427–43.

May, Peter. "The Trinity and Saccidānanda." *Indian Journal of Theology* 7.3 (1958) 92–98.

McCarthy, John F. "On the Procession of the Holy Spirit." *Living Tradition: Organ of the Roman Theological Forum* 66 (1996) 1–10.

McCarthy, Michael C. "An Ecclesiology of Groaning: Augustine, the Psalms, and the Making of Church." *Theological Studies* 66 (2005) 23–48.

McDonnell, Kilian. *The Other Hand of God: The Holy Spirit as the Universal Touch and Goal*. Collegeville, MN: Liturgical, 2003.

McGuckin, John Anthony. "The Trinity in the Greek Fathers." In *The Cambridge Companion to the Trinity*, edited by Peter Phan, 49–69. Cambridge: Cambridge University Press, 2011.

Meersman, Achilles. "Can We Speak of Indigenization of the Catholic Church in India During the Nineteenth Century? Padroado and Propaganda Compared." *Indian Church History Review* 7.2 (1973) 75–82.

Metz, Johann Baptist. *The Emergent Church*. Translated by Peter Mann. New York: Crossroad, 1981.

———. *Faith in History and Society: Toward a Practical Fundamental Theology*. Translated by David Smith. New York: Seabury, 1980.

Meyendorff, John. *Byzantine Theology: Historical Trend and Doctrinal Themes*. New York: Fordham University Press, 1983.

Minz, Nirmal. "Mission in the Context of Diversity: Mission in Tribal Context." *Religion and Society* 36.1 (1989) 7–21.

———. *Rise Up, My People, and Claim the Promise: The Gospel Among the Tribes of India*. Delhi: ISPCK, 1997.

Moltmann, Jürgen. *The Church in the Power of the Spirit: A Contribution to Messianic Ecclesiology*. Translated by Margaret Kohl. New York: Harper & Row, 1977.

———. *The Crucified God: The Cross of Christ as the Foundation and Criticism of Christian Theology*. Minneapolis: Fortress, 1993.

———. *The Trinity and the Kingdom: The Doctrine of God*. Minneapolis: Fortress, 1993.

Monier-Williams, Monier. *A Sanskrit-English Dictionary: Etymologically and Philologically Arranged, with Special Reference to Cognate Indo-European Languages*. New ed. Oxford: Clarendon, 1960.

Morton, S. Andrew. "The Humanism of Paul D. Devanandan." *Indian Journal of Theology* 30.1 (1981) 9–19.

Mozley, J. K. *The Impassibility of God: A Survey of Christian Thought*. Cambridge: Cambridge University Press, 1926.

Mozoomdar, P. C. *The Oriental Christ*. Boston: Geo Ellis, 1883.

———. *The Spirit of God*. Boston: Geo Ellis, 1894.

Mueller, David L. *Karl Barth*. Waco, TX: Word, 1972.

Mueller, Richard A. *Post-Reformation Dogmatics*. Vol. 4 of *The Triunity of God*. Grand Rapids: Baker, 2003.

Bibliography

Muller, Earl. "The Dynamic of Augustine's *De Trinitate*: A Response to a Recent Characterization." *Augustinian Studies* 26 (1995) 65–91.
Mundadan, A. M. "The Changing Task of Christian History." In *Enlarging the Story: Perspectives on Writing World Christian History*, edited by Wilbert R. Shenk, 22–53. Maryknoll, NY: Orbis, 2002.
———. *History of Christianity in India: From the Beginning up to the Middle of the Sixteenth Century*. Vol. 1. Rev. ed. Bangalore: Church History Association of India, 2001.
———. *Paths of Indian Theology*. Bangalore: Dharmaram College, 1998.
Muricken, Ajit. "S. Kappen: The Man and His Contribution to the Study of Counter Culture." In *Religion, Ideology and Counter-Culture: Essays in Honor of Sebastian Kappen*, edited by Philip Mathew and Ajit Muricken, 9–31. Bangalore: Horizon, 1987.
Naranyan, Pulak. "Bengal Renaissance: A Study in Social Contradictions." *Social Scientist* 15.1 (1987) 26–45.
Narasimhacharya, M. *Sri Ramanuja*. New Delhi: Sahitya Akademi, 2004.
Neill, Stephen. *A History of Christian Christianity in India 1707–1858*. 1985. First paperback ed. Cambridge: Cambridge University Press, 2002.
Netland, Harold A. "Introduction: Globalization and Theology Today." In *Globalizing Theology: Belief and Practice in an Era of World Christianity*, edited by Craig Ott and Harold A. Netland, 14–34. Grand Rapids: Baker, 2006.
Newbigin, Lesslie. "Recent Thinking on Christian Beliefs: viii. Mission and Missions." *Expository Times* 88 (1977) 260–64.
———. *Trinitarian Faith and Today's Mission*. 1963. American ed., Richmond, VA: John Knox, 1964.
Nikhilananda, Swami, ed. *Vedantasara of Sadananda*. Almora, India: Advaita Ashram, 1931.
Nirmal, Arvind P. "Toward a Christian Dalit Theology." In *Frontiers in Asian Christian Theology: Emerging Trends*, edited by R. S. Sugirtharajah, 27–40. Maryknoll, NY: Orbis, 1994.
Nirmal, Arvind P., and V. Devasahayam, eds. *A Reader in Dalit Theology*. Madras: Gurukul Lutheran Theological College, 1992.
Norwood, W. Berry. "The Church Fathers and the Deity of Christ." *American Theological Inquiry* 3.1 (2010) 17–33.
O'Collins, Gerald. *The Tripersonal God: Understanding and Interpreting the Trinity*. New Jersey: Paulist, 1999.
O'Malley, John W. "Mission and the Early Jesuits." *Way Supplement* 79 (1994) 3–10.
Office of the Registrar General & Census Commissioner, India. "Census of India 2011." http://censusindia.gov.in/Census_Data_2001/India_at_glance/scst.aspx.
Ogilive, J. N. *The Apostles of India*. London: Hodder and Stoughton, 1915.
Olson, Roger E. "Pietism: Myths and Realities." In *The Pietist Impulse in Christianity*, edited by Christian T. Collins Winn, et al., 3–16. Eugene, OR: Wipf and Stock, 2011.
Olson, Roger E., and Christopher A. Hall. *The Trinity*. Grand Rapids: Eerdmans, 2002.
Oommen, George. "The Emerging Dalit Theology: A Historical Appraisal." *Indian Church History Review* 34.1 (2000) 19–37.
Ormerod, Neil. "Augustine and the Trinity: Whose Crisis?" *Pacifica* 16 (2003) 17–32.
———. *The Trinity: Retrieving the Western Tradition*. Wisconsin: Marquette University Press, 2005.

Bibliography

Osthathios, Geevarghese Mar. "Divine Sharing: Shape of Mission for the Future." *International Review of Mission* 76.301 (1987) 16–20.

———. "More Cross-currents in Mission." *International Bulletin of Missionary Research* 7.4 (1983) 175–76.

Palamas, Gregory. *The Triads*. Translated by Nicholas Gendle. Edited by John Meyendorff. New York: Paulist, 1983.

Panikkar, Raymond. *The Trinity and World Religions: Icon-Person-Mystery*. Bangalore: CISRS and Madras: CLS, 1970.

———. *The Unknown Christ of Hinduism: Towards an Ecumenical Christophany*. Rev. and enlarged edition. Bangalore: Asian Trading, 1982.

Pannenberg, Wolfhart. *Basic Questions in Theology: Collected Essays*. Vol. 1. Translated by George H. Kehm. Philadelphia: Fortress, 1971

———. *Systematic Theology*. Vol. 1. Grand Rapids: Eerdmans, 1994.

———. *Theology and the Kingdom of God*. Philadelphia, PA: Westminster, 1969.

Pape, W. Roy. "Keshub Chunder Sen's Doctrine of Christ and the Trinity: A Rehabilitation." *Indian Journal of Theology* 25.2 (1976) 55–71.

Paradkar, Balwant A. M. *The Theology of Nehemiah Goreh*. Bangalore: CISRS and Madras: CLS, 1969.

Parappally, Jacob. *Emerging Trends in Indian Christian Theology*. Bangalore: IIS, 1995.

Parekh, Manilal C. *Brahmarshi Keshub Chunder Sen*. Rajkot, India: Oriental Christ House, 1926.

Paswan, Sanjay, and Paramanshi Jaideva, eds. *Encyclopaedia of Dalits in India*. Vol. 3. Delhi: Kalpaz, 2002.

Paul VI. "*Ecclesiam Suam*." Encyclical Letter delivered August 6, 1964. http://w2.vatican.va/content/paul-vi/en/encyclicals/documents/hf_p-vi_enc_06081964_ecclesiam.html

Pecknold, C. C. "How Augustine Used the Trinity: Functionalism and the Development of Doctrine." *Anglican Theological Review* 85.1 (2003) 127–41.

Peters, Ted. *God as Trinity: Rationality and Temporality in Divine Life*. Louisville: Westminster John Knox, 1993.

Phan, Peter. "Mystery of Grace and Salvation: Karl Rahner's Theology of the Trinity." In *The Cambridge Companion to the Trinity*, edited by Peter Phan, 192–207. Cambridge: Cambridge University Press, 2011.

Philip, T. V. *Edinburgh to Salvador: Twentieth Century Ecumenical Missiology*. Delhi: ISPCK, 1999.

———. *Krishna Mohan Banerjea: Christian Apologist*. Bangalore: CISRS and Madras: CLS, 1982.

Ployd, Adam. *Augustine, the Trinity, and the Church: A Reading of the anti-Donatist Sermons*. New York: Oxford University Press, 2015.

Poe, Shelli M. *Essential Trinitarianism: Schleiermacher as Trinitarian Theologian*. London: Bloomsbury, 2017.

Poitras, Edward W. "St. Augustine and the *Missio Dei*: A Reflection on Mission at the Close of the Twentieth Century." *Mission Studies* 16.2 (1999) 28–46.

Powell, Samuel M. *The Trinity in German Thought*. Cambridge: Cambridge University Press, 2001.

Prabhakar, M. E., ed. *Towards a Dalit Theology*. Delhi: ISPCK, 1988.

Radhakrishnan, S., ed. *The Principal Upaniṣads*. Translated by S. Radhakrishnan. New York: Harper & Brothers, 1953.

Rahner, Karl. *Foundations of Christian Faith: An Introduction to the Idea of Christianity.* Translated by William V. Dych. New York: Seabury, 1978.

———. *The Teaching of the Catholic Church: As Contained in Her Documents.* New York: Alba House, 1967.

———. *Theological Investigations.* Vols. 1, 4, 9, & 18. London: Darton, Longman & Todd, 1961.

———. *The Trinity.* Translated by Joseph Donceel. New York: Crossroad, 2003.

———. "Trinity, Divine." In *Sacramentum Mundi: An Encyclopedia of Theology*, edited by Adolf Darlap, 295. Vol. 6. New York: Herder & Herder, 1970.

———. "Trinity in Theology." In *Sacramentum Mundi: An Encyclopedia of Theology*, edited by Adolf Darlap, 308. Vol. 6. New York: Herder & Herder, 1970.

Raju, P. T. *Structural Depths of Indian Thought.* Albany: State University of New York Press, 1985.

Rāmānuja. *Vedārthasamgraha.* Translated and edited by J. A. B. van Buitenen. Poona: Deccan College Graduate Research Institute, 1956. Quoted in James S. Helfer. "The Body of Brahman According to Rāmānuja." *Journal of Bible and Religion* 32.1 (1964) 43–46.

Ratzinger, Cardinal Joseph. "Concerning the Notion of Person in Theology." *Communio: International Catholic Review* 17.3 (1990) 439–54.

Rauser, Randal. "Rahner's Rule: An Emperor without Clothes?" *International Journal of Systematic Theology* 7.1 (2005) 81–94.

Rea, Michael C. "The Trinity." In *The Oxford Handbook of Philosophical Theology*, edited by Thomas P. Flint and Michael Rea, 403–29. New York: Oxford University Press, 2009.

Richard of St. Victor. *On the Trinity.* Translated and commentary by Ruben Angelici. Eugene, OR: Cascade, 2011.

———. *The Twelve Patriarchs, The Mystical Ark, Book Three of the Trinity.* Translated by Grover A. Zinn. New York: Paulist, 1979.

Richebächer, Wilhelm. "*Missio Dei:* The Basis of Mission Theology or a Wrong Path?" *International Review of Mission* 92.327 (2003) 588–605.

Roberts, Alexander, and James Donaldson, eds. *Ante-Nicene Fathers: The Writings of the Fathers down to AD 325.* Vols. 1–3 & 5. Peabody, MA: Hendrickson, 2004.

Rosario, Jerry. "Mission from the Perspective of Dalits: Some of its Concerns and Options." *Mission Studies* 13.1 (1996) 281–90.

Rosin, H. H. *"Missio Dei": An Examination of the Origin, Contents, and Function of the Term in Protestant Missiological Discussion.* Leiden: Interuniversity Institute for Missiological and Ecumenical Research Department of Missiology, 1972.

Rössel, Jacques. "'From a Theology of Crisis to a Theology of Revolution?' Karl Barth, Mission and Missions." *Ecumenical Review* 21.3 (1969) 204–15.

Roy, Raja Rammnohun. *The Precepts of Jesus: The Guide to Peace and Happiness, Extracted from the Books of the New Testament.* 1820. Reprint, Calcutta: Baptist Mission, 1823.

Rusch, William G., ed. *The Trinitarian Controversy.* Translated by William G. Rusch. Philadelphia: Fortress, 1980.

Sadangi, H. C. *Emancipation of Dalits and Freedom Struggle.* Delhi: Isha, 2008.

Samartha, Stanley J. *Courage for Dialogue: Ecumenical Issues in Inter-religious Relationships.* Geneva: WCC, 1981.

———. *The Hindu Response to the Unbound Christ.* Madras: CLS, 1974.

Bibliography

———. *One Christ—Many Religions: Toward a Revised Christology*. Maryknoll, NY: Orbis, 1991.
The Samkhya Kārika. Translated by Har Dutt Sharma. Poona, India: Oriental, 1933.
Sanders, Fred. *The Image of the Immanent Trinity: Rahner's Rule and the Theological Interpretation of Scripture*. New York: Peter Lang, 2005.
Schaff, Philip, ed. *The Creeds of Christendom*. Vol. 2. Grand Rapids: Baker, 1990.
———, ed. *Nicene and Post-Nicene Fathers*. 14 vols. Series 1. Peabody, MA: Hendrickson, 2004.
Schaff, Philip, and Henry Wace, eds. *Nicene and Post-Nicene Fathers*. 14 vols. Series 2. Peabody, MA: Hendrickson, 2004.
Scherer, James A. "Church, Kingdom, and *Missio Dei*: Lutheran and Orthodox Correctives to Recent Ecumenical Mission Theology." In *The Good News of the Kingdom: Mission Theology for the Third Millennium*, edited by Charles van Engen, et al., 82–88. Maryknoll, NY: Orbis, 1993.
———. *Gospel, Church, and Kingdom: Comparative Studies in World Mission Theology*. Minneapolis: Augsburg, 1987.
Schleiermacher, Friedrich. *The Christian Faith*. Translated and edited by H. R. Mackintosh and J. S. Stewart. Edinburgh: T & T Clark, 1928.
Schmemann, Alexander. "In Memoriam: Vladimir Lossky 1903–1958." *St. Vladimir's Seminary Quarterly* 2.2 (1958) 47–48.
Schultz, Klaus Detlev. *Mission from the Cross: The Lutheran Theology of Mission*. St. Louis: Concordia, 2009.
Schuster, Jürgen. "Karl Hartenstein: Mission with a Focus on the End." *Mission Studies* 19.1–37 (2002) 53–81.
Sen, Keshub Chunder. *Lectures in India*. Vols. 1 & 2. London: Cassell, 1901–04.
Shenk, Wilbert R. "Recasting Theology of Mission: Impulses from the Non-Western World." *International Bulletin of Missionary Research* 25.3 (2001) 98–107.
Shimray, Shimreingam, ed. *Tribal Theology: A Reader*. Jorhat, India: Eastern Theological College, 2003.
Siecienski, A. Edward. *The Filioque: History of a Doctrinal Controversy*. New York: Oxford University Press, 2010.
Singh, Sundar. "At the Master's Feet." In *The Christian Witness of Sadhu Sundar Singh: A Collection of His Writings*, edited by T. Dayanandan Francis, 30–80. Translated by Arthur Parker and Rebecca Parker. Madras: CLS, 1993.
Skreslet, Stanley H. *Comprehending Mission: The Questions, Methods, Themes, Problems, and Prospects of Missiology*. Maryknoll, NY: Orbis, 2012.
Smith, A. Christopher. "The Legacy of William Carey." *International Bulletin of Missionary Research* 16.1 (1992) 2–8.
Sparrow-Simpson, William John. *St. Augustine and African Church Division*. London: Longmans Row, 1910.
Spicer, Malcolm. *The Mystery of Unity: A Commentary on Saint Augustine's De Trinitate*. Québec-Montréal: National Library, 1993.
Stanislaus, L. "Dalits and the Mission of the Church." In *Emerging Indian Missiology: Context and Concepts*, edited by Joseph Mattam and Joseph Valiamangalam, 189–214. Delhi: ISPCK, 2006.
Stott, John, ed. *Making Christ Known: Historic Mission Documents from Lausanne Movement 1974–1989*. Grand Rapids: Eerdmans, 1996.

Bibliography

Streeter, B. H., and A. J. Appasamy. *The Message of Sadhu Sunder Singh: Study in Mysticism on Practical Religion*. New York: MacMillan, 1921.
Studer, Basil. "History and Faith in Augustine's *De Trinitate*." *Augustinian Studies* 28.1 (1997) 7–50.
———. *Trinity and Incarnation: The Faith of the Early Church*. Collegeville: Liturgical, 1993.
Sumruld, William A. *Augustine and the Arians: The Bishop of Hippo's Encounters with Ulfilan Arianism*. Cranbury, NJ: Associated University Press, 1994.
Sundermeier, Theo. "*Missio Dei* Today: On the Identity of Christian Mission." *International Review of Mission* 92.327 (2003) 560–78.
Tanner, Norman P., ed. *Decrees of the Ecumenical Councils*. Washington, DC: Gregorian University Press, 1990.
Teasdale, Wayne. *Catholicism in Dialogue: Conversations Across Traditions*. Maryland: Rowman & Littlefield, 2004.
Tennent, Timothy C. *Building Christianity on Indian Foundations: The Legacy of Brahmabandhav Upadhyay*. Delhi: ISPCK, 2000.
———. "Contextualizing the Sanskritic Tradition to Serve Dalit Theology." *Missiology: An International Review* 25.3 (1997) 344–49.
———. *Invitation to World Missions: A Trinitarian Missiology for the Twenty-first Century*. Grand Rapids: Kregel, 2010.
———. "Listening to Voices Outside the North American Gate: Trinity and Saccidananda in the Writings of Brahmabandhav Upadhyay." In *Antioch Agenda: Essays on the Restorative Church in Honor of Orlando E. Costas*, edited by Daniel Jeyaraj, et al., 67–87. Delhi: ISPCK, 2007.
———. *Theology in the Context of World Christianity: How the Global Church is Influencing the Way We Think About and Discuss Theology*. Grand Rapids: Zondervan, 2007.
Thangasamy, D. A., ed. *The Theology of Chenchiah: With Selections from His Writings*. Bangalore: CISRS and YMCA, 1966.
Thannippara, Alexander. "Saccidananda, Isvara, Avatara: Towards a Re-evaluation of Some Aspects of the Indian Christian Theology." PhD diss., Rheinischen Friedrich-Wilhelms-Universität, 1992.
Thanzauva, K. "Issues in Tribal Theology." In *Tribal Theology: A Reader*, edited by Shimreingam Shimray, 17–39. Jorhat, India: Eastern Theological College, 2003.
———. *Theology of Community: Tribal Theology in the Making*. Bangalore: Asian Trading, 2004.
Thomas, M. M. *The Acknowledged Christ of the Indian Renaissance*. 3rd ed. Madras: CLS, 1991.
———. *Christian Participation in Nation-Building: The Summing Up of a Corporate Study on Rapid Social Change*. Bangalore: NCCI and CISRS, 1960.
———. Foreword to *An Introduction to Indian Christian Theology*, by Robin Boyd, v–vi. Rev. ed. 1979. Reprint, Delhi: ISPCK/ITL, 1991.
———. *Salvation and Humanisation: Some Crucial Issues of the Theology of Mission in Contemporary India*. Bangalore: CISRS and Madras: CLS, 1971.
———. *To the Ends of the Earth*. Translated by T. M. Philip. Tiruvalla, India: CSS, 2005.
Thomas, M. M., and P. T. Thomas. *Towards an Indian Christian Theology: Life and Thought of Some Pioneers*. 1992. Reprint, Tiruvalla, India: CCS, 1998.
Thomas, T. Jacob. "Indian Tribal Culture: A Rediscovery of Gospel Values." *Indian Journal of Theology* 35.2 (1993) 64–79.

Bibliography

———. "Interaction of the Gospel and Culture in Bengal: Part 1." *Indian Journal of Theology* 36.2 (1994) 38–53.

———. "Interaction of the Gospel and Culture in Bengal: Part 2." *Indian Journal of Theology* 37.2 (1995) 47–63.

Thompson, John. *Modern Trinitarian Perspectives*. New York: Oxford University Press, 1994.

Trakatellis, Demetrios. *The Pre-existence of Christ in the Writings of Justin Martyr*. HDR 6. Missoula, MT: Scholars, 1976.

Upadhyay, Brahmabandhab. *The Writings of Brahmabandhab Upadhyay*. 2 vols. Edited and annotated by Julius J. Lipner and George Gispert-Sauch. Bangalore: United Theological College, 1991–2002.

Vanhoozer, Kevin J., ed. *The Trinity in a Pluralistic Age: Theological Essays on Culture and Religion*. Grand Rapids: Eerdmans, 1996.

Verkuyl, Johannes. "The Kingdom of God as the Goal of the Missio Dei." *International Review of Mission* 68.270 (1979) 168–75.

Vettanky, John. "A Patriot, Pioneer of Enculturation." *Vidyajyoti Journal of Theological Reflection* 63 (1999) 657–66.

Vetticatil, Jose. "Brahmabandhav Upadhyaya." *Jeevadhara: A Journal of Christian Interpretation* 17 (1987) 323–24.

Vicedom, Georg F. *The Mission of God: An Introduction to a Theology of Mission*. Translated by Gilbert A. Thiele and Dennis Hilgendozrf. St. Louis: Concordia, 1965.

Walls, Andrew F. *The Cross-Cultural Process in Christian History: The Studies in the Transmission and Appropriation of Faith*. 2002. Reprint, Maryknoll, NY: Orbis, 2005.

———. Foreword to *Theology in the Context of World Christianity: How the Global Church is Influencing the Way We Think About and Discuss Theology*, by Timothy C. Tennent, xv–xvi. Grand Rapids: Zondervan, 2007.

———. *The Missionary Movement in Christian History: Studies in the Transmission of Faith*. Maryknoll, NY: Orbis, 1996.

Wassmer, Thomas A. "The Trinitarian Theology of Augustine and His Debt to Plotinus." *Harvard Theological Review* 53.4 (1960) 261–68.

Webster, John B. *The Dalit Christians: A History*. Delhi: ISPCK, 2000.

———. *Eberhard Jüngel: An Introduction to His Theology*. New York: Cambridge University Press, 1991.

Weedman, Mark. *The Trinitarian Theology of Poitiers*. Leiden: Brill, 2007.

Welch, Claude. *In This Name: The Doctrine of the Trinity in Contemporary Theology*. New York: Scribner's Sons, 1952.

Whaling, Frank. "Indian Christian Theology: The Humanity of Christ and the New Humanity." *Scottish Journal of Theology* 31 (1978) 319–33.

———. "The Trinity and the Structure of Religious Life: An Indian Contribution to Wider Christian Theology." *Scottish Journal of Theology* 32.4 (1979) 359–69.

Wieser, Thomas, ed. *Planning for Mission: Working Papers on the New Quest for Missionary Communities*. New York: US Conference for the World Council of Churches, 1966.

Wilbur, Morse Earl. *History of Unitarianism: Socinianism and its Antecedents*. Vol. 1. Cambridge, MA: Harvard University Press, 1946.

Williams, Robert R. *Schleiermacher the Theologian: The Construction of the Doctrine of God*. Philadelphia: Fortress, 1978.

Wisse, Maarten. *Trinitarian Theology Beyond Participation: Augustine's De Trinitate*. London: T & T Clark, 2011.

Bibliography

Wright, William, ed. *Apocryphal Acts of the Apostles*. Vol. 2. Translated by William Wright. London: Williams and Norgate, 1871.
Ziegenbalg, Bartholomew. *Remarkable Voyage*. n.p., 1710. Quoted in Lehmann, E. Arno. *It Began at Tranquebar*. Translated by Martin J. Lutz. CLS: Madras, 1956.
Zizioulas, John D. *Being as Communion: Studies in Personhood and Church*. New York: St. Vladimir's Seminary, 1985.
———. "Communion and Otherness." *St. Vladimir's Theological Quarterly* 38.4 (1994) 347–61.

Author Index

Aagaard, Johannes, 41
Aleaz, K. P., 115n100, 124
Ambrose, 130, 138
Andersen, Wilhelm, 44
Appasamy, A. J., 69–71
Aquinas, Thomas, 3, 19, 93n10, 96, 100,
    113, 117, 123, 194, 203
Aristotle, 94
Augustine, of Hippo, Saint, ix, x, 1–9,
    11–12n5, 19–20, 38, 127–36,
    138–69, 171–75, 178–79, 183–86,
    189, 192–93, 203–4, 206–10

Baago, Kaj, 4, 94
Balmes, Jaime, 115
Banerjea, Krishna Mohan, 65–66
Banerji, Kalicharan, 91–92
Barth, Karl, 3, 16–18, 21, 24, 30–31,
    39–40, 78n120
Basil the Great, 11, 23n64, 130
Bevans, Stephen, 178
Beyerhaus, Peter, 78n120
Boff, Leonardo, 32–34, 188
Bosch, David J., 39–40, 48, 201
Braaten, Carl, 36, 180
Bulgakov, Sergius, 208

Carey, William, 58–59
Chakkarai, Vengal, 73–74
Chan, Simon, 181–82

Chenchiah, Pandipeddi, 71–73

De Nobili, Robert, 56
Descartes, 16, 112
Devanandan, Paul David, 75–77
Duff, Alexander, 91

Eusebius of Vercelli, 130

Fabricius, John Philip, 58
Flett, John, 39
Freytag, Walter, 43, 45
Frykenberg, Robert, 54

Gandhi, Mohandas Karamchand, 62
Gaudapāda, 114
Gioia, Luigi, 153
Gispert-Sauch, George, 111, 113–14, 121
Goreh, Nehemiah, 66–68, 109
Gregory of Elvira, 130
Gregory of Nazianzus, 11, 23n64, 130,
    188
Gregory of Nyssa, 11, 130
Guder, Darrell, 40
Gunton, Colin, 26–27, 131, 158n136

Hartenstein, Karl, 39–43, 45, 48, 175
Heaton, R., 93
Hedlund, Roger, 87–88
Hegel, George W. F., 14–15

Author Index

Hilary of Poitiers, 12n5, 130, 138
Hill, Edmund, 149n92, 151–52n108, 157n128
Hoekendijk, Johannes Christiaan, 41n154, 43, 48–49
Holmes, Stephen, 142n67

Irenaeus, 137, 149n98

Jenson, Robert, 24–25, 37
Johanns, Pierre, 106n68
John of Damascene (Damascus), 11n4, 23n64, 188
Jüngel, Eberhard, 30–32
Justin Martyr, 137

Kant, Immanuel, 13
Kappen, Sebastian, 82–83

LaCugna, Catherine Mowry, 35–36, 50
Lipner, Julius, 5, 91–93, 109, 118, 124, 200
Lossky, Vladimir, 21–24

Malkovsky, Bradley, 99n35—100n39
Marshman, Joshua, 58–59, 62–63, 202
Meersman, Achilles, 196
Melanchthon, Philipp, 173
Minz, Nirmal, 86
Moltmann, 2, 14, 25, 27–30, 32, 35, 178
Mozoomdar, Pratap Chander, 62, 64–65, 93
Muller, Max, 107
Mundadan, A. M., 54

Newbigin, Lesslie, 37, 207–8
Novatian, 137–38

Osthathios, Geevarghese Mar, 176

Palamas, Gregory, 22
Panikkar, Raymond, 79, 177, 192–93
Pannenberg, Wolfhart, 24–25
Paradkar, Balwant, 67
Pecknold, C. C., 189

Peters, Ted, 24
Phan, Peter, 19
Phoebadius of Agen, 130
Pluetschau, Heinrich, 57
Powell, Samuel M., 15, 25
Prot, 55

Rahner, Karl, 3, 18–20, 23, 50
Rāmānuja, 70, 99, 197, 199
Redman, Joseph, 93
Reimarus, Herman Samuel, 13
Rosin, H. H., 41, 47
Roy, Raja Ram Mohan, 7, 59, 61–62, 93n10, 106–7
Rufinus, 130

Samartha, Stanley Jedidiah, 80–82
Sanders, Fred, 21
Sapor, 55
Schleiermacher, Friedrich, 14, 16
Schulz, Klaus, 173
Sen, Keshub Chunder, 4, 62–64, 92, 106–9, 123, 194, 202
Shankara (Śankara), x, 3, 68, 80, 90, 97, 99, 100, 102, 105–6, 112n89, 114n98, 115, 170, 198
Singh, Sadhu Sunder, 68–69, 195
Stanislaus, Lazar, 86
Sundermeier, Theo, 43

Teasdale, Wayne, 194
Tennent, Timothy C., 5, 95, 202n120
Tertullian, 137–38
Theophilus of Antioch, 137
Thibaut, M., 101
Thomas, (apostle), St., 53–54
Thomas of Cana, 55
Thomas, M. M., 58, 76n105, 77–79

Upadhyay, Brahmabandhab, x, 1–9, 52, 68, 89–98, 100–104, 106, 109, 110–26, 166, 168–72, 178, 183, 189–92, 194–97, 199–200, 202–6, 209–10

Author Index

Vicedom, Georg, 46,
Victorinus, Marius, 12
Vivekananda, Swami, 62, 91
Von Brück, Michael, 192–93

Walls, Andrew, 88, 90, 201
Ward, William, 58
Warren, M.A.C., 42

Wassmer, Thomas, 154n116
Welch, Claude, 14

Xavier, Francis, 55–56

Ziegenbalg, Bartholomew, 57, 59
Zizioulas, John D., 26–27

Subject Index

abandonment (of the Son), 28, 31
Acts of Judas Thomas, 53
adaptation, 111
Adoptionism, 136
Aham Brahmāsmi, 104
analogies, trinitarian, 133–34, 193;
    analogy of love, 134, 135
anthropocentrism, 16, 46, 51;
    anthropocentric, 3, 44, 86, 176;
    anthropology, 75, 78n120
apophasis, apophaticism, apophatic, 21, 22, 98
Arian, Arianism, 8, 11, 131, 138–39, 159, 168, 210
Ārya Samaj, 61
Asanga (unrelated), 97–98, 100, 112–13
Aseity, 30, 97–99, 170
Athanasian Creed, 12, 169
Atman, 80, 103–104
avatār(s), 70, 73

begetting, begetter, 132–33, 144, 160–61
bhakti, 69–70; *bhakti* tradition, 68–70;
    bhakti movement, 70, 74, 83, 199,
    bhakti marga, 70, 74, 80
Bible translation, 58,
Brahman, 67, 97–106, 112, 170, 191–93;
    parabrahman, 99n35, 100n39, 105, 111–15, 119, 121

Brahman, *nirguṇa*, 97–98, 100–102, 112, 118, 170, 195
Brahman, *saguṇa*, 98, 100–102, 170, 195
Brahminical ethnic particularity, 196, 209
Brahminicalism, 125–26
Brahmo Samaj, 61, 92, 194
Brandenburg Missionary Conference, 39
Buddhism, 83, 126, 198

Cappadocian Fathers, 11, 26–27, 154n116
Catholic mission, 55, 57
Chalcedon, council of, 12, 181
Christianity, global expansion of, 51, 88, 125, 180, 196, 200, 205, 210; global/World, 5, 209; Indian, 53–55, 68, 95–96, 125, 128, 167, 169, 200, 203; indigenous, ix, 5, 69, 94, 203
Christianization, 56, 88
Christocentric mission, 2
Christology, 80–81, 176–77, 208; revised Christology, 81; Yahweh Christology, 137
Christophanies, 139
church and Trinity, 6, 9, 27, 38, 41, 43, 157–58, 168, 174, 178, 180–83, 190–91, 194, 204, 208

239

Subject Index

church, 1–2, 6, 9, 27, 37–41, 43–51, 76, 87, 157–58, 177–83, 185, 191–92, 204, 208
Church, Eastern Orthodox, 11n4, 21, 23n64, 160n141, 181n42
Church, East-Syrian (Persian), 53–55
church, mission of the, 2, 6, 37–41, 43, 46–47, 51, 66, 76, 87, 89, 124, 176, 178–80, 183, 186
Church, Western, 129, 139, 160n141
coinherence, 29; *see also* perichoresis, interpenetration
colonialism, 42
Communio Sacramentorum, 179
Communio Sanctorum, 179
communion, *Koinonia*, 26–27, 33–34, 36, 133, 164–65, 175, 178–79, 182, 204, 207
communion/community, trinitarian, 26–28, 30, 32–34, 132, 160, 165, 175, 178–79, 182, 188, 190–91, 194, 204, 207–8
Constantinople, Council of, 11
consubstantial(ity), 11, 119, 129, 136, 144n77, 150, 156–57, 159–61, 163–64, 166, 175, 189
contextualization, 69, 123, 125, 196
counter theology, theologies, 6, 8, 84, 198
creation, 26–27, 30, 34, 36, 41, 43n163, 46–47, 63, 67, 72, 86, 99, 103n52, 113–14, 121–22, 141, 170, 175, 207–8; doctrine of creation, 67, 75, 98; new creation, 34, 71–72, 76, 192
culture, Christianity/mission, 56, 60n31, 90, 124–25, 201–2; counter culture, 83; Greek/Roman culture, 37, 201; Hindu culture, 56, 61; Indian culture, 6, 67, 73, 94, 126, 197, 200, 204; Tribal culture, 86, 88; Western culture, 61

Dalit(s), Dalit theology, 84–87, 125, 186n60, 197–99, 204
dialogue, 6–9, 56, 66, 74–75, 80, 89, 178, 193–95, 200–203, 209; Hindu-Christian dialogue, 52, 61, 73, 78 79, 106, 166, 194, 202; interreligious dialogue, 76, 81
dogma(tic), 1, 16, 19, 32, 36, 96, 124, 193, 196
dualism, 137

ecclesiology, 178, 180–81, 183, 204; western ecclesiology, 40; Augustinian ecclesiology, 157, 179; Pentecostal ecclesiology, 181
energies (*energeia*), 22
Enlightenment, 10–13, 15, 16
Ephesus, council of, 11
equality, 11–12, 23, 46, 62, 129n2, 132, 136, 143–45, 147, 150–51, 156–57, 164–66, 191
eschaton, 46, 77, 208
essence, 14n21, 15, 19, 22–23, 31, 46, 109, 131, 140, 165, 173
evangelical(ism), 49, 69, 180–81n42, 207
evangelism, 49n197, 76, 176, 180
evangelization, 39, 55–57

fellowship, trinitarian, 28–30, 132–33, 156, 158, 180, 182, 208
filiation, 142, 153, 162, 166, 173, 183
filioque, 21, 121

generation (*generatio*), 119–20, 135, 142, 147, 150–53, 160, 162, 165, 169, 173–75, 190
global South, xi, 200–201, 210
global theology, 4, 178
godforsakenness (divine forsakenness), godforsaken, 28–29
godlessness, 28
gospel and contextualization/ indigenization, 89, 125–26, 168, 171, 194–95, 209; gospel and culture 56, 60n31, 68, 88, 94–95, 196–97, 201–3; gospel, proclamation of, 43, 75–77, 207
grace, 148–49, 153, 155
Great Awakening, 58
Great Commission, 44

hermeneutics, logos-centric, 139

Hinduism, 61, 65–67, 69, 75, 78–80, 87, 96, 199, 200
history, God, Trinity in, 14–15, 19–20, 24–25, 28, 35, 36, 47, 72, 76, 144, 150, 175, 185
holistic mission, 9, 57, 176, 207
Holy Spirit, mission of, 2, 34, 135, 142, 144, 146, 149, 153, 162–63, 165, 174–75; Holy Spirit as Christ, 64, 73–74, 177; Holy Spirit as mutual love, 133, 160n141, 164, 184, 188–89
homoousios, homoousion, 14, 119, 195
horizontalization of mission, 48, 207
humanism, 16, 78n120
humanistic theology, 16
humanization, 58, 74, 77–78, 82, 207
hypostasis(ses), hypostatic, 14, 23, 26, 34, 130, 132, 155, 195

image of God, Trinity, 33–35, 119–20, 134, 179, 183, 190, 192
impassibility, divine (*apatheia*), 27, 32
imperialism, 56
incarnation, 8, 19, 64–65, 70, 73, 129, 138, 141–42, 144–48, 150–51, 153–57, 159, 166, 171–75, 193, 207
India, ix–x, xiv, 53–56, 60, 84–85, 91, 123, 183, 186, 194, 198, 200
Indian Christian theology, 4, 52, 61, 71, 78, 82, 84, 166, 176–77, 202
indigenization, 56, 70, 89, 110, 126, 128, 172, 200, 204, 209
indigenous theology/faith, x–xi, 4, 7–8, 52, 57, 59, 61, 69, 88–89, 111, 125, 169, 197, 201–3, 205, 210; indigenous church, 9, 70, 180–81, 183, 204
individualism, 86, 181n40, 183
inseparability, 130–31, 136, 139, 143–44, 147, 150, 152, 165, 169, 175, 189, 208
International Missionary Council, 38, 41, 47, 128
interpenetration, 11n4, 33, 188–89n68; *see also* perichoresis, coinherence

invisibility (of God and Trinity), 136–37, 139–40, 144–46, 151, 153, 159, 165–66, 179
Islam, ix, 62
Īśvara, 100n39, 170

Jainism, 198

Kingdom of God, 43, 72, 77, 87, 176, 182

Latin paradigm, 129
Lausanne, 49
liberation, human, 34, 82, 85–88, 126, 187; liberation theology, 49, 52–53, 83–84, 86, 197–98, 205
Logos, 63, 70, 117, 120, 139, 170, 201
love, x, 28–29, 32, 34, 133–34, 160, 163–64, 171, 175, 182, 184–86, 189, 207

Marcionism, 136
marginalized, x, 9, 58, 83–84, 86, 166, 184, 186, 190–91
missio Dei (missio), 37–42, 45–51, 128, 135, 165–66, 169–78, 180, 183, 191, 193, 201, 203–4, 206, 208
missio Dei generalis, 46
missio ecclesiae, 41, 45, 47
missio hominum, 44, 46
missio Trinitatis, 39, 47
missiology, 3, 5, 88, 95, 176
mission(s) divine, 2, 37, 128, 144, 151, 153, 155, 165–66, 171, 173–75
modalism, 11, 18, 108, 131, 137
Monarchianism, 11
monarchy, monarchia, 23, 33, 130
monotheism, 14, 33
mutual relations (of Trinity), 18, 20, 30, 37, 133
mutuality, 25, 75, 86, 190
mystery of Trinity, God, 20, 22, 33, 36, 103n52, 133, 135, 149, 151, 157, 159, 163, 171–73, 182, 186–87, 207
mysticism, 68–70, 74

nationalism, Indian, 78, 126

Subject Index

natural theology, 93–94, 109
nature of God, Trinity, 11, 15, 22–24, 37–39, 44, 100, 107, 109, 128, 130–31, 134, 140, 165–66, 171, 174–75, 188, 204
Neo-Hinduism, 75, 78–79
Neo-Platonism, 131
Neo-Scholasticism, 19
Nicene Creed, 11, 129, 169

ontology, 26, 27, 30, 130; substance ontology, 35, 187; relational ontology, 35; ontology of the church, 158n136
orthodoxy, Christian, 64, 66, 109, 138, 169
orthodoxy, trinitarian, 11–12
ousia, 22, 130, 195

pantheism, 64, 100
Parousia, 43, 45
participation, 25, 41, 44, 47, 76, 175–76, 179–80, 190
pathos (passion), divine, 25, 28, 30–31
patrology, 208
Pentecost, 73–74, 129, 141–42, 147, 149, 150–51, 159, 163, 177–78
Pentecostal(ism), 178, 180–82; Indian Pentecostal(ism), 181–82, 204; global Pentecostal(ism), 181
perichoresis, 11n4, 18, 23n64, 29–30, 33–34, 131, 188–90, 207; *see also* interpenetration, coinherence
persona, 14, 170, 171, 195
personhood, 26–27, 99n35—100n39, 121, 137
philosophy, Aristotelian, 3, 96, 194, 203; Greek, 95–96, 195; Enlightenment, 13; scholastic, 96; Indian/Hindu, 2, 7, 68–69, 89, 96–97, 114, 126, 169, 172, 196, 203
Pietism, Pietist, 57, 180–81n40
plenitude, 102, 113, 207
pluralism, pluralistic, 6, 9, 81–82, 192
pneumatology, 176, 208

Pneumatomachism (Macedonianism), 11
Portuguese, 53–56, 60n31
Prajāpati, 65–66
principium, 133, 161–62, 174, 177
procession, 121, 133, 135, 142, 147, 150–53n114, 159–62, 165–66, 169, 173–75, 183, 191, 195
Protestant mission, 57, 59
Protestantism, 16, 21, 203

Rahner's Rule, 19, 20
rationalism, 12
reason, human, 12–13, 57, 60, 72n86, 94, 96–97, 99, 103, 117, 172, 193
reciprocity, 25, 29, 117
reconciliation, 75–76, 135, 142, 147, 154, 156–57, 166, 173, 182, 194
redemption, 43n163, 46, 48, 135, 148, 151, 155, 163, 166; *see* salvation
relation, trinitarian, 2, 20, 25, 27, 35, 132–33, 147, 164, 171–75, 188–90, 193
relationality, 27, 30, 32, 178, 183–84, 186–87, 190, 191, 194, 204
relationship, 15, 20, 23, 25–28, 30, 32–33, 75, 117, 132–33, 171, 183–84, 188, 207
Renaissance, 16; Renaissance, Bengal, 59–61, 91; renaissance, trinitarian, 1, 3–4, 21, 24, 174, 192, 206
resurrection, 25, 77, 86, 142, 163
revelation, 13, 16–17, 20, 31, 46, 70, 73, 76, 97, 103, 117–18, 120, 129, 147–49, 154–55, 172; trinitarian revelation, 15, 17, 24, 33, 129, 135, 147–49, 151, 153, 165–66, 189, 193, 195, 207
Roman Catholicism, 21, 194

Sabellianism, 132, 136, 138
saccidānanda, 2–3, 8, 67–68, 98, 102–11, 117, 119, 121, 123–25, 166, 169–72, 183, 191–95, 203–4
sacrament, 34, 71, 179, 180, 182, 208
salvation history, 20, 25, 28, 29, 35, 41, 43, 45, 49, 207

Subject Index

salvation, 20, 50n197, 78, 155, 193; economy of salvation, 20, 36, 128–29, 142, 149n98, 151, 157, 165–66, 173, 183, 207; *see also* redemption
Sanskrit, 56, 92, 124; Sanskritization, 87, 197; Sanskrit(ic) paradigm/thought/tradition, x, 6–9, 65, 82–83, 123, 125–26, 178, 196–200, 204–5, 209
scholastic theology, 20
secularism, 75–76n105
secularization of mission, 48–49, 207
sending, 1–2, 6, 8, 27, 34, 36–41, 46, 128, 135, 142–44, 146, 151, 159, 163, 165–66, 169, 172–78; *see* divine missions
Serampore College, 59
Serampore mission, missionaries, 58–59, 62
shalom, 43, 48–49
spiration (*spiratio*), 135, 142, 159
St. Thomas tradition, 53–55
subalterns, subaltern theology, movement, 53, 84, 86–88, 125–26, 186–87, 191, 197–198
subordination(ism), 18, 23, 136, 139
substance, 46, 81, 108, 116–17, 120, 132, 141, 144–46, 156, 164–65, 187
substantia, 195
suffering, divine, 27–28, 31–32, 156, 166, 191; human, 33, 176, 191–92, 194; Dalit, 84–87
Sufi philosophy, 106

Tamil, 56, 58
Tat tvam asi, 99, 104, 106n68
theism, 94, 96, 99, 109
theocentric, theocentrism, theocentricity, 1, 3, 16, 39, 44, 46–47, 51
theology of mission, 38, 77, 206; trinitarian, 6, 24, 175, 177, 190; ecumenical, 48; Indian, 55, 175–76, 184, 204, 207, 210
theology of religions, 98, 193
theopathy, 28

theophanies, 136–43, 146, 148, 150, 165
Toledo, council of, 12
Tome of Damasus, 12
Tranquebar, 57–59
translatability, cultural, theological, 90, 196, 202, 209
Tribal, tribal theology, 85–86, 88, 125, 186n60, 197–99
trinitarianism, 109, 191, 195, 203; economic Trinitarianism, 149n98; social (trinitarianism), 32, 34, 35
Trinity, doctrine of the, 1–4, 6–8, 11–19, 28, 35, 38, 90, 95, 129, 168–69, 173, 181, 192, 194–95, 207, 210; Trinity, economic, 8, 14–15, 19–20, 22, 25, 30–31, 35, 50, 130, 142, 149n98, 151, 173; essential 14; immanent, 14–15, 19–20, 22, 30–31, 35, 130, 135, 162, 173
Triune God, Triunity, 17–20, 24, 28–30, 32, 36–38, 40–41, 44, 103, 134–35, 151, 153, 155, 157, 160, 165–66, 169, 174, 177–78, 180, 182, 185–86, 207

Unitarianism, Unitarian, 13, 19, 23, 62, 107
unity (of God, the Trinity), 12, 18, 26, 28–29, 33, 121, 130, 132, 136, 144, 150, 154, 157–60, 164–65, 169, 178–79, 188, 190, 192–93
Upanishad, 98, 99n37, 105, 112, 115–16, 170, 198

Vedanta, Advaita, 2–3, 8–9, 67, 90, 94–98, 103, 107, 109, 115, 121–22, 172, 191–92, 194, 196, 200, 203–4, 206, 209
Vedas, 65–66, 103n52, 107, 198–99
Vishishtadvaita, 70, 100, 197

Western theology, 5, 122, 176, 197, 200, 202
World Evangelical Fellowship, 49
worldview, 3, 37, 75, 85–86, 94, 126, 191, 198

Scripture Index

GENESIS
1:26	134
12:1	140
18:1–15	138
18	140

EXODUS
19:18	140
31:18	140

PSALMS
64	156

ISAIAH
9:6	138
48:16	163

WISDOM
7:26	153
7:27	136
8:1	143

SIRACH
24:5	153

MATTHEW
1:18	144, 162
3:16	146
12:28	140
13:47–50	179
22:37–40	184
28:18–20	37
28:20	73

LUKE
4:18	86
11:20	140

JOHN
1:1	143
1:3	34
1:5, 14	147
1:10–11	144
3:17	77
4:11	188
5:26	160–161
7:16	161
7:39	163
10:30	143, 188
10:38	188
12:28	140
13:34–35	184

Scripture Index

JOHN (continued)

13:35	186
14:18	74
14:26	160–61
15:12–13	185
15:26	133, 153, 160–61
16:14	29
16:28	143, 151–52
17:1	29
17:3	149
17:20–21	188
17:21	29
17:21–26	207
17:22	156
17:23	157
20:21	50

ACTS

2:1	140
2:3	146

ROMANS

5:5	163, 186
5:8	155

I CORINTHIANS

1:21	147

GALATIANS

2:20	74
4:4	143, 147–48

EPHESIANS

1:10	34, 207

PHILIPPIANS

2:6	143
2:7	86

COLOSSIANS

1:16	34

1 TIMOTHY

1:17	136
6:15–16	136

HEBREWS

2:1–3	143

1 JOHN

1:3	182
5:7	144
4:13	164
4:8, 16	134, 164
4:7	184

www.ingramcontent.com/pod-product-compliance
Lightning Source LLC
Chambersburg PA
CBHW050437240426
43661CB00055B/2419